Microsoft

Microsoft
Excel 2013 Plain & Simple

Curtis D. Frye

Published with the authorization of Microsoft Corporation by:
O'Reilly Media, Inc.
1005 Gravenstein Highway North
Sebastopol, California 95472

ISBN: 978-0-7356-7243-7

2 3 4 5 6 7 8 9 10 QG 8 7 6 5 4 3

Printed and bound in the United States of America.

Microsoft Press books are available through booksellers and distributors worldwide. If you need support related to this book, email Microsoft Press Book Support at mspinput@microsoft.com. Please tell us what you think of this book at *http://www.microsoft.com/learning/booksurvey*.

Acquisitions and Developmental Editor: Kenyon Brown
Production Editor: Melanie Yarbrough
Editorial Production: Blue Boot Design Studio
Copyeditor: Box Twelve Communications
Technical Reviewer: Andy Pope
Indexer: Box Twelve Communications
Cover Design: Twist Creative • Seattle
Cover Composition: Karen Montgomery
Illustrator: Rebecca Demarest

[2013-05-03]

For Virginia

Contents

6   Using formulas and functions 97

9 | **Printing worksheets** **173**

12 Summarizing data visually using charts. 239

15

Using Excel in a group environment. **311**

About this book

1

If you want to get the most from your computer and your software with the least amount of time and effort—and who doesn't?—this book is for you. You'll find *Microsoft Excel 2013 Plain & Simple* to be a straightforward, easy-to-read reference tool. With the premise that your computer should work for you, not you for it, this book's purpose is to help you get your work done quickly and efficiently so that you can get away from the computer and live your life.

In this section:

- No computerese!
- A quick overview
- A few assumptions
- Adapting task procedures for touchscreens
- A final word (or two)

No computerese!

Let's face it—when there's a task that you don't know how to do but you need to get it done in a hurry, or when you're stuck in the middle of a task and can't figure out what to do next, there's nothing more frustrating than having to read page after page of technical background material. You want the information you need—nothing more, nothing less—and you want it now! It should be easy to find and understand.

That's what this book is all about. It's written in plain language—no jargon. There's no single task in the book that takes more than a couple pages. Just look up the task in the index or the table of contents, turn to the page, and there's the information you need, laid out in an illustrated, step-by-step format. You don't get bogged down by the whys and wherefores: just follow the steps, and get your work done.

Occasionally, you might have to turn to another page if the procedure you're working on is accompanied by a See Also reference. That's because a lot of tasks overlap, and I didn't want to keep repeating myself. I've scattered some useful tips here and there, and I've thrown in a Try This or a Caution occasionally, but by and large, I've tried to remain true to the heart and soul of a *Plain & Simple* book, which is that the information you need should be available to you at a glance.

Useful tasks...

Whether you use Excel 2013 at home or on the road, I've tried to pack this book with procedures for everything I could think of that you might want to do, from the simplest tasks to some of the more esoteric ones.

...And the easiest way to do them

Another thing I've tried to do in this book is to find and document the easiest way to accomplish a task. Excel 2013 often provides a multitude of methods to accomplish a single end result—which can be daunting or delightful, depending on the way you like to work. If you tend to stick with one favorite and familiar approach, I think the methods described in this book are the way to go. If you like trying out alternative techniques, go ahead! The intuitiveness of Excel 2013 invites exploration, and you're likely to discover ways of doing things that you think are easier or that you like better than mine. If you do, great! It's exactly what the developers of Excel 2013 had in mind when they provided so many alternatives.

A quick overview

Your computer probably came with Excel 2013 preinstalled, but if you do have to install it yourself, setup makes installation so simple that you won't need my help anyway. So, unlike many computer books, this one doesn't start with installation instructions and a list of system requirements.

Next, you don't have to read the sections of this book in any particular order. You can jump in, get the information you need, and then close the book and keep it near your computer until the next time you need to know how to get something done. But that doesn't mean I scattered the information about with wild abandon. I've organized the book so that the tasks you want to accomplish are arranged in two levels—you find the general type of task you're looking for under a main section title, such as "Formatting the worksheet," "Summarizing data visually using charts," "Using Excel in a group environment," and so on. Then, in each of those sections, the smaller tasks within the main task are arranged in a loose progression from the simplest to the more complex.

Section 1 (this section) introduces the book, while Section 2, "What's new and improved in Excel 2013," fills you in on the most important new features of Excel 2013, which include the program's seamless integration with Microsoft Windows 8. Excel 2013 also gives you new ways to analyze your data quickly, whether using the Quick Analysis tool, Recommended Charts, Recommended PivotTables, and editing and sharing your data on the web by using SkyDrive and Excel Web App.

Section 3, "Getting started with Excel 2013," and Section 4, "Building a workbook," cover the basics: starting Excel 2013 and shutting it down, sizing and arranging program windows, navigating in a workbook, using the user interface ribbon to have Excel do what you want it to do, and working with multiple Excel documents at the same time. Section 3 also introduces galleries, which are collections of preset formats that you can apply to worksheets, charts, and other Excel objects, and shows you how to get help from within Excel and on the web. Section 4 contains a lot of useful information about entering text and data, including shortcuts you can use to enter an entire series of numbers or dates by typing values in just one or two cells. You'll also learn about using the Office Clipboard to manage items that you cut and paste, running the spelling checker to ensure

that you haven't made any errors in your workbook, and finding and replacing text to update changes in information, such as customer addresses or product names.

Section 5, "Managing and viewing worksheets," is all about using worksheets—the "pages" of a workbook. In this section, you'll find out about selecting, renaming, moving, copying, inserting, and deleting worksheets, rows, columns, and cells. In Section 6, "Using formulas and functions," you'll get to know formulas and functions. You use formulas to calculate values, such as finding the sum of the values in a group of cells. After you're up to speed on creating basic formulas, you'll learn how to save time by copying a formula from one cell and pasting it into as many other cells as you like. Finally, you'll extend your knowledge of formulas by creating powerful statements using the function library in Excel 2013.

	A	B	C	D	E	F	G	H
1								
2		**January**						
3		Hour						
4	**Day**		5:00 AM	6:00 AM	7:00 AM	8:00 AM		
5		1	2117	1989	1544	2408	=SUM(C5:F5)	
6		2	1128	1109	1354	1115		
7		3	1228	1350	1662	1758		
8		4	2295	2496	1964	1793		
9		5	1866	1631	1631	1136		
10		6	1234	1536	2348	1208		
11		7	1608	1825	1851	1037		
12								

Section 7, "Formatting the cell," focuses on making your workbooks' cells look great. Here's where you'll learn techniques to make your data more readable, such as by changing font sizes and font colors and by adding colors and shading to cells. Section 8, "Formatting the worksheet," describes similar techniques you can apply to your worksheets, such as moving,

	A	B	C	D	E	F
1						
2		Customer	Month	Category	Amount	
3		Fabrikam	January	Ground	$ 14,501.98	
4		Fabrikam	January	3Day	$ 3,501.75	
5		Fabrikam	January	2Day	$ 5,599.10	
6		Fabrikam	January	Overnight	$ 35,907.82	
7		Fabrikam	January	Priority Overnight	$ 17,333.25	
8						

inserting, and deleting rows and columns, applying worksheet themes, and coloring sheet tabs to call attention to important information.

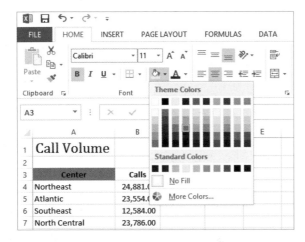

Section 9, "Printing worksheets," is all about printing your Excel documents, whether that means printing all or just a portion of your results. Your productivity should increase after reading Section 10, "Customizing Excel to the way you work," where I'll show you how to add commands to the Quick Access toolbar, customize the tabs on the ribbon user interface, control which error messages appear, define rules that Excel uses to replace often-misspelled words, create workbooks from built-in templates, and create custom workbook templates that you can use to create new workbooks based on those formats.

Section 11, "Sorting and filtering worksheet data," provides you with techniques that you can use to limit the data displayed in a worksheet and determine the order in which it is presented. Do

you need to see all of the sales for a specific product but don't want to bother with the rest of the data for the moment? No problem.

A picture is worth ten thousand words (according to Confucius; the modern version of the saying shorts you by nine thousand words), and in Section 12, "Summarizing data visually using charts," I'll show you how to use the Excel 2013 charting engine to create and use charts—including sparkline charts—to

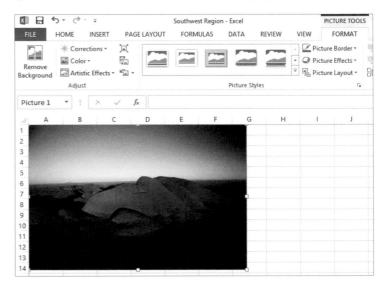

summarize your data visually. In Section 13, "Enhancing your worksheets with graphics," you'll learn just how easy it is to insert clip art, add a special text effect, or resize a photo that you added to a worksheet.

Section 14, "Sharing Excel data with other programs," and Section 15, "Using Excel in a group environment," are all about sharing the data in your Excel worksheets—whether it's with your colleagues, on the Internet, or with other programs. Section 14 shows you how to make Excel 2013 interact with other Microsoft Office 2013 programs, such as by embedding documents from other programs in your Excel workbooks, exchanging data between Excel and Word, or importing a text file into an Excel worksheet. In Section 15, you'll learn how to use Excel

in a group environment, to add comments to your worksheets, and to accept or reject the comments made by others. You'll also learn how to publish a worksheet to the web as well as how to pull information from the Internet directly into your worksheets and to share and edit your workbooks using Excel Web App. This section also introduces XML (an abbreviation for Extensible Markup Language), a handy technology that enables you to exchange data between spreadsheet applications.

A few assumptions

I had to make a few educated guesses about you, my audience, when I started writing this book. Perhaps you just use Excel for personal reasons, tracking your household budget, doing some financial planning, or recording your times for weekend bike races. Maybe you run a small, home-based business, or you're an employee of a corporation where you use Excel to analyze and present sales or production data. Taking all these possibilities into account, I assumed that you need to know how to create and work with Excel workbooks and worksheets, summarize your data in a variety of ways, format your documents so that they're easy to read, and then print the results or share them over the web or distribute your data both ways.

Another assumption I made is that—initially, anyway—you use Excel 2013 just as it came, meaning that you'd be working with the standard user interface. I've written the procedures and captured the graphics throughout this book based on the Excel 2013 user interface as it was installed on my computer.

Adapting task procedures for touchscreens

In this book, we provide instructions based on traditional keyboard and mouse input methods. If you're using Excel on a touch-enabled device, you might be giving commands by tapping with your finger or with a stylus. If so, substitute a tapping action any time we instruct you to click a user interface element. Also note that when we tell you to enter information in Excel, you can do so by typing on a keyboard, tapping in the entry field under discussion to display, and using the onscreen keyboard, or even speaking aloud, depending on your computer setup and your personal preferences.

A final word (or two)

I had three goals in writing this book:

1 Whatever you want to do, I want the book to help you get it done.

2 I want the book to help you discover how to do things you didn't know you wanted to do.

3 And, finally, if I've achieved my first two goals, I'll be well on the way to the third, which is for my book to help you enjoy using Excel 2013. I think that's the best gift I could give you to thank you for buying my book.

I hope you'll have as much fun using *Microsoft Excel 2013 Plain & Simple* as I've had writing it. The best way to learn is by doing, and that's how I hope you'll use this book.

Jump right in!

What's new and improved in Excel 2013

2

This section of the book introduces a selection of the new and improved features in Excel 2013: using Excel 2013 in Windows 8, analyzing data by using the Quick Analysis tool, entering data quickly by using Flash Fill, creating recommended charts, formatting charts by using the new formatting tools, filtering Excel tables by using slicers, creating a recommended PivotTable, and editing a workbook in SkyDrive and the Excel Web App.

In this section:

- Using Excel 2013 in Windows 8
- Analyzing data instantly by using the Quick Analysis tool
- Entering data quickly by using Flash Fill
- Creating the right chart using chart recommendations
- Formatting charts by using the new tools interface
- Filtering Excel tables using slicers
- Creating a recommended PivotTable
- Editing a workbook in SkyDrive and Excel Web App

Using Excel 2013 in Windows 8

After you install Excel on your computer, you can start it from the Start screen in Windows 8, which opens the program with a new, blank workbook. You can also start Excel in Windows 8 by pinning it to the taskbar and clicking it when viewing your computer in Desktop mode.

Launch Excel 2013 in Windows 8

1 If necessary, press Ctrl+Esc to display the Start screen.

2 If necessary, scroll to the Start screen to display the Excel 2013 tile.

3 Click the Excel 2013 tile.

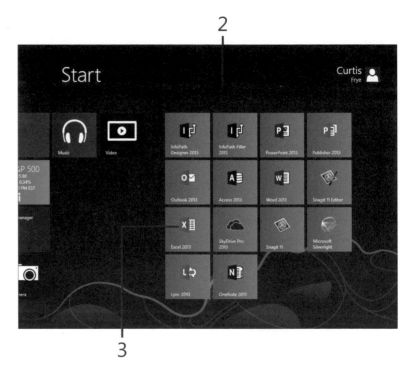

Analyzing data instantly by using the Quick Analysis tool

One of the refinements in Excel 2013 is the Quick Analysis Lens, which brings the most commonly used formatting, charting, and summary tools into one convenient location. You have a wide range of tools available to you, including the ability to create an Excel table or PivotTable, insert a chart, or add conditional formatting. You can also add total columns and rows to your data range. For example, you can click Totals and then Running Total for columns, identified by the icon labeled Running Total and the yellow column at the right edge of the button, to add a column that calculates the running total for each row.

Summarize data by using Quick Analysis

1 Select the cell range that you want to summarize.

2 Click the Quick Analysis action button to display the Quick Analysis tools available to you.

3 Click the label representing the category of tools that you want to use.

4 Click the button representing the summary that you want to create.

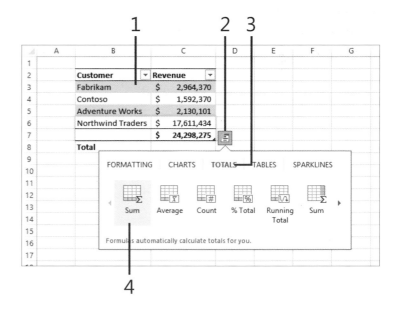

> **TIP** You can add one summary column and one summary row to each data range. If you select a new summary column or row when one exists, Excel displays a confirmation dialog box to verify that you want to replace the existing summary. When you click yes, Excel makes the change.

Entering data quickly by using Flash Fill

Your data sets might contain values in a single cell that you'd like to divide into separate cells. For example, your worksheet might contain a list of names where the first name, middle initial, and last name all appear in the same cell. If you need to separate the first name, middle initial, and last name into separate cells, you can do so by using Flash Fill, which is new in Excel 2013.

To use Flash Fill, click a cell to the right of the list that contains the data that you want to work with, and then type the correct value for that cell. For example, your list might contain the name Mark Hassall. If you want to store the person's first name in one cell and last name in another, you would type **Mark** in the first cell and **Hassall** in the second. You then repeat the process for the second row of the list, at which point Flash Fill recognizes the data pattern and offers to fill in the remaining values.

If your data set contains rows with additional data, such as a middle initial, you can correct the first example of that differing pattern to update similar rows in the new columns.

Separate data by using Flash Fill

1 Click the cell to the right of the first row that you want to work with.

2 Type the value that you want to extract from the row, and press Enter.

3 In the cell directly below the first, start typing the extracted value for the row.

4 Press Enter to accept the suggested Flash Fill values for the remaining rows.

5 If desired, repeat the process in the cell to the right of the first cell in the new column to extract another value from the row's original data.

Creating the right chart by using chart recommendations

You can create a chart manually, or you can create a chart that the program recommends. The Recommended Charts gallery, which is new in Excel 2013, displays a set of charts that you can create based on your data. All you need to do is click the chart that you want and confirm your choice. In either case, you can then change a chart's appearance with no trouble at all.

Create a recommended chart

1 Click a cell in the data list that you want to summarize.

2 Click the Insert tab.

3 Click Recommended Charts.

4 Click the chart that you want to create.

5 Click OK.

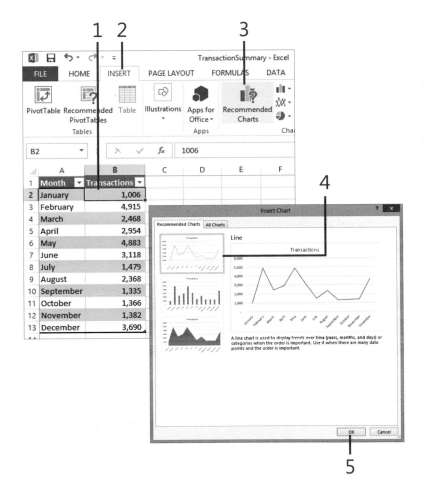

Filtering Excel tables by using slicers

In versions of Excel prior to Excel 2013, the only visual indication that you had applied a filter to an Excel table column was the indicator added to the column's filter arrow. The indicator told users that there was an active filter applied to that column but provided no information about which values were displayed and which were hidden. In Excel 2013, slicers provide a visual indication of which items are currently displayed or hidden in an Excel table field.

Add a slicer

1 Click any cell in the Excel table that you want to filter.

2 Click the Insert tab.

3 Click Slicer.

4 Select the check box next to each column by which you want to filter the table.

5 Click OK.

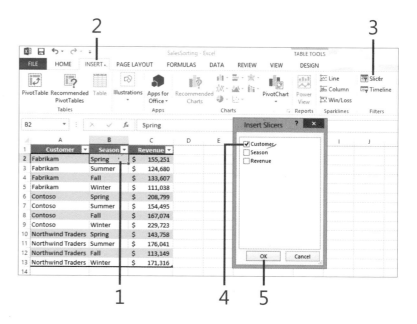

Define a filter by using a slicer

1 In the slicer, do any of the following:

a Click an item to display just its related values.

b While pressing the Ctrl key, select multiple items to display those items' related values.

c While pressing the Shift key, click two items to display related values for every value from the first selected item to the second selected item in the slicer's list.

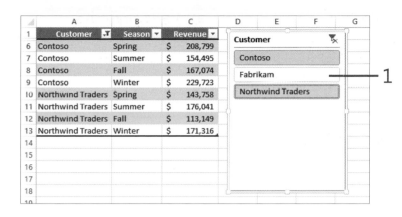

Creating a recommended PivotTable

Excel workbooks enable you to store and summarize large data collections effectively. As versatile as Excel tables and formulas are, they are static. After you create a data arrangement or summary in a standard worksheet, you can change it only by copying, pasting, or moving your data and altering your

formulas. You can extend those capabilities by creating Pivot-Tables. PivotTables are powerful and versatile tools that let you rearrange, sort, and filter your data dynamically, without editing your data or changing any formulas.

Create a recommended PivotTable

1 Click any cell in the Excel table or data list that you want to summarize.

2 Click the Insert tab.

3 Click Recommended PivotTables.

4 Click the PivotTable that you want to create.

5 Click OK.

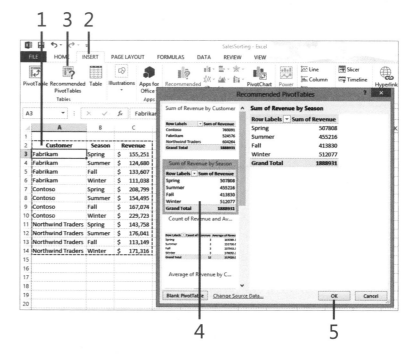

Editing a workbook in SkyDrive and the Excel Web App

The SkyDrive service and Microsoft Office 365 provide access to the Office Web Apps, which let you create and edit Office documents in your web browser. The Microsoft Excel Web App provides a rich set of capabilities that you can use to create new workbooks and edit workbooks that you created in the desktop version of the application. If you find that you need some features that aren't available in the Excel Web App, you can open the file in the Excel 2013 desktop application.

Edit a file in the Excel Web App

1 In your web browser, navigate to *http://www.skydrive.com*.

2 Navigate to the folder that contains the file that you want to edit.

3 Click the tile of the file that you want to edit.

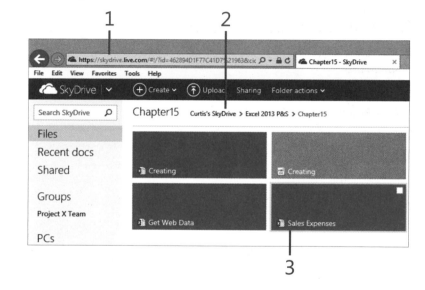

Formatting charts by using the new tools interface

Charts summarize data visually, so every chart has a particular arrangement and presentation of its elements. The overall arrangement of a chart's elements is its *layout*, whereas the overall appearance of the chart's elements is its *style*. You can apply predefined layouts and styles to your charts. As with any formatting that you apply, you can always fine-tune your choices later.

Change a chart's style

1 Click the chart that you want to change.

2 Click the Chart Styles button.

3 In the Chart Styles gallery that appears, click the new style.

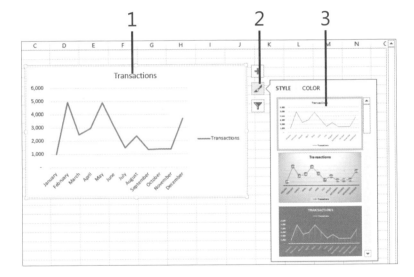

Getting started with Excel 2013

3

Microsoft Excel 2013 is designed to help you store, summarize, and present data relevant to your business or home life. You can create spreadsheets to track products and sales or—just as easily—build spreadsheets to keep track of your personal investments or your kids' soccer scores. Regardless of the specific use that you have in mind, Excel is a versatile program that you can use to store and retrieve data quickly.

Working with Excel is pretty straightforward. The program has a number of preconstructed workbooks that you can use for tasks such as tracking work hours for you and your colleagues or computing loan payments, but you also have the freedom to create and format workbooks from scratch, giving you the flexibility to build any workbook that you need.

This section of the book covers the basics: how to start Excel and shut it down, how to open Excel documents, how to change the Excel window's size and appearance, and how to get help from within the program. There's also an illustrated overview of the Excel window, with labels for the most important parts of the program, and a close-up look at the new user interface. You can use the images in this section as touchstones for learning more about Excel.

In this section:

- Surveying the Excel program window
- Starting Excel in Windows 8
- Adding Excel 2013 to the Start screen
- Starting Excel 2013 in Windows 7
- Opening, searching for, and assigning properties to workbooks
- Creating a new workbook
- Working with multiple workbooks
- Sizing, viewing, and zooming windows
- Saving Excel workbooks
- Closing workbooks and exiting Excel
- Using the Excel Help system

Surveying the Excel program window

In many ways, an Excel worksheet is like the ledger in your checkbook. The page is divided into rows and columns, and you can organize your data by using these natural divisions as a guide. The box formed by the intersection of a row and a column is called a cell. You can identify an individual cell by its column letter and row number. This combination, which identifies the first cell in the first column as cell A1, is called a cell reference. The following graphic shows you the important features of the Excel 2013 screen.

Working with the user interface

Excel 2013 incorporates the ribbon user interface. In Excel 2013, you can find what you need in one place: the ribbon at the top of the screen.

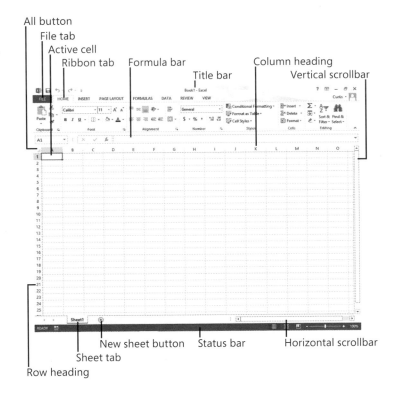

Working with galleries

After you enter your data in a worksheet, you can change the appearance of data and objects within the worksheet by using galleries that appear on the user interface. The ribbon has three types of galleries: galleries that appear in a dialog box, galleries that appear as a drop-down menu when you click a user interface item, and galleries that appear within the user interface itself. The following graphic shows a styles gallery.

Excel 2013 lets you see how formatting will appear before you apply a formatting change. Rather than make you apply the change and then remove it if you don't like how it turned out, when you hover your mouse pointer over a style in a gallery, Excel 2013 generates a live preview of how your data or object will appear if you apply that style. All you need to do is move your mouse to see what your objects will look like when you're finished.

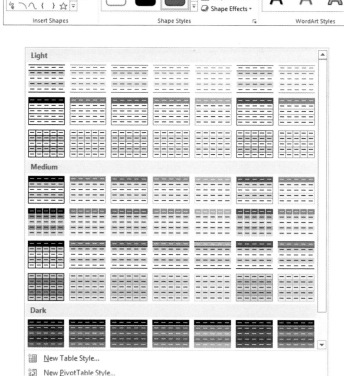

TIP If positioning your mouse pointer over an icon in a gallery doesn't result in a live preview, that option might be turned off in your copy of Excel 2013. To turn Live Preview on, click the File tab, and then click Options to display the Excel Options dialog box. Click General, select the Enable Live Preview check box, and click OK.

Starting Excel

After you install Excel on your computer, you can start it from the Start page in Windows 8, which opens the program with a new, blank workbook. You can also start Excel in Windows 8 by pinning it to the taskbar and clicking it when viewing your computer in Desktop mode.

Start Excel 2013 in Windows 8

1 If necessary, press Ctrl+Esc to display the Start screen.

2 If necessary, scroll to the Start screen to display the Excel 2013 tile.

3 Click or tap the Excel 2013 tile.

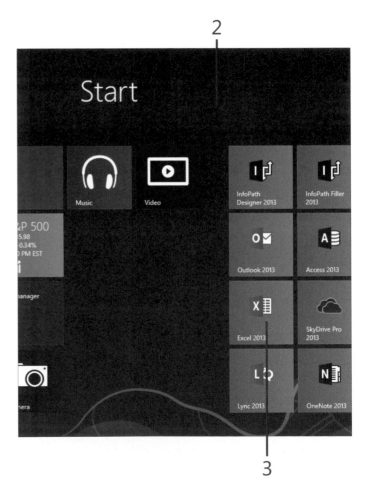

Pin Excel 2013 to the taskbar

1 If necessary, press Ctrl+Esc to display the Start screen.

2 If necessary, scroll to the Start screen to display the Excel 2013 tile.

3 Right-click the Excel 2013 tile.

4 Click Pin To Taskbar.

 TIP To hide the action bar at the bottom of the screen without making any changes, press Esc.

Adding Excel 2013 to the Start screen

The Windows 8 Start screen provides a solid base of operations for your work in Excel. Running a program from the Start screen is as easy as clicking or tapping its tile. If for some reason Excel 2013 doesn't appear on your Start screen, you can add it quickly.

Add Excel 2013 to the Start screen

1 Open File Explorer.

2 Navigate to the folder that contains the Excel.exe program file.

3 Right-click the Excel.exe file.

4 Click Pin to Start.

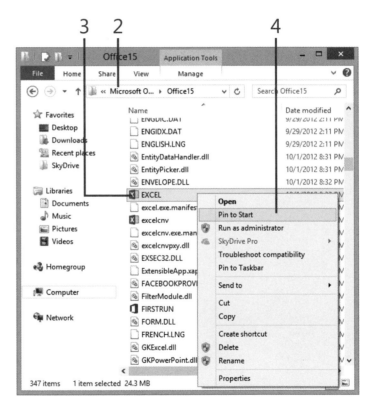

Starting Excel 2013 in Windows 7

If your computer uses the Microsoft Windows 7 operating system, you can run Excel 2013 by opening the Start menu, displaying the Microsoft Office 2013 programs, and clicking

Excel 2013. You can display the Start menu by clicking the Start button or by pressing Ctrl+Esc, whichever is faster for you.

Start Excel 2013 in Windows 7

1 Click the Start button on the taskbar.

2 Click All Programs.

3 Click Microsoft Office 2013.

4 Click Excel 2013.

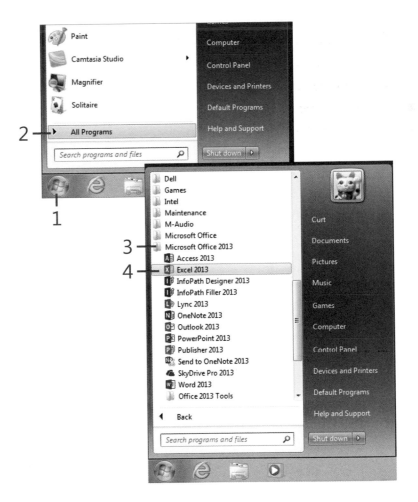

Opening existing workbooks

After you create an Excel workbook, you will probably want to open it again, whether to verify the contents, add or update data, or copy data from one workbook to another. If you know where in your file system your workbook is stored, you can use the Open dialog box within Excel to locate and open your file. If you worked with your file recently, you can probably also find it in the Recent Workbooks list in the Backstage view that you display by clicking the File tab.

Open a workbook

1　Click the File tab.

2　Click Open.

3　Click Computer.

4　Click Browse.

(continued on next page)

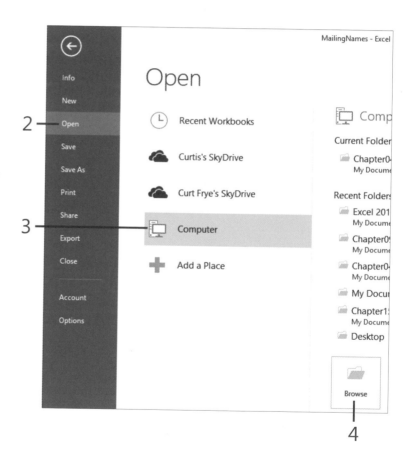

Open a workbook (continued)

5 Navigate to the folder that contains the workbook that you want to open.

6 Click the workbook.

7 Click Open.

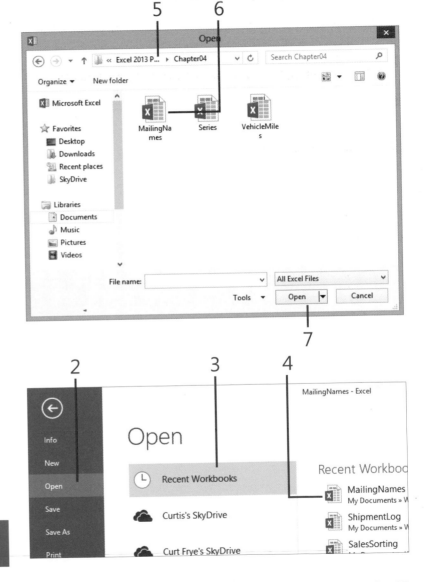

Open a recently used workbook

1 Click the File tab.

2 Click Open.

3 Click Recent Workbooks.

4 Click the workbook that you want to open.

TIP You can also display the Open page of the Backstage view by pressing Ctrl+O.

Using file properties

Finding files can be difficult on computers that you share with your colleagues or if you've been using the same computer for a long time and have created a lot of workbooks. You can make it easier to find your files by adding descriptive terms to their

Properties fields. If you enter a term in a Properties field, you can search using that term, even if it doesn't occur within the body of the workbook.

Set file properties

1 Open the file to which you want to assign property values.

2 Click the File tab.

3 Click Info.

4 Click Properties.

5 Click Show Document Panel.

6 Add information describing your file.

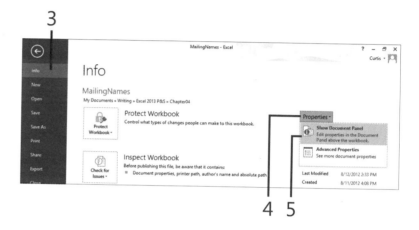

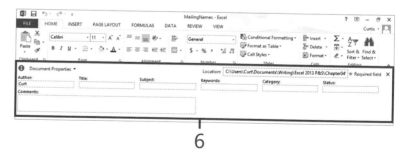

Define custom properties

1 Open the file to which you want to assign property values.

2 Click the File tab.

3 If necessary, click Info.

4 Click Properties.

5 Click Advanced Properties.

6 Click the Custom tab.

7 Type the name of the custom property.

8 Select the type of data contained in the property.

9 Type a value for the property.

10 Click Add.

11 Click OK.

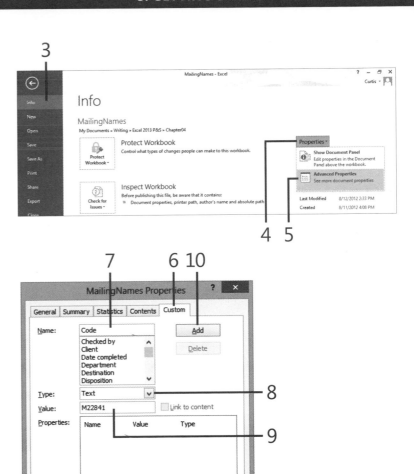

TRY THIS Excel comes with a set of predefined custom properties, such as Checked By and Date Completed. To use an existing custom property, display the Custom tab of the Properties dialog box, click the name of the custom property, type a value for the property in the Value box, and click OK.

Creating a new workbook

As a general rule, you should create a new workbook any time that you need a place to store data on a new subject. For example, you might track your company's sales in one workbook, the products your company offers in another, and your employees' personal information and salaries in another.

Create a new workbook

1 Click the File tab.

2 Click New.

3 Click Blank Workbook.

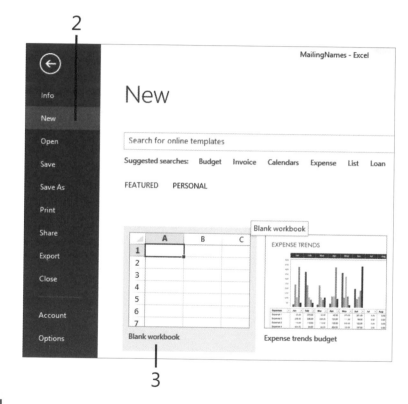

Working with multiple workbooks

When you create an Excel workbook for each subject of your business, you sometimes need to look at data from more than one workbook to make your decisions. In cases like this, you can switch between workbooks by choosing the workbook's name from the list displayed when you click the Switch Windows button on the View tab. You can also choose one of several arrangements so that you can work with your workbooks effectively.

Switch between open workbooks

1 Click the View tab.

2 Click Switch Windows.

3 Click the name of the workbook that you want to display.

Show more than one workbook

1 Click the View tab.

2 Click Arrange All.

3 Select the arrangement that you want.

4 Click OK.

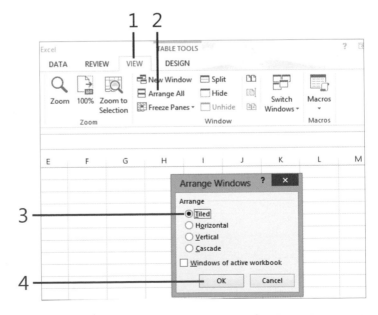

Sizing and viewing windows

You work with windows in the Excel program the same way you work with windows on your desktop. You can make a workbook's window as large as the screen itself. If you have more than one workbook open at a time, you can choose from several display arrangements to order the windows most effectively.

Resize a window

1 Click the Maximize button to make the window take up the entire screen.

2 Click the Minimize button to represent the window as a button on the taskbar.

3 Click the Restore button to return the window to its previous size.

4 Drag the left or right border of the window to resize it horizontally.

5 Drag the top or bottom border of the window to resize it vertically.

6 Drag a corner to resize the window both horizontally and vertically.

7 Drag the window's title bar to change its position.

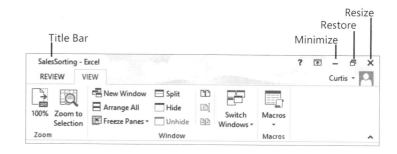

TIP The Maximize and Restore buttons are actually two states of the same "window size" button, so you never see them on a window at the same time.

Zooming in or out on a worksheet

If you are not satisfied with how much of your worksheet you can see, you can make the worksheet larger or smaller without changing the window size. When you zoom out on a worksheet, you can see the overall layout, but it might be difficult to read the data in individual cells. To get a better look at the data in your cells, you can zoom in on your worksheet.

Zoom in or out

1 Click the Zoom In control to make your window's contents 10 percent larger per click.

2 Click the Zoom Out control to make your window's contents 10 percent smaller per click.

3 Drag the Zoom slider control to the left to zoom out or to the right to zoom in.

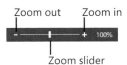

Zoom out Zoom in

Zoom slider

Zoom in or out to a custom zoom level

1 Click the View tab.

2 Click Zoom.

3 Select the Custom option.

4 Type a new zoom level in the Custom field.

5 Click OK.

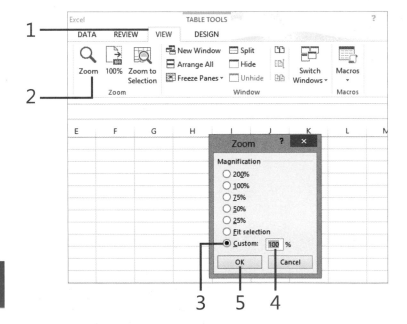

 TIP The maximum zoom level is 400 percent; the minimum zoom level is 10 percent.

Saving Excel workbooks

There's nothing more frustrating than losing a few minutes or even hours of work because you forget to save your file. When you close your workbook, Excel checks to see whether it has changed since the last time you saved it. If it has been changed, you're asked whether you want to save your workbook before you close it. If you want to save multiple versions of the same workbook, you can create a copy of your file by saving it with a different name.

Save a workbook

1 Click the Save button on the Quick Access toolbar.

Save a workbook with a new name

1 Click the File tab.

2 Click Save As.

3 Click Computer.

4 Click Browse.

(continued on next page)

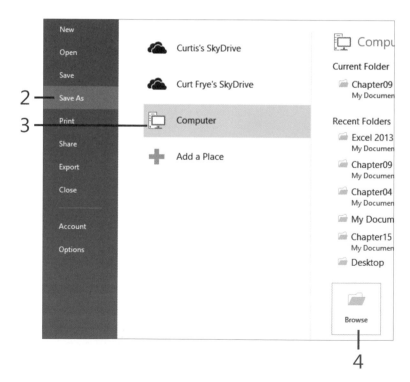

Save a workbook with a new name *(continued)*

5 Navigate to the directory where you want to save your file.

6 Type a new file name.

7 Click Save.

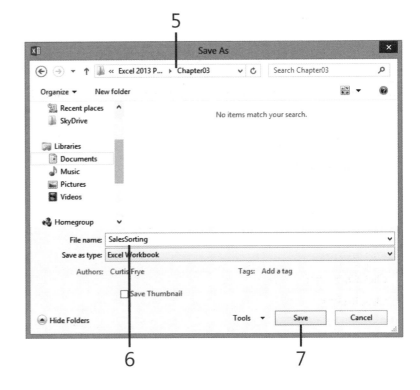

Changing the default file folder

When you display the Open, Save, and Save As dialog boxes in Excel, the program opens to its default folder, which is usually your Documents folder. If you frequently open workbooks that are saved in folders other than Documents, you can change the folder that Excel displays by default.

Change the default file folder

1 Click the File tab.

2 Click Options.

3 Click Save in the Excel Options dialog box.

4 In the Default Local File Location box, type the path for the folder that you want to appear by default.

5 Click OK.

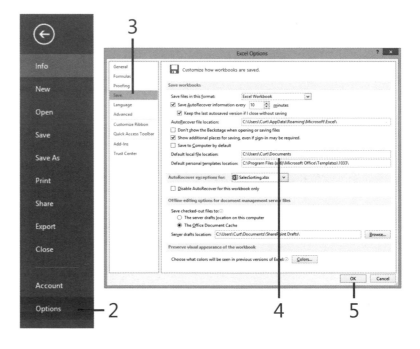

Closing workbooks and exiting Excel

When you're done working with an Excel workbook, you can close it to reduce the clutter on your desktop and the amount of memory that your computer uses to manage its programs.

You can also exit the Excel program when you've completed your work and are ready to move on to other tasks.

Close a workbook

1 Click the File tab.

2 Click Close.

3 If a dialog box appears asking whether you want to save any unsaved changes, you can do any of the following:

a Click Save to save the workbook using the same name and location.

b Click Don't Save to discard all the changes made since the workbook was last saved.

c Click Cancel to return to the workbook.

Exit Excel

1 Click the Close button at the top-right corner of the program window.

Using the Excel Help system

If you need to get help for using Excel, you can look in a number of places. One option is to right-click an object (such as a worksheet or a graphic) to see a list of things that you can do with the object. You can also open the Excel Help files and browse through them to find the answer to a specific question or just to explore.

Get Microsoft Excel Help

1 Click the Microsoft Excel Help button.

Get suggested commands from shortcut menus

1 Right-click any Excel object to see the shortcut menu of commands.

2 Click a command.

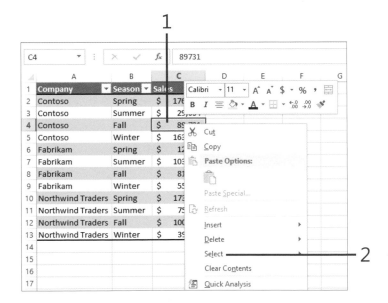

Finding Excel Help on the web

The Excel Help system extends well beyond the files installed with your program. There are a multitude of helpful resources on the web, which you can search for from within the Excel Help system.

Get help on the web

1 Click the Microsoft Office Excel Help button.

2 Type your search terms.

3 Click the Search button.

4 Browse the topics displayed for help and resources.

TIP You can visit the Microsoft Office Online site directly by opening your web browser and typing **office.microsoft.com/** in the address box. You can find numerous links to help and how-to files on that page.

Searching for a workbook

When you work in Excel for a while, it's likely that you'll create lots of workbooks and save them in many different places. If you don't know the exact name of the file that you want to open or its location, but you do know part of its name or some of the data it contains, you can search for the file and open it after you locate it.

Search for a workbook

1 Press Windows+C to display the charms.

2 Click Search.

3 Click Files.

4 Type a search term.

5 Click the file that you want to open.

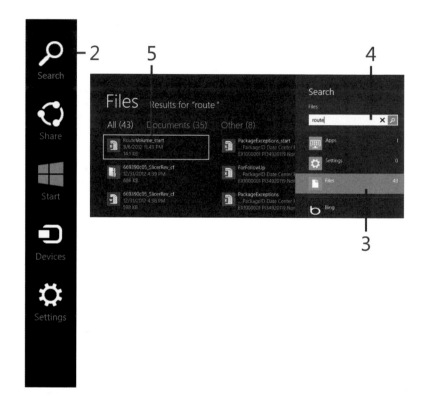

Building a workbook

4

One of the real strengths of Microsoft Excel 2013 is that the program makes it easy for you to enter large quantities of data. When you type text, Excel remembers what you entered in previous cells in the same column and offers to complete the current entry for you. The good news is that you need to type *Arkadelphia* only once. After the first time, typing the first few letters gives Excel enough information to guess the city's name. Entering a series of numbers, dates, or days also goes quickly and smoothly. If you want to enter a long series of numbers, dates, or even weekdays, you can type one or two values and have Excel fill in the remaining values in the series! These techniques, combined with formatting and other skills you'll learn elsewhere in this book, make data entry nearly painless.

In this section:

- Understanding how Excel interprets data entry
- Navigating the worksheet and selecting cells
- Entering text, numbers, dates, and times in cells
- Entering data using fills, Flash Fill, and other shortcuts
- Creating an Excel table
- Editing cell contents and inserting symbols into a cell
- Creating hyperlinks
- Cutting, copying, pasting, finding, and replacing cell values
- Undoing or redoing an action
- Checking the spelling in your worksheet

Selecting cells

Whenever you make changes to cells in a worksheet, you can save time by applying the changes to similar cells at the same time. In Excel 2013, you can select groups of cells that aren't even next to each other. If your worksheet stores dates in cells with other information in cells in between, you can select all the date cells and apply a format to them at the same time.

Select a contiguous group of cells

1 In the group that you want to select, drag from the upper-left cell to the lower-right cell.

Select a noncontiguous group of cells

1 Drag from the upper-left cell you want to select to the lower-right cell to select the first set of cells.

2 Hold down the Ctrl key, and drag to select another set of cells.

Select rows or columns

1. Click the header for the first row or column you want to select.

2. Hold down the Shift key, and click the header for the last row or column you want to select.

	B	C	D	E	F	G	H	I
			Day					
	VehicleID	Monday	Tuesday	Wednesday	Thursday	Friday	Saturday	
	V101	159	144	124	108	125	165	
	V102	113	106	111	116	119	97	
	V103	87	154	124	128	111	100	
	V104	137	100	158	96	127	158	
	V105	86	132	154	97	154	165	
	V106	159	163	155	101	89	160	
	V107	111	165	155	92	91	94	
	V108	101	162	123	87	93	140	
	V109	164	159	116	97	149	120	
	V110	100	107	143	144	152	132	

1 2 Column header

Select noncontiguous rows or columns

1. Click the header of the first row or column you want to select, hold down the Ctrl key, and click the headers of the other rows or columns.

1

	A	B	C	D	E	F	G	H
1								
2			Day					
3		VehicleID	Monday	Tuesday	Wednesday	Thursday	Friday	Saturday
4		V101	159	144	124	108	125	165
5		V102	113	106	111	116	119	97
6		V103	87	154	124	128	111	100
7		V104	137	100	158	96	127	158
8		V105	86	132	154	97	154	165
9		V106	159	163	155	101	89	160
10		V107	111	165	155	92	91	94
11		V108	101	162	123	87	93	140
12		V109	164	159	116	97	149	120

 TIP To cancel the selection of a group of cells, rows, or columns, click any cell in the worksheet.

Entering text in cells

No workbook worthy of the name stays empty for long. You can type any sort of text you want directly in a cell, whether the text is a label identifying the data in a row or column or an explanation reminding you and your colleagues of any limitations on the data to be entered in a cell. Most text entered in Excel workbooks is short enough to fit on one line, but if you want to have the text in a cell appear on two or more lines and break at a specific location, you can easily insert a line break.

Enter text as one line

1 Click the cell in which you want to enter text.

2 Type the text that you want to appear.

3 Press Enter.

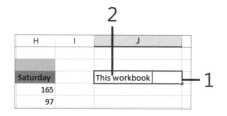

Enter text with forced line breaks

1 Click the cell in which you want to enter text.

2 Type the text that you want to appear on the first line. Press Alt+Enter to insert a line break.

3 Type the text that you want to appear on the second line, and then press Enter.

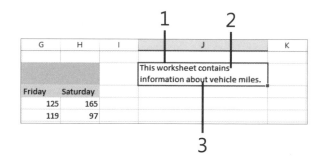

> **TIP** In Excel 2013, the formula bar doesn't automatically expand to display all the information in a cell. To scroll through the contents of the formula bar one line at a time, use the scroll buttons at the right edge of the formula bar. To display the formula bar's entire contents, click the Expand Formula Bar control to the right of the formula bar. When you expand the formula bar, the Expand Formula Bar control changes to the Collapse Formula Bar control; clicking it returns the formula bar to its original one-line height.

> **SEE ALSO** For information about how to make your columns wider to allow more text to appear within a cell, see "Resize a column" on page 160.

Entering numbers in cells

The backbone of any workbook is the numerical data in its worksheets, whether that data reflects sales, employee salaries, or the quantity of a given product that you have in inventory. Entering numbers in Excel is as simple as clicking the cell and typing, but you can also enter very large or very small numbers using scientific notation. In scientific notation, a number with a positive exponent is written as 1.00E+06, which is read as "one times ten to the sixth power." Numbers that are less than one can be written with negative exponents. For example, the number .001 would be written as 1.00E-03 and read as "one times ten to the negative third power."

Enter numbers

1 Click the cell in which you want to enter a number.

2 Type a numerical value.

3 Press Enter.

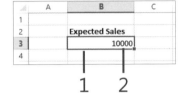

Enter numbers using scientific notation and exponents

1 Click the cell in which you want to enter a number.

2 Type the base number you want.

3 Type **E**.

4 Type the exponent you want.

5 Press Enter.

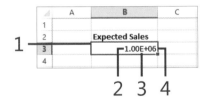

> **TIP**   You can type a number but have it interpreted as a text value by typing ' (an apostrophe) before the number value. The apostrophe will not appear in the cell, but a green icon will appear in the corner of the cell; clicking the cell exposes formatting options you can apply to the data.

> **SEE ALSO**   For information about applying number formatting such as dollar and percent signs instead of typing them, see "Formatting cells containing numbers" on page 126.

Entering dates and times in cells

Dates are extremely important in any business or personal situation, so Excel takes care to get them right. Excel understands dates no matter how you type them, so feel free to type them as needed. You can always change the formatting later.

Enter a date

1 Click the cell in which you want to enter a date.

2 Type the month, day, and year, with each number separated by a slash (/) or a hyphen (-).

3 Press Enter.

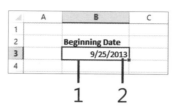

Enter a time

1 Click the cell in which you want to enter a time.

2 Type the hour, a colon (:), and the minutes. Press the spacebar, and type **a** or **p** for A.M. or P.M.

3 Press Enter.

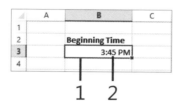

> ⚠ **CAUTION** Your regional settings affect which entries Excel interprets as dates. In countries that represent dates using the Day/Month/Year format, 9/25/2013 would be interpreted as a text entry because there are only 12 months in a year.

Enter a date and time

1 Click the cell in which you want to enter a date and time.

2 Type a date, press the spacebar, and then type a time.

3 Press Enter.

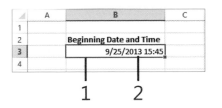

Enter the current date and time

1 Click the cell in which you want to enter the current date and time.

2 Type **=NOW()**.

3 Press Enter.

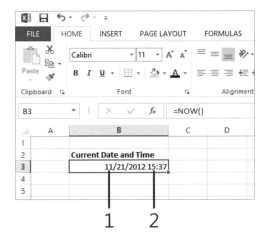

TIP You can enter the current date by pressing Ctrl-; and the current time by pressing Ctrl-Shift-;. These values are entered as static values and won't change when Excel recalculates the worksheet where they're entered.

CAUTION Different countries have different customs for writing dates. For example, 07/04/13 could mean July 4, 2013, or April 7, 2013, depending on where you live.

Entering data using fills

Entering a long series of data, such as the days in the month, weekdays, or a series of numbers with a definite progression, is tedious. As you type or paste the data, it's easy to forget which months have 31 days or on which day of the week the first of a month falls. Excel makes entering such series simple: Using

AutoFill, you can type a label or value in one cell and assign it to many other cells; type labels or values in two or more cells and have Excel extend the series based on the relationship of the cell entries; or even extend dates by a day, a month, or a year.

Fill data using AutoFill

1 Type the label or value that you want to appear in multiple cells.

2 Drag the Fill handle down or across the cells you want to fill.

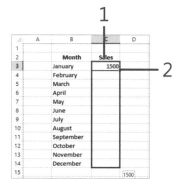

TRY THIS Type **1/1/2013** in cell A1 and then drag the Fill handle across the cells you want to fill. Excel fills your cells by increasing the day for every entry. Now click the AutoFill Options button that appears, and click Fill Years.

TIP If you hold down the Ctrl key as you drag the Fill handle, Excel changes how it fills in your series. For example, if dragging the Fill handle would normally copy a single value into the cells that you drag over, dragging while holding down the Ctrl key causes the value to increment (for example, dragging the Fill handle of a cell that contains the value "1" increments the value to 2, then 3, and so on).

Use AutoFill to enter a series of values

1 Type the first label or value for your list.

2 Type the second label or value for your list.

3 Select the two cells.

4 Drag the Fill handle to the cell containing the last label or value in the series.

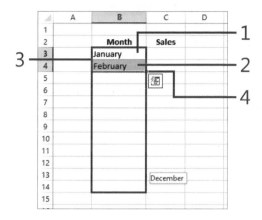

Entering data by using Flash Fill

Your worksheet might contain a list of names where the first name, middle initial, and last name all appear in the same cell. If you need to separate the first name, middle initial, and last name into separate cells, you can do so using Flash Fill, which is new in Excel 2013.

To use Flash Fill, click a cell to the right of the list that contains the data you want to work with and then type the correct value for that cell. For example, your list might contain the name Mark

Hassall. If you want to store the person's first name in one cell and last name in another, you would type **Mark** in the first cell and **Hassall** in the second. You then repeat the process for the second row of the list, at which point Flash Fill recognizes the data pattern and offers to fill in the remaining values.

If your data set contains rows with additional data, such as a middle initial, you can correct the first example of that differing pattern to update similar rows in the new columns.

Combine data by using Flash Fill

1 Click the cell to the right of the first row you want to work with.

2 Type the combined value for the row's data in the active cell, and press Enter.

3 In the cell directly below the first, start typing the combined value for the row.

4 Press Enter to accept the suggested Flash Fill values for the remaining rows.

5 If necessary, click a cell to the right of a row that contains data with a different pattern.

6 Type the combined value for that row's data in the active cell, and press Enter.

✓ **TIP** Start Flash Fill by typing a target value for a row that contains the simplest data pattern, such as a row with just a first and last name. Then you can create a pattern for more complex rows, such as those that also have a middle initial.

Separate data by using Flash Fill

1 Click the cell to the right of the first row you want to work with.

2 Type the value you want to extract from the row, and press Enter.

3 In the cell directly below the first, start typing the extracted value for the row.

4 Press Enter to accept the suggested Flash Fill values for the remaining rows.

5 If desired, repeat the process in the cell to the right of the first cell in the new column to extract another value from the row's original data.

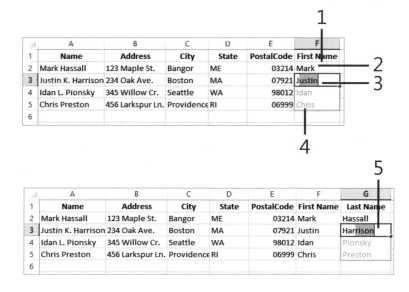

Entering data with other shortcuts

Excel gives you lots of ways to enter data quickly. The less time you spend typing data, the more time you have to analyze and make decisions based on what the data tells you. One way Excel offers to help you enter data is to recognize whether the first few characters of the text that you're typing matches text from another cell in the same column; if the text matches, Excel offers to complete the rest of that text. If it's the text that you want, you can accept it and move on. If not, just keep typing.

A similar way Excel simplifies data entry is by letting you pick the value for the active cell from a list of existing values in a column. This technique is not that important for a small worksheet, but when you're working with page after page of data, seeing a sorted list of possible values is a real help.

Enter data with AutoComplete

1 Type the beginning of an entry.

2 Press Tab to accept the AutoComplete value.

	A	B	C	D	E	F
1						
2		Customer	Month	Category	Amount	
3		Fabrikam	January	Ground	$ 14,501.98	
4		Fabrikam	January	3Day	$ 3,501.75	
5		Fabrikam	January	2Day	$ 5,599.10	
6		Fabrikam	January	Overnight	$ 35,907.82	
7		Fabrikam	January	Priority Overnight	$ 17,333.25	
8		Fabrikam				
9						

— 1

Pick data from a list

1 Right-click a cell in a column with existing values and then click Pick From Drop-Down List from the shortcut menu.

2 Click the item in the list you want to enter.

> ⚠ **CAUTION** AutoComplete works only if the text or data you are entering is similar to text already in the same column.

> ✓ **TIP** You can also display the Pick From Drop-Down List items by selecting the cell in which you want to enter the value and pressing Alt+Down arrow.

	A	B	C	D	E	F
1						
2		Customer	Month	Category	Amount	
3		Fabrikam	January	Ground	$ 14,501.98	
4		Fabrikam	January	3Day	$ 3,501.75	
5		Fabrikam	January	2Day	$ 5,599.10	
6		Fabrikam	January	Overnight	$ 35,907.82	
7		Fabrikam	January	Priority Overnight	$ 17,333.25	
8		Fabrikam	February			
9				2Day		
10				3Day		
				Ground		
11				Overnight		
				Priority Overnight		
12						

— 1

— 2

Understanding how Excel interprets data entry

Excel makes it easy for you to enter data in a worksheet by guessing the type of data you're entering and applying the appropriate formatting to that data. It's important to remember that because Excel is a computer program, it has some limitations. For example, Excel performs calculations by using decimal values, such as .5, rather than fractions, such as ½; however, if you do want to express some of your data as fractions and not as decimal values, you can do so by changing the cell's format to Fraction. In either case, you can save the data in your preferred format.

Another aspect of this bias toward decimal values is that entering dates and times is much easier than it would be if you had to type out a full date, such as February 3, 2013. For example, if you have U.S. regional settings and type 2/3 in a cell and press Enter, Excel recognizes the text as an abbreviation for the third day of the month of February and displays the data as 3-Feb. In the U.K. and other regions where the day is entered first, 2/3 is interpreted as 2-Mar.

You can choose the format you want for dates and times by selecting the cells that will hold dates or times, clicking the Home tab on the ribbon, and then clicking the Number dialog box launcher to display the Number tab of the Format Cells dialog box. Inside the dialog box, click Date in the list of categories. The available date formats appear on the right. From there, just click the format you want, and click OK.

Selecting a number format changes the way data is displayed in a cell but doesn't affect the underlying value. For example, if you want a numerical value in a cell to appear as a fraction, such as representing 0.5 as ½, click the Number tab, click the Fraction category, specify the type of fraction on the right, and click OK.

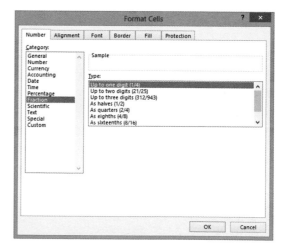

Creating an Excel table

One popular way to maintain data in Excel is by creating a data list. A list describes one type of object, such as orders, sales, or contact information. Structurally, a list consists of a header row, which contains labels describing the data in each column, and data rows, which contain data about a particular instance of the list's subject. For example, if you use a list to store your customer's contact information, you could have a separate column for the customer's first name, last name, street address, city, state, postal code, and telephone number. Each row in a list would contain a particular customer's information.

In Excel 2013, you can store your data lists in an Excel table. An Excel table is an object that you can refer to in your formulas and use to summarize your data.

Create an Excel table

1 Type your table headers in a single row.

2 Type your first data row directly below the header row.

3 Click any cell in the range in which you want to create a table.

4 On the Home tab, click Format As Table.

5 Click the table style to use.

6 Verify that Excel identified the data range correctly.

7 If your table has headers, select the My Table Has Headers check box.

8 Click OK.

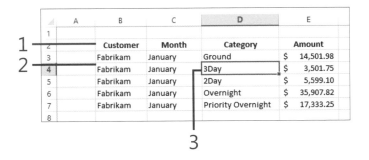

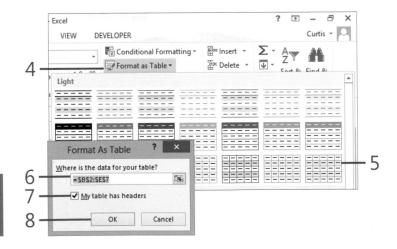

> **TIP** You can display the Create Table dialog box by clicking any cell in an existing cell range and pressing Ctrl+L. If you click OK, Excel 2013 creates an Excel table using the default Excel table style.

Add data to an Excel table

1 Click the cell at the lower-right corner of the Excel table, and press Tab to create a new table row.

2 As an alternative to step 1, type data in the cell below the lower-left corner of the Excel table, and press Tab. Excel makes the new row part of the Excel table.

Next row   Bottom row

TRY THIS Display an Excel table that takes up more than one screen vertically, and scroll down the workbook page. When the table's header row reaches the top of the screen, it freezes in place, but the data rows continue scrolling. Now you don't have to remember which column is which; the labels are right there!

Editing an Excel Table

When you create an Excel table, you design it with the best structure to store your data. If the data you want to store in your Excel table changes, you can resize the table to fit your new collection.

If you'd like to copy an entire column of data from an Excel table, you can do so by positioning the mouse pointer over the column's header. When the mouse pointer changes to a downward-pointing black arrow, click the left mouse button to select the column. You can then press Ctrl+C to copy the data and paste it elsewhere in your workbook.

Rename an Excel table

1 Click any cell in the Excel table.

2 On the ribbon, under Table Tools, click the Design tab.

3 In the Properties group, type a new name for your Excel table, and press Enter.

Resize an Excel table

1 Drag the resize handle at the lower-right corner of the Excel table to add or remove table rows or columns.

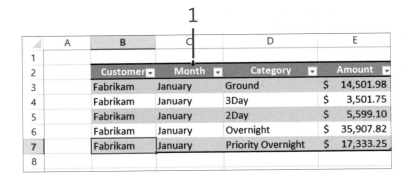

Select an Excel table column

1 Position the mouse pointer over the header cell of an Excel table column. When the pointer changes to a downward-pointing black arrow, click the header of the column that you want to select.

⚠ **CAUTION** Be sure not to click the filter arrow at the right edge of an Excel table's column header; doing so displays the column's filter options, which, although useful, don't enable you to select the entire column.

Editing cell contents

You're not stuck with the first data you enter in a cell. In fact, you can change the value completely, delete it, or update it to reflect a supplier's new business name or a customer's new address. You also are not stuck with only one way to edit the data; you can edit the data either in the formula bar or directly in the cell.

Edit cell contents in the formula bar

1 Click the cell that you want to edit.

2 Select the text that you want to edit in the formula bar.

3 Type the new text, and press Enter.

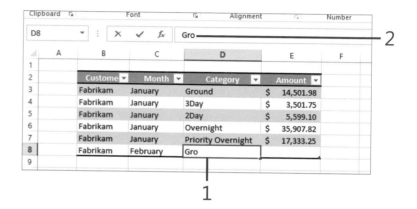

Edit cell contents directly in the cell

1 Double-click the cell that you want to edit.

2 Select the text that you want to edit.

3 Type the new text, and press Enter.

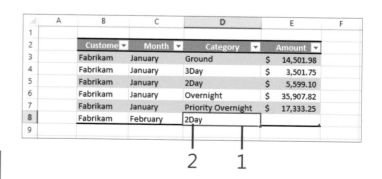

> **TIP** If you double-click a cell but cannot edit its contents, another user might have turned off this option. To turn on in-cell editing, click the File tab, and click Options. In the Excel Options dialog box, click Advanced to display the Advanced page of the dialog box. In the Editing Options group, select the Allow Editing Directly In Cells check box, and click OK.

> **TIP** If you're editing a cell and decide you don't want to keep your edits, press the Esc key to return the cell to its previous state.

Inserting a symbol in a cell

Not every bit of information can be communicated effectively by using text. If your worksheet is meant for public consumption and you mention another company's products, you might want to include a trademark (™) or another symbol to recognize that company's intellectual property. Excel—and the other Office programs—have lots of symbols that you can use. If you use a symbol in the course of your everyday business, you can probably find it in Excel.

Add a symbol to a cell

1 Click the Insert tab.

2 Click Symbols.

3 Click Symbol.

4 Click the Font down arrow.

5 Select the font from which you want to pick the symbol.

6 Click the symbol that you want to insert.

7 Click Insert.

8 Click Close.

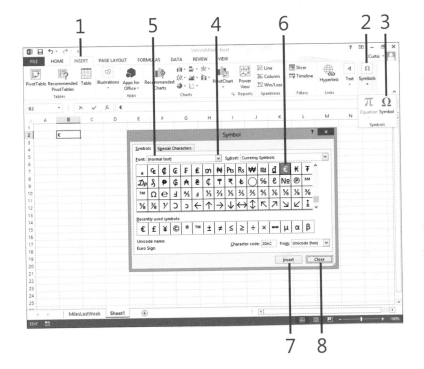

TIP If you want to insert more than one symbol consecutively (in the same cell), click the first symbol, click the Insert button, click the next symbol, click the Insert button again, and so on. When you're done inserting symbols, click the Close button.

Creating hyperlinks

One of the hallmarks of the World Wide Web is that documents published on the web can have references, or hyperlinks, to points in the same document or to other web documents. One great way to take advantage of this feature is to create a workbook in which you track sales by product and have a cell at the end of each product's row with a hyperlink to in-depth product information. That information could be on another worksheet in the same workbook, in another file on your computer, or in a file on another computer.

Add a hyperlink to files

1 Click the cell where you want to place a hyperlink.

2 Click the Insert tab.

3 Click Hyperlink.

4 Click Place In This Document.

5 Click the element to which you want to link.

6 Type the cell reference of the cell to which you want to link.

7 Type a short phrase to describe the hyperlink's target.

8 Click OK.

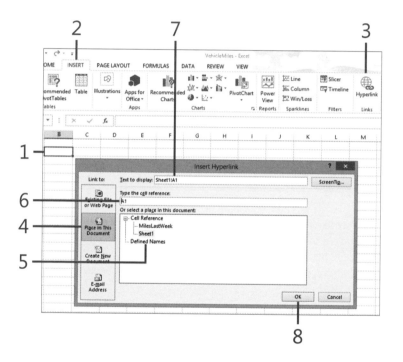

 TIP Excel 2013 also enables you to create links to any named ranges or Excel tables in your workbook.

Add a hyperlink to another file

1 Click the cell in which you want to place a hyperlink.

2 Click the Insert tab.

3 Click Hyperlink.

4 Click Existing File Or Web Page.

5 Click Current Folder.

6 Click the file to which you want to link.

7 Type a short phrase to describe the hyperlink's target.

8 Click OK.

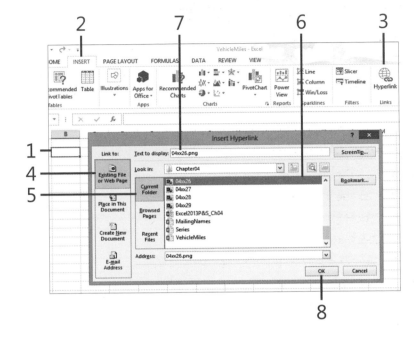

TIP You can view recently used files by clicking Recent Files in the Look In pane.

Creating hyperlinks to web and email resources

Many home businesses and larger organizations make information available on websites. If your workbook references products, services, or other information that's available on a web page, you can create a hyperlink to that information. You can also create a mailto hyperlink, which, when clicked, lets you send an email message to the address referred to in the link.

Add a hyperlink to a webpage

1 Click the cell in which you want to place a hyperlink.

2 Click the Insert tab.

3 Click Hyperlink.

4 Click Existing File Or Web Page.

5 Click Browsed Pages.

6 Click the webpage to which you want to link.

7 Type a short phrase to describe the hyperlink's target.

8 Click OK.

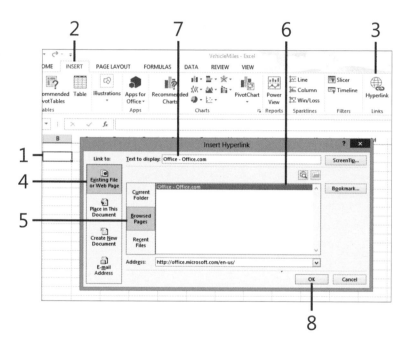

 CAUTION When you click Browsed Pages, the Insert Hyperlink dialog box displays all the web pages you visited recently.

Add a mailto hyperlink

1 Click the cell in which you want to place a hyperlink.

2 Click the Insert tab.

3 Click Hyperlink.

4 Click E-Mail Address.

5 Type the email address to which you want to link.

6 Type text describing the hyperlink.

7 Type a default subject for the email message.

8 Click OK.

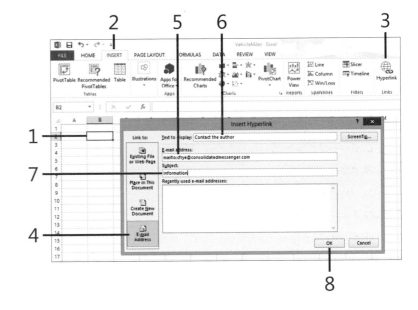

TIP You can type just the target email address in the E-mail Address field. Excel adds the mailto: prefix for you.

Cutting, copying, and pasting cell values

After you enter values in one or more cells, you can copy the values and paste them into another cell, remove the values from the cells and paste them elsewhere, or just cut the values and leave them on the Clipboard. Excel 2013 lets you control how the pasted values appear in your worksheet. When you click the Paste button's down arrow, you can hover your mouse

pointer over any of the icons to display a live preview of how the pasted data will appear if you select that paste formatting option. Pointing to another icon displays the result of selecting that paste option, and clicking an icon pastes your copied items using the icon's paste options.

Cut a cell value

1 Select the cells that you want to cut.

2 Click the Home tab.

3 In the Clipboard group, click the Cut button.

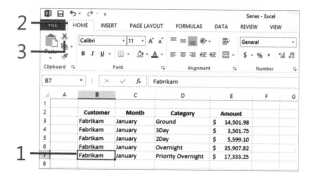

Copy a cell value

1 Select the cells that you want to copy.

2 Click the Home tab.

3 In the Clipboard group, click the Copy button.

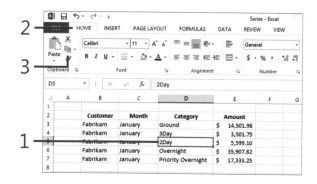

Undoing or redoing an action

One of the strengths of Excel is how easily it lets you change the formatting, layout, and structure of your workbooks. However, sometimes you might not have made the exact change that you wanted. If that's the case and you haven't closed the workbook since you made the change you want to get rid of, you can easily undo your changes by clicking the Undo button on the Quick Access Toolbar. Excel keeps a record of your changes, which you can see by clicking the down arrow at the right edge of the Undo button. When you reverse a change by clicking the Undo button, Excel displays the Redo button. Clicking the Redo button, as you might expect, reapplies the last change you undid. If you have made a change but haven't clicked the Undo button, Excel displays the Repeat button, which you can click to apply the last change to a new selection.

Undo or redo an action

1 Click the Undo button.

2 Alternatively, click the Redo button.

Undo   Redo

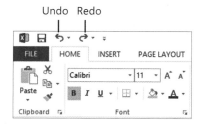

Pasting values with more control

When you cut or copy cells, you write a copy of the cells' contents and formatting to the Clipboard. When you paste the cells back into a worksheet, Excel pastes the values, formulas, and formatting associated with the cells. However, you're not limited to such simple pasting behavior; you can choose to paste just the cell's formula, just a formula's result, paste everything except the cells' borders, or even paste an image of the item, which you can click to display the item you copied.

Table 4-1 lists the advanced paste options you can use.

Paste values with more control

1 Cut or copy a value.

2 Click the cell into which you want to paste your values.

3 Click the Home tab.

4 In the Clipboard group, click the Paste button's down arrow.

5 Select the action that you want to take.

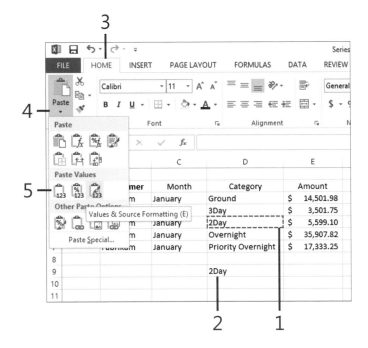

Table 4-1   Paste special options

Option	Action
Paste	Performs the standard paste operation.
Formulas	Pastes the formulas from the cells you copied.
Formulas & Number Formatting	Pastes the formulas and number formatting from the cells you copied.
Keep Source Formatting	Pastes the contents of the cells you copied and retains the copied cells' formatting.
Keep Source Column Widths	Pastes the contents of the cells you copied and makes the columns into which you paste the copied data the same width as the source columns.
Values	If the copied cell contains a formula, pastes the result of the formula into the target cell.
Values & Number Formatting	If the copied cell contains a formula, pastes the result of the formula and the cell's number formatting into the target cell.
Values & Source Formatting	If the copied cell contains a formula, pastes the result of the formula and the cell's formatting into the target cell.
Formatting	Pastes the copied cell's formatting into the target cell.
No Borders	Pastes the contents of the copied cells without including any borders drawn around the cells.
Transpose	Exchanges the rows and columns of the copied data.
Paste Link	Creates a link to the copied item; does not create a new copy of the item.
Paste Special	Displays the Paste Special dialog box.
Paste As Hyperlink	Pastes a text hyperlink to the copied item.
Linked Picture	Pastes an image that, when clicked, activates a hyperlink to the copied item.
Picture	Pastes an image of the copied item's appearance (for example, pasting a picture of a chart doesn't create a new chart).
Copy As Picture	Copies an image of the selected item's appearance to the Clipboard.

Clearing cell contents

If you're lucky, you won't have to replace the data and formatting you've entered in a workbook; however, there might be times when you want to clear the data, formatting, or contents of a group of cells. Clearing is like cutting, but clearing differs because you have the option to leave the formatting in the cell from which you remove the data. When you cut a cell's contents, Excel removes the cell's contents and formatting.

Clear a cell

1 Select the cell that you want to clear.

2 Click the Home tab.

3 In the Editing group, click the Clear button.

4 Select the type of clearing that you want.

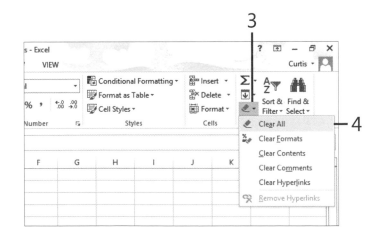

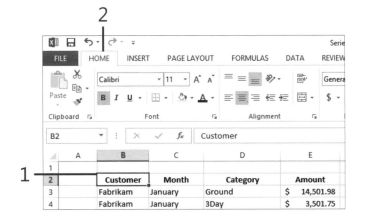

TIP If all you want to do is clear the cell contents, click the cell that you want to clear and then press Delete.

Navigating the worksheet

Using the mouse and keyboard, you can move from cell to cell in a worksheet, move up or down a page at a time, or move to the first or last cell in a row. Table 4-2 lists the keyboard shortcuts you can use in addition to the scroll bars and sheet tabs that you use with your mouse.

Table 4-2 Worksheet navigation keyboard shortcuts

Key	Action
Left arrow	Move one cell left.
Right arrow	Move one cell right.
Up arrow	Move one cell up.
Down arrow	Move one cell down.
Enter	Move one cell down.
Tab	Move one cell to the right.
Ctrl+Home	Move to cell A1.
Ctrl+End	Move to the last used cell in the worksheet.
Page Up	Move up one page.
Page Down	Move down one page.
Ctrl+arrow key	Move to the next cell with data in the direction of the arrow key. If there is not another cell with data in that direction, you move to the last cell in the worksheet in that direction.

Using the Office Clipboard

When you work in Excel, you can take advantage of the flexibility that comes with its place in the Office suite by using the Office Clipboard. The Office Clipboard keeps track of the last 24 items you've cut or copied from any Office document. You can open the Office Clipboard and then paste any of its contents into your workbook. If an item that you know you won't use again resides on the Office Clipboard, you can always remove it.

Display the contents of the Office Clipboard

1 Click the Home tab.

2 Click the Clipboard dialog box launcher.

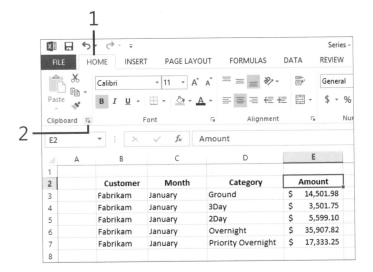

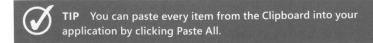
TIP You can paste every item from the Clipboard into your application by clicking Paste All.

Paste an item from the Office Clipboard

1 Click the cell into which you want to paste a Clipboard item.

2 Click the down arrow next to the Clipboard item that you want to paste.

3 Click Paste.

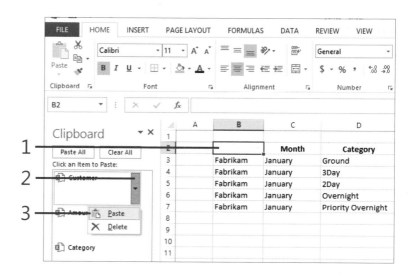

Clear an item from the Office Clipboard

1 Point to the Clipboard item that you want to delete.

2 Click the down arrow that appears next to the item.

3 Click Delete.

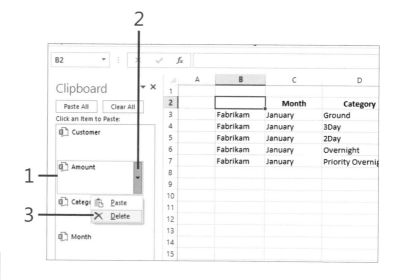

 TIP You can remove all entries from the Office Clipboard by clicking Clear All.

Finding and replacing text

After you enter data into a workbook, you might need to search the document for a particular word or, if one of your suppliers changes the name of a product, replace some or all instances of a word or phrase. You can do that by using the Find and Replace features in Excel.

Find a word or value

1 Click the Home tab.

2 In the Editing group, click Find & Select.

3 Click Find.

4 Type the text you want to find.

5 Click Find Next.

6 Click Close.

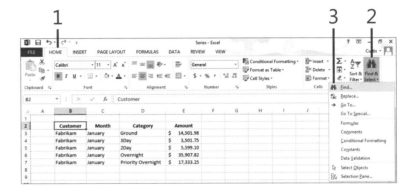

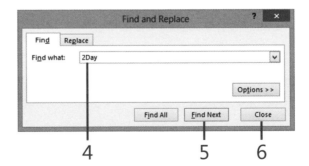

Replace a word or value

1 Click the Home tab.

2 In the Editing group, click Find & Select.

3 Click Replace.

4 Type the text that you want to replace.

5 Type the text that you want to take the place of the existing text.

6 Click Find Next, and then click the associated button in the Find And Replace dialog box to perform any of the following actions:

   a Click Replace to replace the text.

   b Click Find Next to skip this instance of the text and move to the next time it occurs.

   c Click Replace All to replace every instance of the text.

7 Click Close.

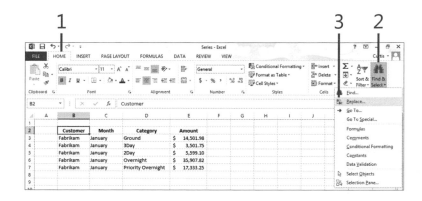

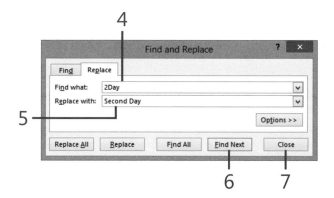

> ⚠️ **CAUTION** Clicking Replace All is a quick way to change every occurrence of one value to another value, but it can also have unintended consequences. For example, changing "ear" to "bear" would change "hearing" to "hbearing." It's much safer to use Find Next and verify each change.

Checking the spelling in your worksheet

After you create a workbook and fill it with data, labels, and explanatory text, you should always use the Excel spelling checker to check your text for misspellings. If Excel finds a word it doesn't recognize, the spelling checker asks you whether it's correct and might suggest alternatives. You can have Excel ignore a word once or for the entire document, choose one of the program's suggestions, or even add new words to the dictionary. Products are often given unique names, so adding them to the dictionary that Excel uses to check all documents can save you a lot of time.

Check spelling

1 Click the Review tab.

2 In the Proofing group, click Spelling. If you are asked whether you want to save your work, do so.

3 Follow any of these steps:

a Click Ignore Once to ignore the current misspelling.

b Click Ignore All to ignore all instances of the misspelled word.

c Click Add To Dictionary to add the current word to the dictionary.

d Click AutoCorrect to create an AutoCorrect entry that replaces the misspelled word with the word highlighted in the Suggestions list.

e Click the correct spelling, and then click Change to replace the current misspelling with the correct word.

f Click the correct spelling, and then click Change All to replace all instances of the current misspelling with the correct word.

g Click Cancel to stop checking spelling.

4 Click OK to clear the dialog box that appears after the spelling check is complete.

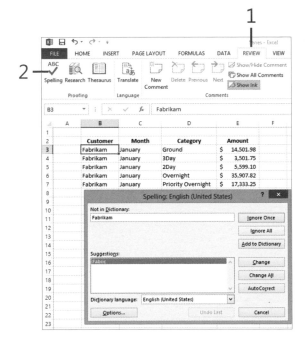

> **TIP** If you don't start checking spelling with cell A1 selected, Excel checks spelling to the end of the worksheet and then displays a dialog box asking whether you want to continue checking from the beginning of the worksheet. Click Yes to continue.

Managing and viewing worksheets

5

After you build your workbook, you can reorganize it as needed. If you use data in a specific worksheet often, you can move the worksheet to the front of the workbook. Similarly, if you often switch between two worksheets, you can put their sheet tabs next to each other so that you don't have to spend as much time moving from one worksheet to the other. Another way that you can save time is to enter the same data or apply the same formatting to multiple cells in several worksheets at the same time.

Finally, you can change how Excel displays your data in a workbook. If you have a series of headings in the first row of a worksheet, they don't have to disappear when you scroll down. Instead, you can have Excel freeze the rows at the top of the screen and then you can scroll down as far as you want without losing your guides at the top.

In this section:

- Viewing and selecting worksheets
- Renaming worksheets
- Moving and copying worksheets within a workbook or between workbooks
- Inserting and deleting worksheets
- Inserting and deleting columns, rows, and cells
- Hiding and unhiding columns and rows
- Freezing worksheet rows and columns
- Splitting a worksheet into independent areas
- Saving custom worksheet views

Viewing and selecting worksheets

Every Excel workbook should hold data on a given subject, such as products you carry, your customers, or your sales. By the same token, every page, or worksheet, in a workbook should store part of the workbook's data. One way to divide your data is by time. For example, if you track your sales by the hour, you could easily fit a month's worth of data in a worksheet; at most, you would need 31 rows to cover every day and, if your store is open around the clock, 24 columns to take care of the hours. You can view individual worksheets quickly, and it's simple to work with more than one worksheet at a time.

Select multiple worksheets

1 Click the sheet tab of the first worksheet that you want to select.

2 Hold down the Ctrl key, and click the sheet tabs of additional worksheets that you want to select.

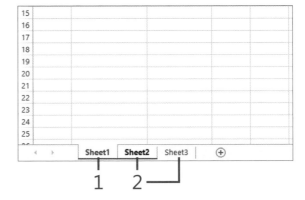

Renaming worksheets

When you create a workbook, Excel includes a worksheet named Sheet1. If you add worksheets, they are named Sheet2, Sheet3, and so on. Those names are fine when you first create a workbook, but after you add data to several worksheets, naming the sheet tabs helps you and your colleagues find the data that you're looking for. As always, if you think of a better name for your worksheets or want to change the name of a worksheet temporarily to make it stand out, you can rename a worksheet any time that you want.

Change the name of a worksheet

1 Double-click the sheet tab of the worksheet that you want to rename.

2 Type the new name of the worksheet, and press Enter.

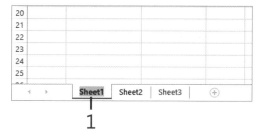

Moving worksheets

Business needs change—the data that was so important yesterday might be of only passing significance today. In fact, if a new customer sends a big order your way, you might spend most of your time adding to and reading from a worksheet that you haven't looked at more than twice in the previous month. If that worksheet is at the back of your workbook, you can move it to the front to make it easier to find in the workbook. Or, if you keep every other worksheet relating to that customer in a separate workbook, you can move the worksheet from its current spot to its rightful place in the other workbook.

Move worksheets within the workbook

1 Drag the sheet tab of the worksheet that you want to move.

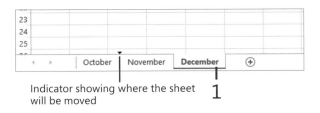

Indicator showing where the sheet will be moved

Move worksheets to another workbook

1 Open the workbook that will receive the worksheets.

2 Switch to the workbook that contains the worksheets that you want to move, hold down the Ctrl key, and click the sheet tabs of the worksheets that you want to move.

3 Right-click the selection.

4 Choose Move Or Copy from the shortcut menu.

5 Click the To Book down arrow.

6 Click the workbook to which you want to move the worksheets.

7 Click OK.

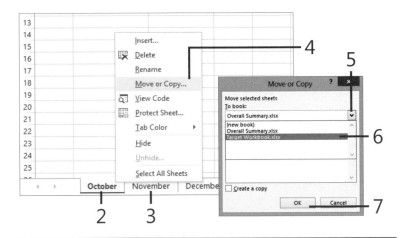

> **TIP** If you want to position a worksheet last in a workbook, right-click the worksheet that you want to move, choose Move Or Copy from the shortcut menu, click Move To End, and click OK.

> **TIP** If the destination workbook has a different Office theme applied to it, selecting the Match Destination Theme check box causes the copied worksheet to take on the target workbook's formatting.

Copying worksheets

After you finish adding data to a worksheet—such as at the end of a calendar month, when you create a new worksheet to store data for the next month—you might want to include the entire worksheet as part of a monthly overview presentation to your general manager. Rather than keep all the worksheets in their original workbooks and flip from document to document when you create your presentation, you can copy the worksheet from the current workbook (and any other worksheets with data that you want to include) to a central document. Going from worksheet to worksheet is much easier than going from workbook to workbook!

Copy worksheets within the workbook

1 Hold down the Ctrl key, and drag the worksheet that you want to copy to the new location.

Copy worksheets to another workbook

1 Open the workbook that will receive the new worksheets.

2 Switch to the workbook that contains the worksheets that you want to copy, hold down the Ctrl key, and click the sheet tabs of the worksheets that you want to copy.

3 Right-click the selection.

4 Choose Move Or Copy from the shortcut menu.

5 Select the Create A Copy check box.

6 Click the To Book down arrow.

7 Click the workbook to which you want to copy the worksheet(s).

8 Click OK.

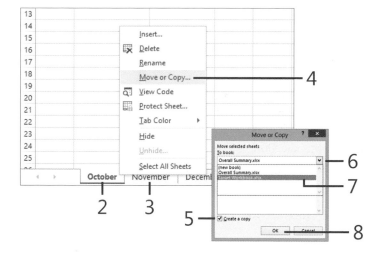

 TIP Select the New Book option from the To Book list to copy the selected worksheet or worksheets to a new workbook.

⚠ **CAUTION** If you don't hold down the Ctrl key while you drag the sheet tab of the worksheet that you want to copy, you just move the worksheet to a new location in the workbook.

Inserting and deleting worksheets

If you haven't changed Excel from the way it was installed, any workbooks that you create will contain one worksheet. One worksheet provides plenty of room if you're working at home and is perhaps all you need for small projects, but you'll run out of space quickly if you're tracking products or monthly sales. Adding or deleting a worksheet takes just a moment, but if you want to delete a worksheet, be sure you're getting rid of the right one!

Insert a blank worksheet

1 Right-click the sheet tab of the worksheet that follows the location where you want to insert a worksheet.

2 Choose Insert from the shortcut menu.

3 Double-click Worksheet.

TIP If you want to insert a worksheet at the end of the workbook, click the New Sheet, which looks like a plus sign in a circle, at the right edge of the tab bar.

Delete one or more worksheets

1 Hold down the Ctrl key, and click the sheet tabs of the worksheets that you want to delete.

2 Right-click the selection.

3 Choose Delete from the shortcut menu.

4 Click Delete to confirm that you want to delete the worksheets.

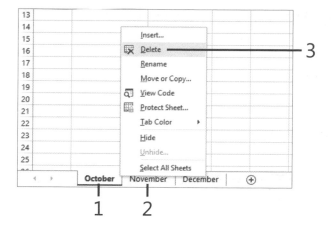

⚠ **CAUTION**   If you have data in the worksheet that you want to delete, deleting the worksheet erases all the data in that worksheet. This operation is not reversible.

Hiding or showing a worksheet

If you build a workbook that contains a lot of worksheets, you might find it easier to navigate the workbook if you can't see the sheet tabs of the worksheets that you're not using. You can hide the sheet tabs of worksheets so that they don't appear in the Excel window, reducing clutter and letting you find the worksheets that you are using, with no trouble.

Hide a worksheet

1 Hold down the Ctrl key, and click the sheet tabs of the worksheets that you want to hide.

2 Right-click any selected worksheet tab and then choose Hide.

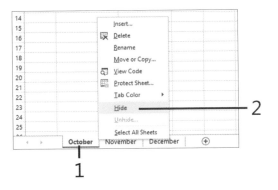

Unhide a hidden worksheet

1 Right-click any worksheet tab.

2 Click Unhide.

3 Click the worksheet that you want to unhide.

4 Click OK.

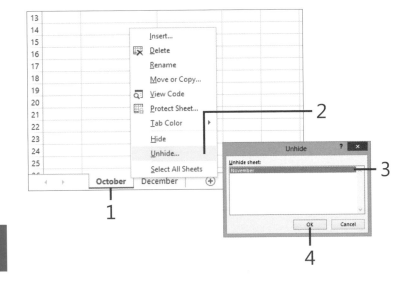

 TIP After you unhide a worksheet, Excel displays that worksheet immediately.

Changing worksheet tab colors

A great way to make any worksheet element stand out is to change it to a color that contrasts with the other colors used in the worksheet. In Excel, you can change the color of sheet tabs. For example, you can change the color of a sheet tab in a workbook in which you track sales for a year with a worksheet for each month. Rather than move the current worksheet to the front of the list, which would put the worksheets out of order, you can change the color of the sheet tab to make it stand out. When the month ends, you can remove the color from that sheet tab and apply it to the new month's sheet tab.

Color a sheet tab

1 Hold down the Ctrl key, and click the sheet tabs that you want to color.

2 Right-click the selection, and point to Tab Color on the shortcut menu.

3 Select the color that you want.

 TIP If you don't see the tab color you want in the Tab Color palette, click More Colors to display the Colors dialog box.

Inserting, moving, and deleting cells

There's very little that's more frustrating than creating a large worksheet and discovering that you forgot to enter data in a few cells. If you're new to Excel, you might be tempted to cut the existing cells and paste them a few cells below their current location to make room for the new data. But that's too much like work; there's an easier way to insert a few cells to give you

the room that you need. Similarly, it's not that difficult to move a group of cells to a new location in your worksheet or to delete a group of cells that contains data that you entered by accident. After you insert or delete cells, you can choose how to move existing cells to make room for the new cells or to fill in the space left by the deleted cells.

Inserting cells in a worksheet

1 Select the cells in the spot where you want to insert new cells.

2 Click the Home tab.

3 In the Cells group, click the Insert button's down arrow.

4 Click Insert Cells.

5 Select the option button representing how you want to move the existing cells to make room for the inserted cells.

6 Click OK.

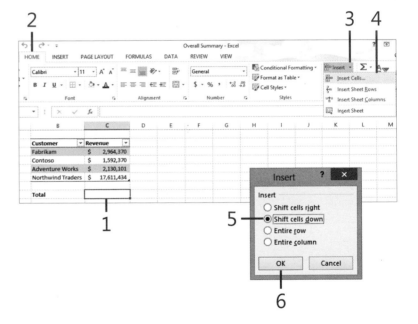

Move cells in a worksheet

1 Select the cells that you want to move.

2 Move the mouse pointer over the outline of the selected cells.

3 Drag the cells to the new location.

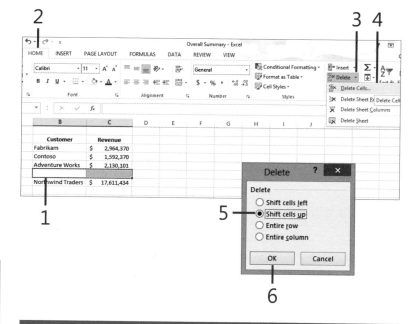

Delete cells in a worksheet

1 Select the cells that you want to delete.

2 Click the Home tab.

3 In the Cells group, click the Delete button's down arrow.

4 Click Delete Cells.

5 Select the option button representing how you want the remaining cells to fill in the deleted space.

6 Click OK.

⚠ **CAUTION** Because Excel doesn't highlight an entire row or column when you click a single cell, it is possible to be a bit inaccurate if you attempt to delete a row or column by clicking a cell and then clicking the Entire Row or Entire Column option in the Delete dialog box. It's better to follow the procedure listed in the following section, where you click the row or column header so that you can see the entire row or column to be deleted.

✓ **TIP** As you drag the cells in the worksheet, Excel displays an outline where the cells would go when you release the mouse button.

Inserting, moving, and deleting cells: Delete cells in a worksheet **83**

Inserting columns and rows

After you create a worksheet and begin filling in your data, you might decide to insert a row or column to add data that you didn't think to include when you started. For example, a customer might want to add a product to an order. To accommodate this new data, you can insert a blank row below the last row in their existing order and add the new item there.

There might be times when you no longer need to use a particular row or column. Whether you placed an extra column to add some white space between the main body of data and a summary calculation or a row holds the contact information of a customer who asked to be removed from your list, you can delete the row or column quickly and easily. Or, if you want to change a column or row's position, you can move a group of columns or rows to another location in the worksheet.

Insert a row in a worksheet

1 Right-click the row header below where you want the new row to appear.

2 Choose Insert from the shortcut menu.

Insert a column in a worksheet

1 Right-click the column header to the right of where you want the new column to appear.

2 Choose Insert from the shortcut menu.

> **TIP** If you want to insert more than one row or column at a time, select the number of adjacent rows or columns equal to the number that you want to insert and then choose the appropriate command from the Insert menu.

Setting insert options

When you insert columns or rows into a worksheet, Excel checks the rows above and below or the columns to the left and right of the insertion for any formatting that you've applied to those rows or columns. If it finds any formatting, Excel displays the Insert Options action button, which you can click to apply the same formatting to the inserted rows or columns.

Set insert options

1 After inserting rows or columns, click the Insert Options button.

2 Select the type of formatting that you want the new cells to have.

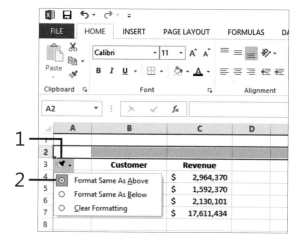

 TIP The Insert Options button appears only if the cells above or below the insertion point have special formatting.

Deleting rows or columns

Rows and columns serve definite purposes in worksheets, so there might be times when you no longer need to use a particular row or column. Whether you placed an extra column to add some white space between the main body of data and a summary calculation or a row holds the contact information of a customer who asked to be removed from your list, you can delete the row or column quickly and easily.

Delete rows or columns

1 Select the rows or columns that you want to delete.

2 Right-click a header in the selection, and choose Delete from the shortcut menu.

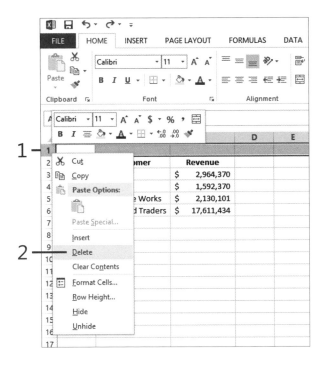

> ⚠ **CAUTION** Formulas that reference cells in the columns or rows that you delete will no longer work. The Error action tells you that there is an Invalid Cell Reference Error and gives you options to fix the problem. #REF! appears in the damaged cell.

Moving rows or columns

No matter how carefully you design your worksheets, you might need to rearrange its contents by repositioning rows and columns without deleting their data. Moving rows and columns is a lot like cutting and pasting cells or cell values—you just need to know how to select the elements you want to move.

Move one or more rows

1 Select the rows that you want to move.

2 Click the Home tab.

3 Click the Cut button.

4 Click the first cell in the row where you want the rows to be moved.

5 Click Paste.

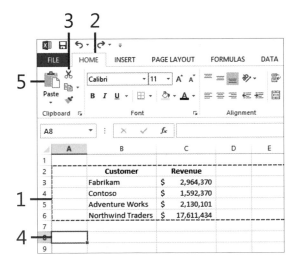

Move one or more columns

1 Select the columns that you want to move.

2 Click the Home tab.

3 Click the Cut button.

4 Click the first cell in the column where you want to move the columns.

5 Click Paste.

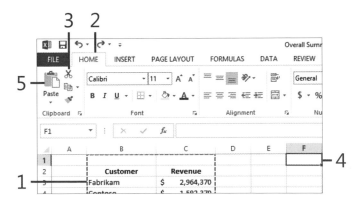

Hiding and unhiding columns and rows

If you're working with a worksheet that contains lots of data, you might need to refer to the contents of rows or columns that aren't close enough on the worksheet to appear on the same screen. Rather than scroll back and forth to access the data that you need, you can hide any intervening rows or columns so that everything that you need to see is displayed on the screen at the same time. The rows or columns that you hide are gone only temporarily. The data hasn't been deleted; it's just been moved out of your way while you don't need it.

Hide rows or columns

1 Select the rows or columns that you want to hide.

2 Right-click a row or column header in the selection, and choose Hide from the shortcut menu.

Unhide rows or columns

1 Click the row or column header of the row above or the column to the left of the rows or columns you want to unhide.

2 Hold down the Shift key, and click the row or column header of the row below or the column to the right of the rows or columns you want to unhide.

3 Right-click the selection, and choose Unhide from the shortcut menu.

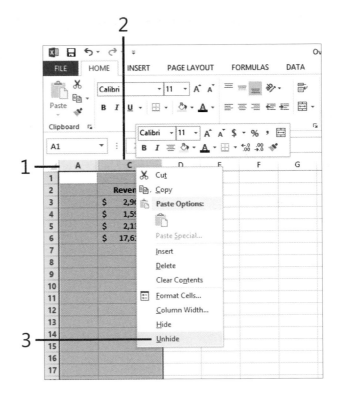

TIP There are two ways that you can tell that hidden rows or columns are in a worksheet. First, whenever rows or columns are hidden, row numbers or column letters are missing. For example, if rows 2, 3, and 4 are hidden, the first two visible rows of the worksheet are labeled row 1 and row 5. The other way you can tell that a worksheet contains hidden rows or columns is by the thick line that appears on the border of the row header or column header where the rows or columns would otherwise appear.

Entering data and formatting on many worksheets at the same time

After you work with Excel for a while, you'll probably develop standard worksheets that you use over and over. When working with worksheets that follow a common layout, you might want to enter a set of data across multiple worksheets. For example, you might have a set of column headers that you want to appear on several worksheets, and you would like to

avoid creating them from scratch for each individual worksheet. In Excel 2013, you can save lots of time by entering data and formatting in equivalent blocks of cells on multiple worksheets. If you have existing data that you want to paste into several worksheets at the same time, you can do that as well.

Enter and format data on several worksheets at one time

1 Hold down the Ctrl key, and click the sheet tabs of the worksheets that you want to edit.

2 Select the cell or cells in which you want to enter the data.

3 Type the data that you want to appear in the same cell or cells on the worksheets that you selected.

4 Right-click the selected cells.

5 Using the Mini toolbar, specify the formatting options that you want.

6 Press Enter.

7 Click the sheet tab of any unselected worksheet.

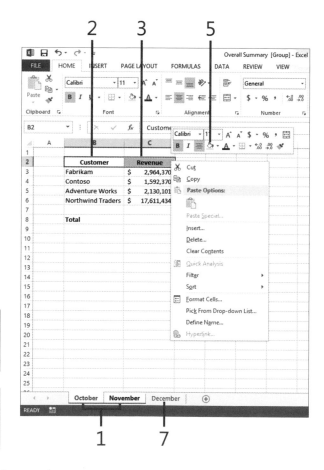

> **→ TRY THIS** To format your cells by using controls that aren't available on the Mini toolbar, right-click the cell(s) and choose Format Cells to display the Format Cells dialog box.

> **✓ TIP** If you select all of your workbook's worksheets, you can ungroup them by right-clicking any selected worksheet's sheet tab and then clicking Ungroup Sheets.

Copy cells from one worksheet to a group of worksheets

1 Click the Home tab.

2 Select the cells that you want to copy.

3 Click the Copy button.

4 Hold down the Ctrl key, and click the sheet tabs of the worksheets that you want to receive the copied data.

5 Click the cell that you want to receive the data.

6 Click Paste.

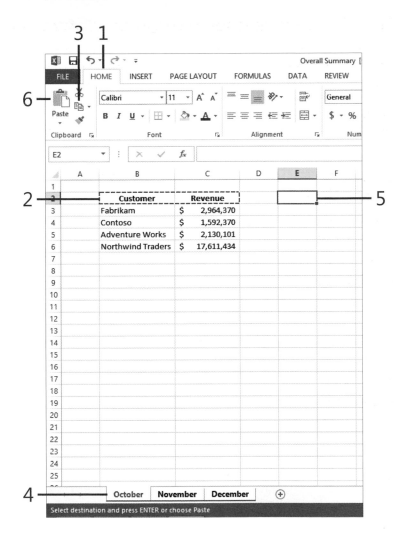

Changing how you look at Excel workbooks

When you're examining your Excel data to make a business decision, you might need to look at data from more than one worksheet or even from more than one workbook. Hourly sales totals can help determine when you need more staff on the floor, but if you keep track of the number of customers in the store as well, you might find that your great sales on Monday mornings come from landscape architects loading up for the week. In that case, you would be better off having your warehouse staff and not your counter clerks show up to handle the load.

You can open more than one workbook at a time and arrange them on the screen so that you can read data from both sources at the same time. You can do something similar if you have relevant data in two parts of the same worksheet. If you can't see everything you need to see, you can split the worksheet into two or four units, all with independent scroll bars.

View different parts of one worksheet at the same time

1 Click the cell where you want to split the worksheet.

2 Click the View tab.

3 In the Window group, click Split.

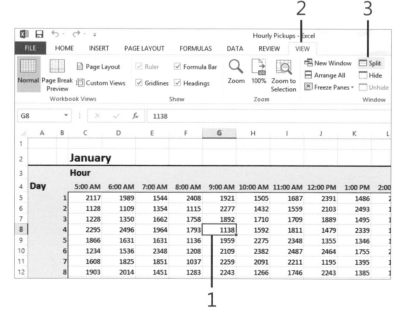

TIP To remove a worksheet split, click the View tab and then, in the Window group, click Split.

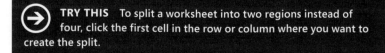

TRY THIS To split a worksheet into two regions instead of four, click the first cell in the row or column where you want to create the split.

View multiple workbooks at the same time

1 Open all the workbooks that you want to view.

2 Click the View tab.

3 Click Arrange All.

4 Select the option representing the target arrangement.

5 Click OK.

> ⚠ **CAUTION**   All the workbooks will be arranged like this unless you select the Windows Of Active Workbook check box, which applies the arrangement only to the active workbook.

View multiple parts of a worksheet by freezing panes

1 Click the cell below and to the right of where you want to freeze the worksheet.

2 Click the View tab.

3 In the Window group, click Freeze Panes.

4 Click one of the following items:

   a Freeze Panes, which keeps the cells above or to the left of the current selection visible at all times

   b Freeze Top Row, which keeps the top row visible at all times

   c Freeze First Column, which keeps the leftmost column visible at all times

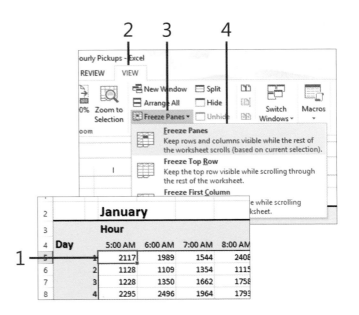

Naming and using worksheet views

After you set up your Excel worksheets so that you can read them effectively, you don't need to re-create the arrangement every time you run Excel. Instead, you can record the arrangement—which includes splits, frozen rows and columns, and hidden cells—in a view. Views are especially handy for worksheets that are used by different people, all of whom need different information. Different views can be created for each person, so if the data that one person views spans many columns, you can set the print settings to Landscape mode for that view.

Name the current view of the worksheet

1 Arrange your Excel window as you would like it to appear.

2 Click the View tab.

3 In the Views group, click Custom Views.

4 Click Add.

5 Type the name of the view.

6 Select what you want to include in the view.

7 Click OK.

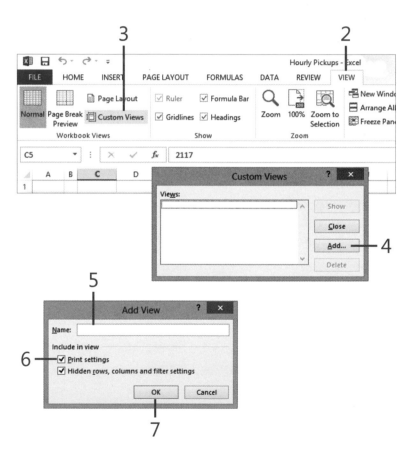

Switch to another view of the worksheet

1 Click the View tab.

2 Click Custom Views.

3 Click the view that you want.

4 Click Show.

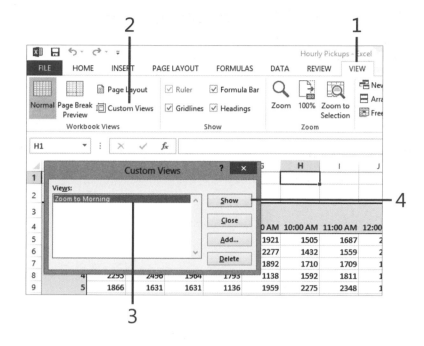

Using formulas and functions

6

Microsoft Excel 2013 workbooks let you do much more than simply store and organize your data. One important task that you can perform in Excel is to summarize the values in related cells. Whether those cells represent the sales for a day at your store, the returns from your personal investments, or your times in bicycle races, you can find the total or average of the values, identify the minimum or maximum value in a group, or perform dozens of other calculations on your data. Many times you can't access the information that you want without referencing more than one cell; it's also often true that you'll use the data in the same group of cells in more than one calculation. Excel makes it easy to reference a number of cells at once, letting you build your calculations quickly.

In this section:

- Understanding formulas and cell references in Excel
- Creating and editing formulas
- Creating, editing, and deleting named ranges
- Using named ranges in formulas
- Summarizing the values in groups of cells
- Creating formulas that reference cells in other workbooks
- Analyzing data using the Quick Analysis Lens
- Summing with subtotals and grand totals
- Exploring the Excel function library
- Creating conditional functions
- Exploring new functions in Excel 2013

Creating simple cell formulas

Building calculations in Excel is pretty straightforward. If you want to find the sum of the values in two cells, you just type an equal sign (=), the reference of the first cell, a plus sign (+), and the reference of the second cell. The formula that you enter appears on the formula bar, where you can examine and edit it.

Build a formula

1 Click the cell in which you want to enter a formula.

2 Type =.

3 Type the expression representing the calculation that you want to perform.

4 Press Enter.

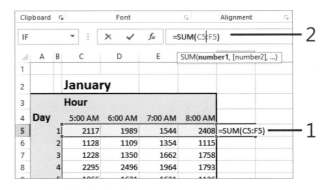

Edit a formula

1 Click the cell that you want to edit.

2 Select the part of the formula that you want to edit in the formula bar.

3 Make any changes that you want.

4 Press Enter.

TRY THIS Click the Excel Help button. Then, in the Excel Help dialog box, type common formulas in the Search box, press Enter, and click Examples Of Commonly Used Formulas in the list of available topics. The Help file that appears has quite a few examples of formulas that you might want to create.

CAUTION Be sure that there's no space before the equal sign in your formula. If there is, Excel interprets the cell's contents as text, not as a formula.

Understanding formulas and cell references in Excel

When you build a formula, you need to identify the worksheet cells that provide the values for the formula and the operations that you want to perform on those values. To identify a cell, you give its cell a reference. The first cell in the first column is cell A1, meaning column A, row 1. If you examine a formula, you sometimes see a cell reference written as $A$1, rather than just A1. The difference is that cell references written with the dollar signs are absolute references, meaning that the reference doesn't change when the formula is copied to another cell. Cell references written without the dollar signs are relative references, which do change when the formula with the reference is copied to another cell.

The benefit of relative references is that you can write a formula once, copy it to as many other cells as you like, and have Excel update the formulas to reflect the new cells. For example, consider the worksheet in the following figure, which tracks the number of hourly package pickups for a month.

The cells in column P contain formulas that calculate the sum of the hourly pickup values in column C through column O. The formula in cell P5, =SUM(C5:O5), finds the sum of cells in row 5, corresponding to January 1. When you copy the formula from cell P5 to cell P6, the formula changes to =SUM(C6:O6). Excel notices that you copied the formula to a new row and assumes that you want the formula to work on that data. Had you written the formula as =SUM($C$5:$O$5), however, Excel would notice that the formula used absolute references and would copy the formula as =SUM($C$5:$O$5).

If you want to reference a value from a cell in another workbook, you can do that. Excel uses 3D references, which means that any cell in any workbook can be described by three pieces of information: the name of the workbook, the name of the worksheet, and the cell reference.

Here's the reference for cell Q38 on the January worksheet in the Y2013ByMonth workbook:

[Y2013ByMonth.xlsx]January!$Q$38

The good news is that you don't need to remember how to create these references yourself. If you want to use a cell from another workbook in a formula, all that you need to do is click the cell where you want to use the value, start the formula, and then click the cell in the other workbook. Excel fills in the reference for you.

	=SUM(C5:O5)										
	H	I	J	K	L	M	N	O		P
0 AM	10:00 AM	11:00 AM	12:00 PM	1:00 PM	2:00 PM	3:00 PM	4:00 PM	5:00 PM		
1921	1505	1687	2391	1486	2075	1626	1326	1612		23,687
2277	1432	1559	2103	2493	1317	1519	1836	1439		20,681
1892	1710	1709	1889	1495	1405	1513	1493	1997		21,101
1138	1592	1811	1479	2339	1839	2416	1838	1403		24,403
1959	2275	2348	1355	1346	1947	2098	1163	1410		22,165
2109	2382	2487	2464	1755	2086	1261	1989	2338		25,197
2259	2091	2211	1195	1395	1727	1171	1753	1029		21,152
2243	1266	1746	2243	1385	1414	1675	2274	1765		22,662
1942	1639	2018	2468	2247	2493	1827	2261	1861		26,294
2278	1044	1936	1233	1677	1988	1690	1649	1784		21,266
2434	2181	1721	2235	1534	1407	1187	1581	2355		21,915
2426	1514	1526	1086	1478	1943	1028	1988	1892		22,061
1459	1703	1706	2083	2305	2348	1662	2218	2257		25,764
1164	2115	1469	1629	2398	1970	1665	1343	1471		22,357

Assigning names to groups of cells

When you work with large amounts of data, it's easy to lose track of which cells contain which data. In addition, it can be difficult to locate data in workbooks that you didn't create. Although you might always store product prices in one worksheet column, there's no guarantee that your colleagues will follow the same pattern! One way to prevent confusion is to define a named range for any cell group that holds specific information. For example, in a worksheet with customer order data, you can define the Totals named range to represent the cells in which the total for each order is stored. After you define the named range, you can display its contents, rename it, or delete it.

Create a named range

1 Select the cells that you want to name.

2 Click the Name Box on the formula bar.

3 Type the name that you want for the range.

4 Press Enter.

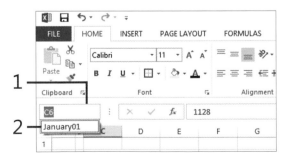

Go to a named range

1 Click the Name Box down arrow.

2 Click the range to which you want to go.

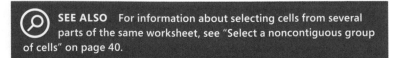

SEE ALSO For information about selecting cells from several parts of the same worksheet, see "Select a noncontiguous group of cells" on page 40.

Delete a named range

1 Click the Formulas tab.

2 Click Name Manager.

3 Click the named range that you want to delete.

4 Click Delete.

5 Click OK to clear the confirmation dialog box that appears.

6 Click Close.

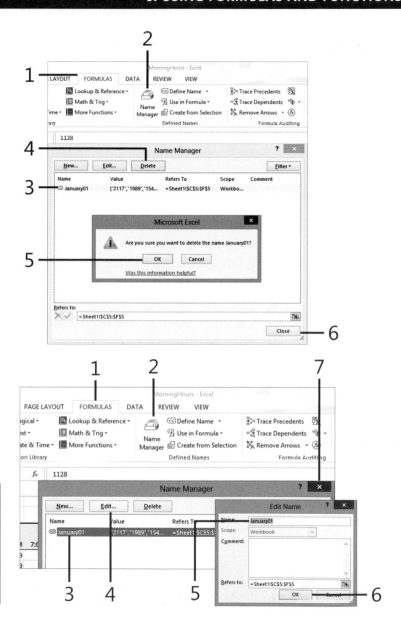

Rename a named range

1 Click the Formulas tab.

2 Click Name Manager.

3 Click the named range that you want to rename.

4 Click Edit.

5 Type a new name for the range.

6 Click OK.

7 Close the Name Manager dialog box.

> ⚠ **CAUTION** The name that you give your named range shouldn't duplicate a potential cell address. For example, typing DAY1 in a formula would reference cell DAY1. To avoid this problem, either ensure that your ranges have names that begin with at least four letters (the last column is XFD) or use an underscore to separate the letters from the rest of the name. The name DAY1 isn't valid, but the name DAY_1 is.

Using names in formulas

When you define a named range, you create a shortcut that you can use to refer to a group of cells. A great way to use named ranges is in formulas. Instead of entering the references of every cell that you want to use in your calculation, you can type the name of the range. When you reference named ranges in formulas, your formulas are shorter and easier to understand. Rather than seeing a series of cell references that you need to examine, you and your colleagues can rely on the named ranges to understand the goal of a calculation.

Excel 2013 further streamlines formula creation with Formula AutoComplete. Remember that when you start typing a value into a cell, Excel examines the previous values in that column and offers to let you complete the entry by pressing Tab or Enter. Now, when you start typing a named range's name into a formula, Excel recognizes that you might be entering a named range and displays a list of named ranges (as well as built-in functions) available in the active workbook. All you have to do is click the named range that you want, and it's included in the formula immediately.

Create a formula with a named range

1 Click the cell in which you want to enter a formula.

2 Type = followed by the formula that you want. When you want to use a range that has a name, start typing the name instead of the cell address.

3 Click the named range in the Formula AutoComplete list that appears.

4 Press Enter.

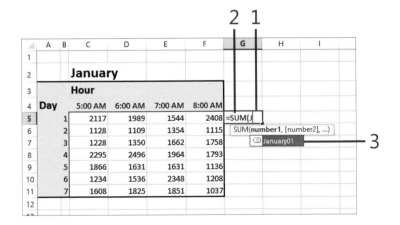

 TIP If you change the name of a range of cells, Excel automatically makes the name change in every one of your formulas.

Creating a formula that references values in an Excel table

In previous versions of Excel, it was a challenge to create named ranges that included an entire column in a data list. Suppose that you created a named range that encompassed the existing cells in a data column, such as the cell range A3:A44; if you added data to cell A45, you would need to change the cells in the named range's definition. Yes, there is a complicated way to create a dynamic named range in Excel 2003 and earlier versions, but you don't have to worry about it in Excel 2013. All you need to do is create an Excel table (as shown in "Creating an Excel table" on page 52) and select the headers of the columns that contain the data that you want to summarize in your formulas.

Create a formula with an Excel table reference

1 Click the cell in which you want to create the formula.

2 Type =, followed by the function to include in the formula and a left parenthesis; for example, =SUM(would be a valid way to start.

3 Type the name of the Excel table.

4 Type a left square bracket.

5 Click the name of the table column.

6 Type a right square bracket, a right parenthesis, and press Enter.

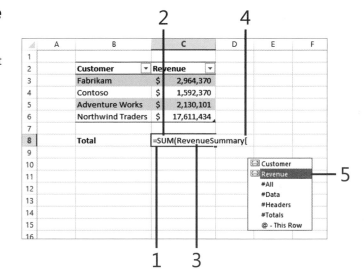

> **TIP** To include more than one table column in a formula, either hold down the Shift key, select the column header of the first column to use in the formula, and then click another column to select everything in the span between the two columns, or hold down the Ctrl key and click the other column headers that you want to use. Excel includes the references in the formula.

Creating formulas that reference cells in other workbooks

One of the strengths of Excel is that you aren't limited to using cells from the current workbook in your formulas. If you want, you can use data from any other workbook in your calculations. For example, you might have a workbook in which you track monthly advertising sales for your newsletter. If you want to create a new workbook to summarize all income and expenses for your publication, you can do so. By letting you create formulas that reference cells from more than one workbook, Excel makes it easy for you to organize your workbooks so that each workbook holds data about a specific subject. Not only can you find the data easily, you can reference it anywhere else.

After you create links between workbooks, you can have Excel update your calculation if the data in the linked cell changes. You can also change the cell to which you linked, or if the workbook with the cell to which you linked has been moved or deleted, you can delete the link and have Excel store the last value from the calculation.

Use cells from other workbooks in a formula

1 Open the workbook with the cell that you want to reference in your formula.

2 Display the workbook where you want to create the formula.

3 In the workbook cell where you want to create the formula, type = followed by the first part of the formula.

4 Click the View tab.

5 Click Switch Windows.

6 Click the name of the workbook with the cell that you want to include in the formula.

7 Select the cells with the values that you want to use in the formula.

8 Press Enter.

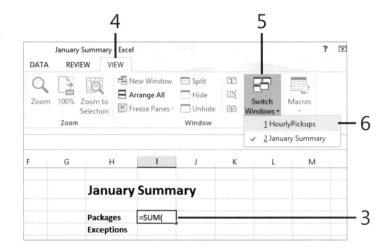

Break links to other workbooks and convert to values

1 Click the cell that contains the formula that you want to edit.

2 Select the part of the formula representing the link that you want to break.

3 Press F9.

4 Press Enter.

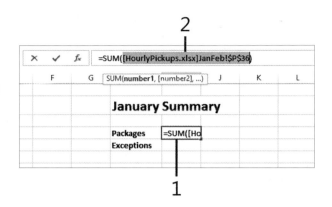

Refresh links

1 Click the Data tab.

2 In the Connections group, click Refresh All.

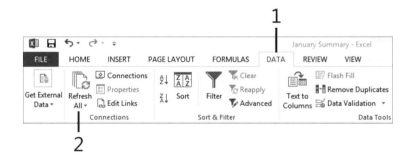

TIP You can use the techniques here to link to a cell on a different worksheet in the same workbook. Just create the formula, and when you want to put in the cell reference, move to the target worksheet and click the appropriate cell.

Changing links to different workbooks

If you create a link to a value in another workbook, you might find that the other workbook's structure changes. You can update the properties of a link by using the Edit Links dialog box, which you can open using the controls on the Data tab of the ribbon.

Change links to different workbooks

1 Click the Data tab.

2 In the Connections group, click Edit Links.

3 Click the link that you want to change.

4 Click Change Source.

5 Click the workbook with the new cell to which you want to link.

6 Click Open.

7 Select the sheet from which to update values.

8 Click OK.

9 Click Close.

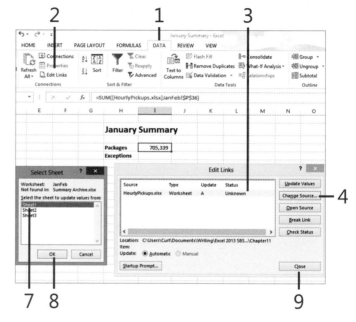

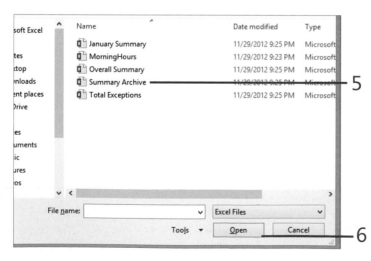

> **TIP** Under certain circumstances, such as when the new target workbook contains a single worksheet, the option to select a sheet might not appear.

Analyzing data by using the Quick Analysis lens

One of the refinements in Excel 2013 is the Quick Analysis lens, which brings the most commonly used formatting, charting, and summary tools into one convenient location. You have a wide range of tools available to you, including the ability to create an Excel table or PivotTable, insert a chart, or add conditional formatting. You can also add total columns and rows to your data range. For example, you can click Totals and then Running Total for columns, identified by the icon labeled Running Total and the yellow column at the right edge of the button, to add a column that calculates the running total for each row.

Summarize data by using Quick Analysis

1 Select the cell range that you want to summarize.

2 Click the Quick Analysis action button to display the Quick Analysis tools available to you.

3 Click the label representing the category of tools that you want to use.

4 Click the button representing the summary that you want to create.

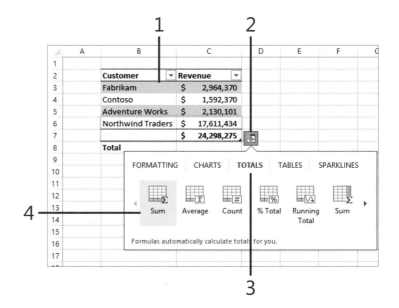

TIP You can add one summary column and one summary row to each data range. If you select a new summary column or row when one exists, Excel displays a confirmation dialog box to verify that you want to replace the existing summary. When you click Yes, Excel makes the change.

SEE ALSO For information about creating a chart by using the Quick Analysis lens, see Section 12, "Summarizing data visually using charts."

Summing a group of cells without using a formula

Sometimes, such as when you're entering data into a worksheet or you're curious to find out the sum or average of the values in a few cells, it's too much work to find a blank cell and write a formula to calculate the sum or average for the cells. Rather than make you create a separate formula, Excel counts the number of cells selected, calculates a running total and average

for the currently selected cells, and displays the results on the status bar. Finding the sum, average, and count of the values in the selected cells are the most commonly used operations, so Excel calculates those values by default. However, you can choose from several other operations, or you can even tell Excel not to calculate a running total for any selected cells.

Summarize data in a group of cells

1   Select the cells that you want to summarize to have the summary appear on the status bar.

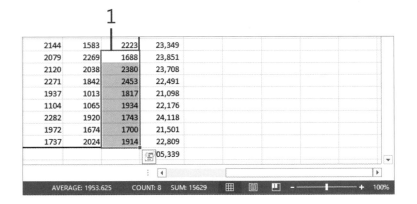

Find the total, average, or other values of cell data

1   Right-click the status bar, and choose the summary operations that you want from the shortcut menu.

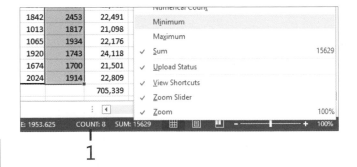

> **TIP**   Active summary operations are checked on the shortcut menu. Clicking a checked summary operation turns off that operation.

Creating a summary formula

After you enter data into a worksheet, you can create formulas to summarize the values and display the result of the calculation. You can summarize the values in a group of cells in many ways: You can find the total or average of the cell values, identify the maximum or minimum value in the group, or simply count the number of cells containing values. You can create these formulas by clicking the cell below or to the right of the cells that you want to summarize, displaying either the Home tab or the Formulas tab, and clicking the AutoSum button. (The button appears on both tabs.) Clicking the AutoSum button creates a SUM formula, which finds the arithmetic sum of the values, but you can choose other calculations by clicking the AutoSum button's down arrow. After you create the formula that you want, you can use the result in other calculations.

Create an AutoSum formula

1 Click the cell where you want the summary value to appear.

2 Click the Home tab.

3 Click the AutoSum down arrow.

4 Click the AutoSum function that you want to use.

5 If necessary, select the cells with the data that you want to summarize.

6 Press Enter.

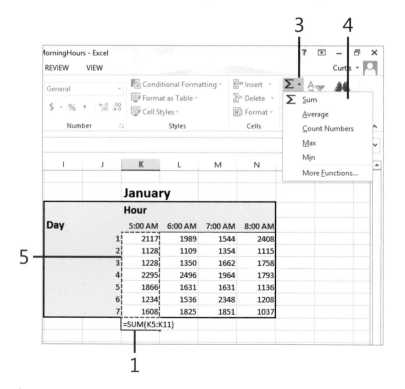

SEE ALSO   For information about finding a running total for a group of cells without creating a formula, see "Summing a group of cells without using a formula" on the previous page.

Summing with subtotals and grand totals

You frequently need to organize the data in an Excel worksheet by one or more criteria. For example, you might have a worksheet in which you list yearly sales for each product that you offer, with the products broken down by category. If your data is organized this way, you can have Excel calculate a subtotal for each category of products. When you create a subtotal, you identify the cells with the values to be calculated and the cells that identify the change from one category to the next. Excel updates the subtotal and grand total for you if the value of any cell changes.

Create a subtotal

1 Click any cell in the range that you want to subtotal.

2 Click the Data tab.

3 In the Outline group, click Subtotal.

4 Click the At Each Change In down arrow.

5 Click the value on which you want to base the subtotals.

6 Click the Use Function down arrow.

7 Click the subtotal function that you want to use.

8 Select which columns should have subtotals calculated.

9 Click OK.

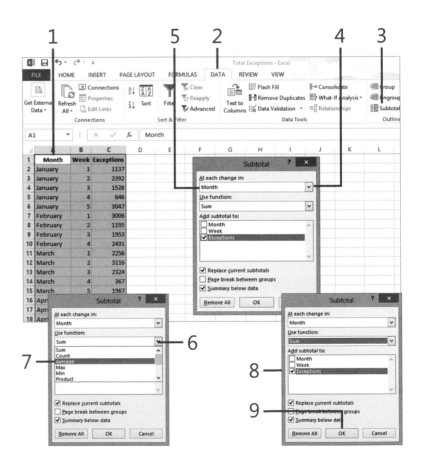

Remove a subtotal

1 Click any cell in the subtotaled range.

2 Click the Data tab.

3 Click Subtotal.

4 Click Remove All.

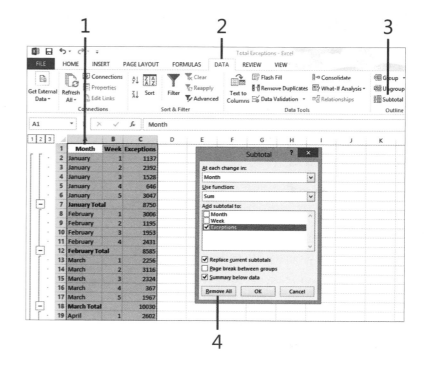

Exploring the Excel function library

You can create dozens of different functions in Excel. You can use Excel functions to determine mortgage payments, perform scientific calculations, or find the square root of a number. The best way to become familiar with the formulas available in Excel is to display the Insert Function dialog box and move through the listed functions, clicking the ones that look interesting. When you click a function, its description appears at the bottom of the dialog box.

Another way to get information about a function is to view the ScreenTip that appears next to the function. If you double-click a cell with a function, a ScreenTip with the function's structure and expected values appears below it. Clicking an element of the structure points to the cell or cells providing that value.

List functions available from the Excel library

1 Click the Insert Function button on the formula bar.

2 Display the drop-down list, and click the function category that you want to view.

3 Click the function that you want to examine.

4 Click OK.

5 Click Cancel to close the Function Arguments dialog box.

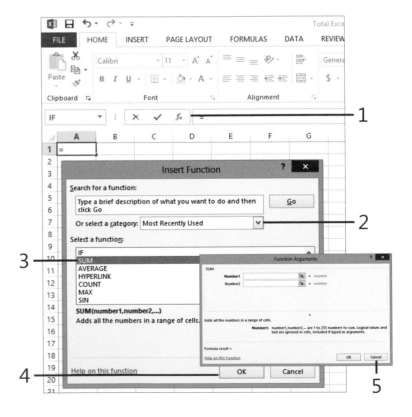

Use function ScreenTips

1 Double-click a cell that contains a formula.

2 In the ScreenTip, click the function name to open the Help file entry for the function.

3 Click the Close button to close the Help window.

4 Click an argument to select the cells to which it refers.

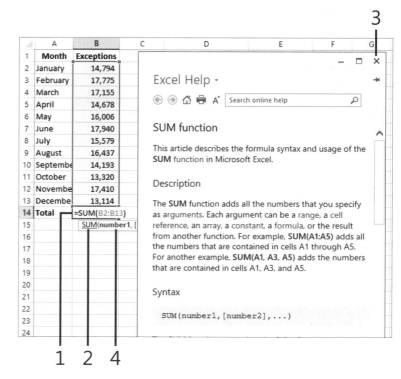

Using the IF function

In addition to calculating values based on the contents of other cells, you can have Excel take different actions based on the contents of those other cells by using the IF function. For example, if you create a workbook to track the times of riders in a bicycle racing club, you can create a formula to compare each rider's time to their previous times. When someone's most recent time is the lowest time in the group, you can have Excel display Personal Best in the cell with the formula, alerting you to congratulate the rider in your next club newsletter.

Create an IF function

1 Click the cell in which you want to enter an IF function.

2 Click the Formulas tab.

3 Click Logical.

4 Click IF.

5 Type a conditional statement that evaluates to true or false.

6 Type the text that you want to appear if the condition is true.

7 Type the text that you want to appear if the condition is false.

8 Click OK.

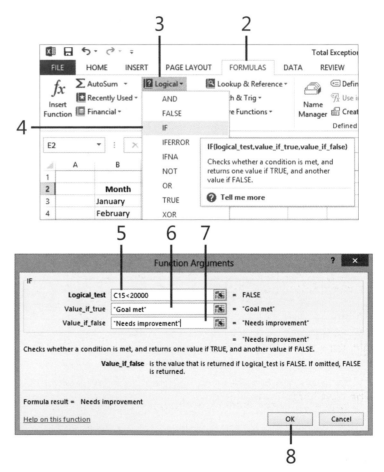

CAUTION The text message must be enclosed in quotation marks.

TIP You can also create an expression in the Value_If_True and Value_If_False boxes. Excel displays the result of the expression in the appropriate box.

Checking formula references

When you create a formula that draws values from several different places in your workbook—or from other workbooks—it can be difficult to see what's going wrong if your formula isn't producing the expected results. Excel helps you locate a cell's precedents (the cells that the formula uses in its calculation) and dependents (the cells that depend on the current cell to calculate their own values). To help you find what you need to check your formulas, Excel groups all the tools that you need on the Formula Auditing group on the Formulas tab.

Find cell precedents and dependents

1 Click the cell that you want to examine.

2 Click the Formulas tab.

3 Using the controls in the Formula Auditing group, follow either of these steps:

   a Click Trace Precedents.

   b Click Trace Dependents.

Remove tracer arrows

1 Click the Formulas tab.

2 Click the Remove Arrows down arrow, and follow any of these steps:

   a Click Remove Arrows to remove all arrows.

   b Click Remove Precedent Arrows to remove the precedent arrows.

   c Click Remove Dependent Arrows to remove the dependent arrows.

> ✓ **TIP** Tracer arrows are particularly effective when they're used to examine formulas that include named ranges. When you refer to a named range, you know what the indicated cells are supposed to represent.

Debugging your formulas

When you share a workbook with your colleagues, some of the values in that workbook might change rapidly as new data is entered. For example, workbook data probably will change quickly if you are evaluating stock prices. Stock market values change frequently, so your data will as well. You can monitor the value in a cell even while you're using another workbook by setting a watch. When you set a watch, the values of the cells you're monitoring appear in the Watch Window.

Another way that you can monitor your data is to check the result of part of a calculation by using the Evaluate Formula dialog box. When you click the Evaluate Formula button, Excel displays the formula in the active cell and the subtotal for part of the calculation. You can move through the formula bit by bit, with Excel showing you the result of each piece of the formula.

Monitor a formula for changes

1 Click the Formulas tab.

2 Click Watch Window.

3 Click Add Watch.

4 Select the cells that you want to watch.

5 Click Add.

6 Click Watch Window.

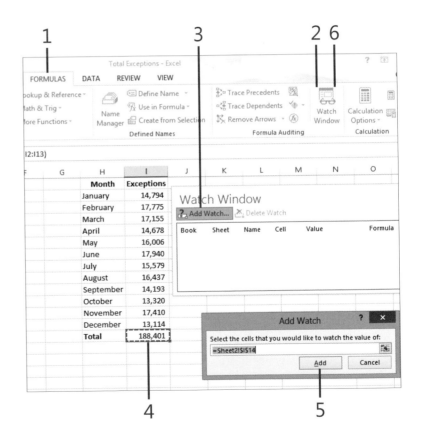

Delete a watch

1 Click the Formulas tab.

2 Click Watch Window.

3 Click the watch that you want to delete.

4 Click Delete Watch.

5 Click the Close button.

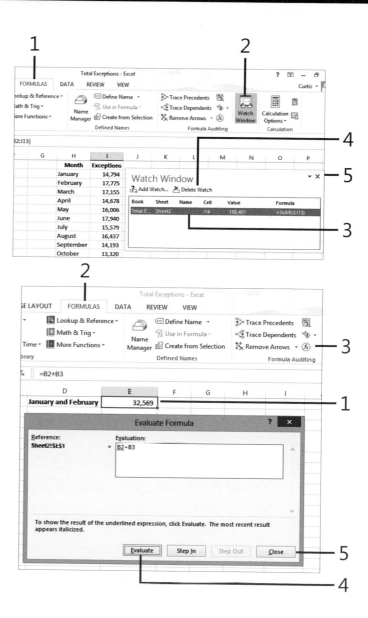

Evaluate parts of a formula

1 Click the cell with the formula that you want to evaluate.

2 Click the Formulas tab.

3 Click Evaluate Formula.

4 Click Evaluate (one or more times) to move through the formula's elements.

5 Click Close.

New functions in Excel 2013

Excel 2013 includes 51 new functions that you can use for dates, statistics, engineering, and even web data.

Table 6-1 lists all of the functions and describes what they do.

Table 6-1   New functions in Excel 2013

Category	Function Name	Description
Date and Time	DAYS	Calculates the number of days between two dates.
Date and Time	ISOWEEKNUM	Returns the number of the ISO week number of the year for a given date.
Engineering	BITAND	Returns a bitwise AND of two numbers.
Engineering	BITLSHIFT	Returns a numbered generated by shifting the bits in a number to the left by a specified number of places.
Engineering	BITOR	Returns a bitwise OR of two numbers.
Engineering	BITRSHIFT	Returns a number generated by shifting the bits in a number to the right by a specified number of places.
Engineering	BITXOR	Returns a bitwise XOR of two numbers.
Engineering	IMCOSH	Returns the hyperbolic cosine of a complex number.
Engineering	IMCOT	Returns the cotangent of a complex number.
Engineering	IMCSC	Returns the cosecant of a complex number.
Engineering	IMCSCH	Returns the hyperbolic cosecant of a complex number.
Engineering	IMSEC	Returns the secant of a complex number.
Engineering	IMSECH	Returns the hyperbolic secant of a complex number.
Engineering	IMSINH	Returns the hyperbolic sine of a complex number.
Engineering	IMTAN	Returns the tangent of a complex number.

Category	Function Name	Description
Financial	PDURATION	Calculates the number of periods that an investment will take to reach a value.
Financial	RRI	Calculates the equivalent interest rate for the growth of an investment.
Information	ISFORMULA	Returns TRUE if a cell contains a formula.
Information	SHEET	Returns the sheet number of a sheet.
Information	SHEETS	Returns the number of sheets in a reference.
Logical	IFNA	Returns a value that you specify if an expression results in an #N/A error; otherwise, it returns the value of the expression.
Logical	XOR	Returns the logical exclusive OR of all arguments (that is, it returns TRUE if exactly one argument is true).
Lookup and Reference	FORMULATEXT	Returns the formula in the referenced cell as text.
Math and Trigonometry	ACOT	Returns the arccotangent of a number.
Math and Trigonometry	ACOTH	Returns the hyperbolic arccotangent of a number.
Math and Trigonometry	ARABIC	Converts a number written as a Roman numeral into an Arabic number.
Math and Trigonometry	BASE	Converts a number into a text representation of the number in a given base.
Math and Trigonometry	CEILING.MATH	Rounds a number up to the nearest integer or to the nearest significant multiple.
Math and Trigonometry	COT	Returns the hyperbolic cosine of a number.
Math and Trigonometry	COTH	Returns the cotangent of an angle.
Math and Trigonometry	CSC	Returns the cosecant of an angle.
Math and Trigonometry	CSCH	Returns the hyperbolic cosecant of an angle.
Math and Trigonometry	DECIMAL	Converts a text representation of a number in a given base to a decimal number.
Math and Trigonometry	FLOOR.MATH	Rounds a number down to the nearest integer or to the nearest significant multiple.

Category	Function Name	Description
Math and Trigonometry	ISO.CEILING	Returns a number that is rounded up to the nearest integer or to the nearest significant multiple.
Math and Trigonometry	MUNIT	Returns the unit matrix of the specified dimension.
Math and Trigonometry	SEC	Returns the secant of an angle.
Math and Trigonometry	SECH	Returns the hyperbolic secant of an angle.
Statistical	BINOM.DIST.RANGE	Calculates the probability of a result using the binomial distribution.
Statistical	COMBINA	Returns the number of combinations for a given number of items, allowing replacement.
Statistical	GAMMA	Returns the Gamma function value.
Statistical	GAUSS	Returns 0.5 less than the standard normal cumulative distribution.
Statistical	PERMUTATIONA	Returns the number of permutations for a given number of items, allowing replacement.
Statistical	PHI	Returns the value of the density function for a standard normal distribution.
Statistical	SKEW.P	Returns the skewness of a distribution based on the population instead of a sample from the population.
Text	NUMBERVALUE	Converts text to a number.
Text	UNICHAR	Returns the Unicode character referenced by a number.
Text	UNICODE	Returns the Unicode number of the first character of a text string.
Web	ENCODEURL	Returns a URL-encoded string.
Web	FILTERXML	Returns specific data from XML content using a user-supplied xpath value.
Web	WEBSERVICE	Returns data from a web service.

Formatting the cell 7

Microsoft Excel 2013 helps you manage large quantities of data with ease. One of the ways you can accomplish this is by changing how the program displays the data in your worksheet. For example, you can easily change the size of characters displayed in a cell, add color to emphasize important cells, or change the orientation of text within a cell. Excel 2013 also enables you to change a cell's formatting based on the contents of the cell by creating conditional formats, including color scales, data bars, and icon sets.

In this section:

- Formatting cells and cell contents
- Adding cell backgrounds and formatting cell borders
- Defining cell styles
- Aligning and orienting cell contents
- Applying conditional formatting
- Displaying data bars, icon sets, or color scales based on cell values
- Copying formats with format painter
- Merging or splitting cells or data

Formatting cell contents

Some cells have values that need to stand out. Whether the value is a grand total for a year's sales or a label that lets your colleagues know that data they enter in the worksheet must be within certain limits, you can change the font used to display the data; make the text larger or smaller; or make the text appear bold, italicized, or underlined. You can apply these settings by using the controls on the Home tab of the ribbon or on the mini toolbar.

Change font and font size

1   Select the cells that you want to format.

2   Click the Home tab.

3   Click the Font down arrow.

4   Click the font that you want.

5   Click the Font Size down arrow.

6   Click the font size that you want.

TIP   You can display the Format Cells dialog box, which contains a wider range of cell formatting controls, by selecting a group of cells, right-clicking any selected cell, and choosing Format Cells. You can also display the Format Cells dialog box by clicking the Font group's dialog box launcher.

Change text appearance

1 Select the cells that you want to format.

2 Click the Home tab.

3 Use the tools in the Font, Alignment, and Number groups to change your text's appearance.

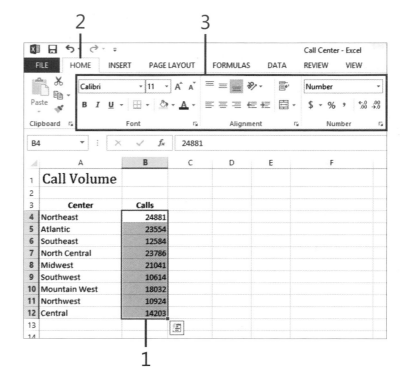

⚠ **CAUTION** When you select multiple cells to change their appearance, the range you select might have a combination of cells that already have formatting applied to them and cells that have no formatting applied. If this is the case, you might have to click the buttons multiple times until all the cells are formatted how you want them.

Formatting part of a cell's contents

Most Excel worksheets contain numbers that summarize business operations, personal finance, or hobby activities. Other cells might contain labels or other explanatory text that helps you and your colleagues interpret the data in the worksheet.

You can apply formatting to the entirety of a cell's contents, but you can also format a portion of the a cell's contents to emphasize a particular word, phrase, or portion of a value.

Format part of a cell's contents

1 Click the cell with the data that you want to format.

2 In the formula bar, select the contents of the cell that you want to format.

3 If necessary, click the Home tab.

4 Use the controls in the Font group on the ribbon to apply the changes that you want.

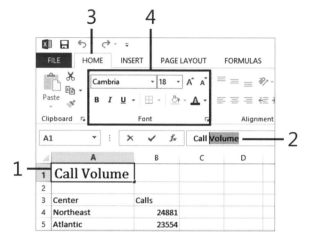

Formatting cells containing dates

In many cases, knowing when something happened is just as important as knowing what happened. For example, if you run a garden supply store or nursery, it's useful to know that you get most of your customers on the weekends but that you make most of your large sales (most likely to landscape architects and other stores) during the week. Excel recognizes when you enter a date in a cell and applies the program's default format to the date. There are many date formats to choose from—pick the one you like the best!

Set a date format

1 Select the cells that you want to format as a date.

2 Click the Home tab.

3 In the Number group, click the Format Cells dialog box launcher.

4 Click the Number tab.

5 Click Date.

6 Click the date format you want.

7 Click OK.

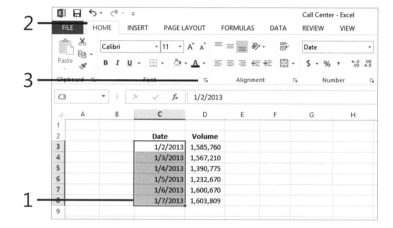

> ✓ **TIP** You can apply the Short Date or Long Date format to a cell by selecting the cell and then, on the Home tab, in the Number group, clicking the Number Format box's list arrow and selecting Short Date or Long Date. If the cell you format contains the date August 2, 2013, the Short Date format displays it as 8/2/2013 and the Long Date format displays it as Monday, August 2, 2013.

Formatting cells containing numbers

Numerical data plays a central role in Excel workbooks; therefore, it stands to reason that you have lots of options for choosing how you want your numbers to appear. Two frequently used formats are the Accounting number style, which displays a cell's contents as a monetary value, and Percent, which multiplies a value by 100 and adds a percent sign to the end. The two biggest benefits of formatting data as a percent are that you save a lot of time (and avoid mistakes) by not typing the decimal point or percent sign yourself and that you can tell the values are percentages at a glance.

Two other options for formatting your numbers are to display the values in a cell with commas every third digit and to increase or decrease the number of digits to the right of the decimal point. Although two decimal places are sufficient for most financial data, you might need to track currency exchange amounts to three or four decimal places.

Display numerical values as currency and percentages

1 Select the cells that you want to format.

2 Click the Home tab.

3 Using the tools in the Number group, follow any of these steps:

  a Click the Accounting Number Format button to apply the currency style with two decimal places. You can choose a currency symbol other than your default (which is the $ sign in the United States) by clicking the down arrow at the right edge of the Accounting Number Format button.

  b Click the Percent Style button to add a percent sign with no decimal places.

  c Click the Comma Style button to add a comma format with two decimal places.

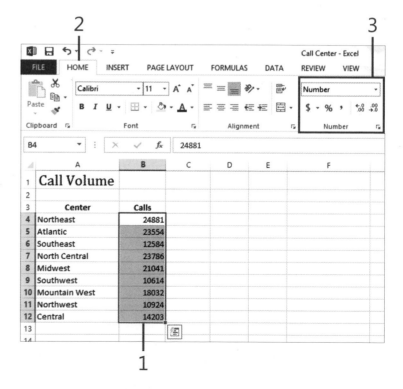

Set the number of decimal places

1 Select the cells that you want to format.

2 Click the Home tab.

3 Follow either of these steps:

   a Click the Increase Decimal button in the Number group on the ribbon.

   b Click the Decrease Decimal button in the Number group on the ribbon.

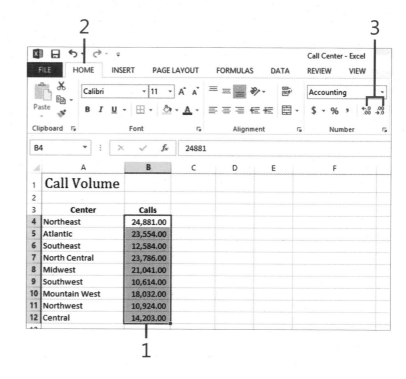

TIP When you create a worksheet, you should apply the numerical formatting that you want to all the cells in which you'll store numbers of a certain type. That way, when you type the data later (or copy it from another document), it will be formatted correctly.

Adding cell backgrounds and shading

Sometimes creating or applying a workbook theme is too much work. If all you want to do is highlight the value in a cell by changing the cell's background to red, you don't need to go to the trouble of finding the theme that includes red as one of its colors. Instead, you can simply change the background color of cells to make those cells stand out. However, be sure there's enough contrast between the background and text colors. Very little is worse than having to squint at the monitor to read text that blends in with the background color.

Add background color

1 Select the cells that you want to change.

2 Click the Home tab.

3 In the Font group, click the Fill Color down arrow.

4 Select the background color that you want.

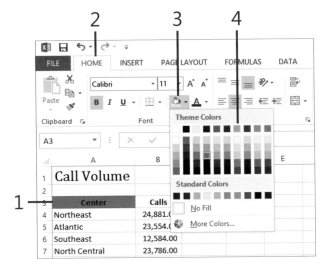

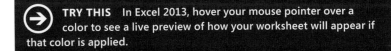

TIP After you apply a color, the Fill Color button changes to reflect your most recent choice. Clicking the button, rather than the down arrow at the right edge of the button, applies the previous choice to the active selection.

TRY THIS In Excel 2013, hover your mouse pointer over a color to see a live preview of how your worksheet will appear if that color is applied.

Change background shading

1 Select the cells that you want to change.

2 Right-click the selection, and click Format Cells on the shortcut menu.

3 Click the Fill tab.

4 Click the Pattern Color down arrow and then select the color that you want.

5 Click the Pattern Style down arrow and then select the pattern that you want.

6 Click OK.

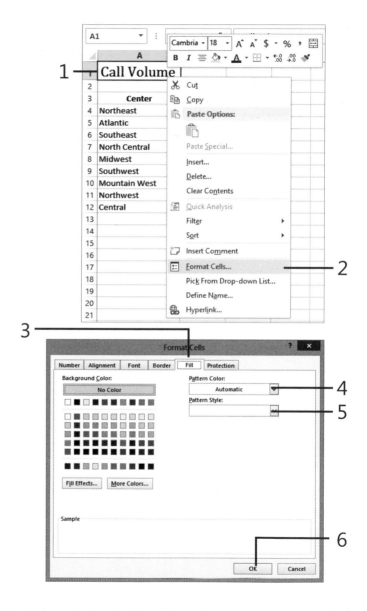

Formatting cell borders

The grid that appears on the standard worksheet uses light gray lines to mark cell boundaries, but those boundary lines don't distinguish one area of the worksheet from another. One way you can make a group of cells stand out from other groups is to draw a border on the edge of the cells. You can also change the color of any border that you add to your worksheet.

Draw borders

1 Select the cells around which you want to draw a border.

2 Click the Home tab.

3 Click the Border button's down arrow.

4 Click the type of border that you want to apply.

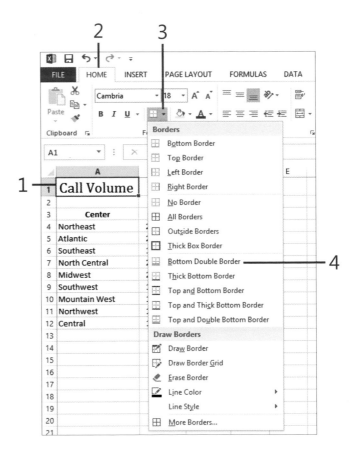

Format cell borders

1 Click the cell that you want to format.

2 Click the Home tab.

3 Click the Font group's dialog box launcher.

4 Click the Border tab.

5 Select the line style.

6 Click the Color down arrow.

7 Click the color that you want to use for the borders.

8 Select the borders that you want to use.

9 Click OK.

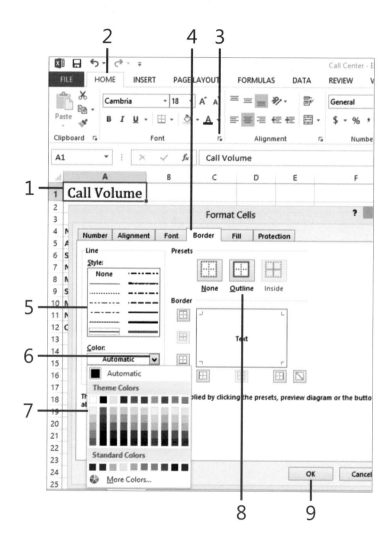

Defining cell styles

When you develop a worksheet, you will probably create a set of formats you want to apply consistently to certain parts of it. For example, you might always want your column headings to be slightly larger and in a different font from the body of the worksheet. You can save the formatting you want for a worksheet element as a style, which you then can apply to appropriate parts of your worksheets. Excel 2013 makes it easy to format your cell contents using styles.

Apply a style

1 Select the cells that you want to change.

2 Click the Home tab.

3 In the Styles group, click Cell Styles.

4 Click a style.

TIP When you hover the mouse pointer over a style, the selected cells change their appearance to preview how the cells will appear if you apply that style.

Create a style

1 Click the Home tab.

2 In the Styles group on the ribbon, click Cell Styles.

3 Click New Cell Style.

4 Type a new style name.

5 Click Format.

6 Specify the formatting that you want this style to contain.

7 In the Format Cells dialog box, click OK.

8 In the Style dialog box, click OK.

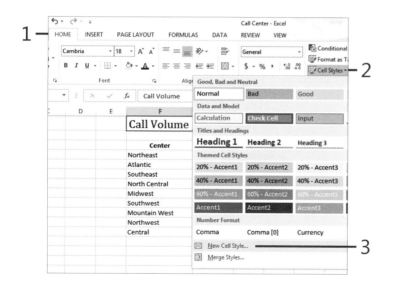

TIP Any custom styles that you create appear at the top of the Cell Styles gallery.

Modifying and deleting cell styles

Excel 2013 includes a wide range of styles that you can use to format your cell contents quickly. If you want to define a heading, emphasize data, or highlight explanatory text, you can probably find a style that works. If one of the built-in cell styles is close to the formatting that you want to apply to a cell, you can modify an existing style instead of creating a new one. Later, if you decide you no longer need a custom style, you can always delete it.

Modify a style

1 Click the Home tab.

2 In the Styles group on the ribbon, click Cell Styles.

3 Right-click the style that you want to modify.

4 Click Modify.

5 Click Format.

6 Specify the formatting that you want.

7 Click OK twice.

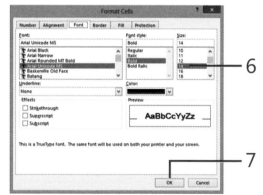

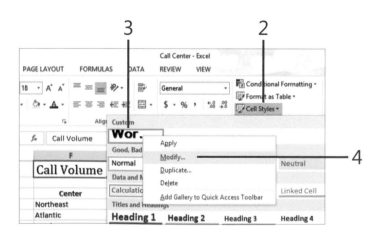

Delete a style

1 Click the Home tab.

2 In the Styles group on the ribbon, click Cell Styles.

3 Right-click the style that you want to delete.

4 Click Delete.

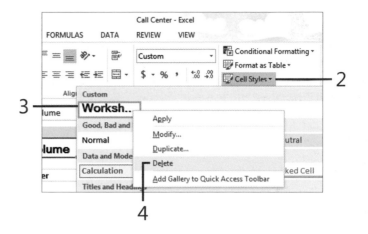

Aligning and orienting cell contents

Most of the time you will want your text to be square with the left edge of a cell, but headings are much easier to read (and stand out better) when they're centered in a cell, and numbers are easier to read when the last digit of every number is flush with the right edge of a column. Similarly, if you want to create a tall, thin cell with text written in a vertical line, you can do so by typing your text in a cell and then changing the content's orientation. When your data doesn't fit neatly within the width of a cell, you can choose to have the text displayed on a new line in the same cell. This setting, called text wrapping, treats a cell like a small text box with narrow margins.

Change text alignment

1 Select the cells that you want to align.

2 Click the Home tab.

3 Using the controls in the Alignment group on the ribbon, follow any of these steps:

  a Click the Align Left button to align the text with the left edge of the cell.

  b Click the Center button to center the text horizontally within the cell.

  c Click the Align Right button to align the text with the right edge of the cell.

  d Click the Top Align button to align the text with the top of the cell.

  e Click the Middle Align button to center the text vertically within the cell.

  f Click the Bottom Align button to align the text with the bottom edge of the cell.

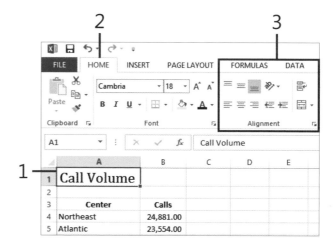

Set text orientation and wrapping

1 Select the cells that you want to orient.

2 Click the Home tab.

3 Using the controls in the Alignment group on the ribbon, follow either or both of these steps:

   a Click the Orientation button and then select the orientation for your cell text.

   b Click the Wrap Text button to wrap the text to fit inside the column width.

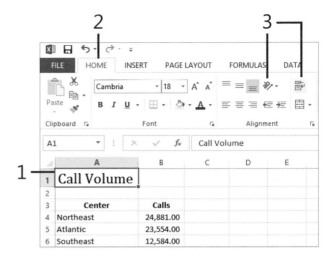

TIP If you want more control over how to rotate the text within a cell, right-click the cells that you want to orient and choose Format Cells from the shortcut menu. In the Format Cells dialog box, click the Alignment tab, type the number of degrees that you want to rotate the baseline of your text, and then click OK.

Formatting a cell based on conditions

Another way you can make your data easier to interpret is to change the appearance of your data based on the value in a cell. This kind of formatting is called conditional formatting because the data must meet certain conditions to have a format applied to it. For example, if you use a worksheet to track your customers' credit lines, you could have a customer's outstanding balance appear in red if they are within 10 percent of their credit limit.

Change the format of a cell based on its value

1   Select the cells that you want to change.

2   Click the Home tab.

3   In the Styles group on the ribbon, click Conditional Formatting.

4   Click New Rule.

5   Click Format Only Cells That Contain.

6   Click the Comparison Phrase down arrow.

7   Click the comparison phrase that you want.

8   Type the constant values or formulas that you want evaluated.

9   Click Format.

10 Specify the formatting that you want, and click OK.

11 Click OK.

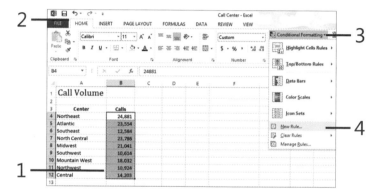

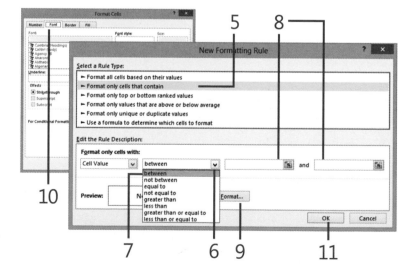

> ⚠ **CAUTION**   The layout of the Edit The Rule Description pane changes to reflect the rule type that you choose. Don't be surprised if you see a different number of fields than are shown here.

Change the format of a cell based on the results of a formula

1 Select the cells that you want to change.

2 Click the Home tab.

3 In the Styles group on the ribbon, click Conditional Formatting.

4 Click New Rule.

5 Click Use A Formula To Determine Which Cells To Format.

6 Type the formula that you want evaluated.

7 Click Format.

8 Specify the formatting that you want, and click OK.

9 Click OK.

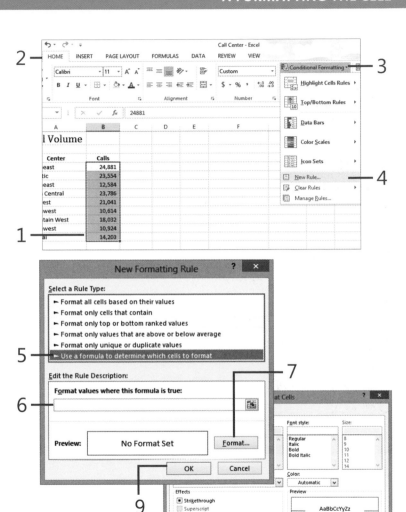

TRY THIS In a blank worksheet, click cell A1, click the Home tab, click the Conditional Formatting button, and then click New Rule. Define a condition that applies when a cell value is between 400 and 1,000. Specify that bold formatting be applied to the cells. Click OK. Define a second condition that applies when a cell value is less than 400. Specify that italic formatting be applied to the cells. Click OK. Type 450 in cell A1, and press Enter. The cell's contents are displayed in bold type. Click cell A1, type 350, and press Enter. The cell's contents are now displayed in italics.

Editing and deleting conditional formats

Excel 2013 makes it easy for you to manage conditional formatting rules that you create in your worksheets. You can change the properties of a rule (such as the formatting applied or the conditions themselves), change the order in which the rules are applied, or delete a rule entirely.

Edit a conditional formatting rule

1 Select the cells that contain the rule you that want to edit.

2 Click the Home tab.

3 In the Styles group, click Conditional Formatting.

4 Click Manage Rules.

5 Click the rule that you want to change.

6 Click Edit Rule.

7 Use the controls to make your changes.

8 Click OK twice to save your changes.

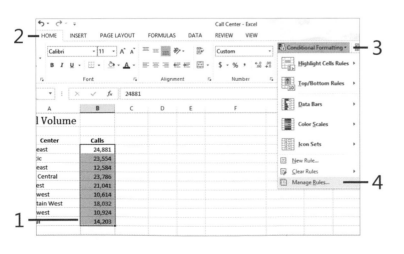

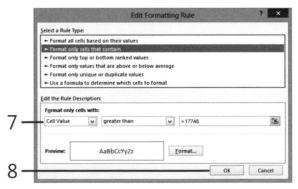

Delete a conditional formatting rule

1 Select the cells that contain the rule that you want to delete.

2 Click the Home tab.

3 In the Styles group, click Conditional Formatting.

4 Click Manage Rules.

5 Click the rule that you want to delete.

6 Click Delete Rule.

7 Click OK.

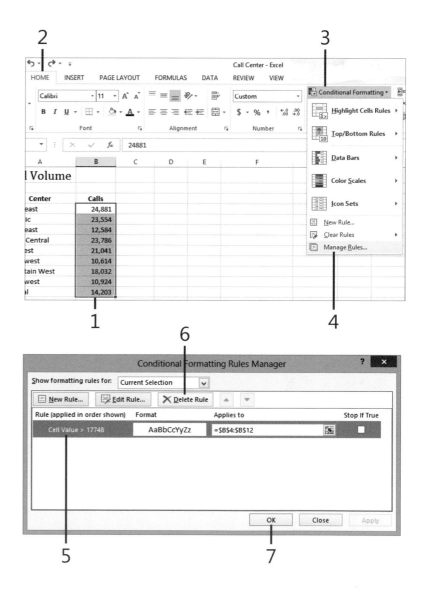

Changing how conditional formatting rules are applied

Excel 2013 enables you to create powerful conditional formatting rules and to control how those rules are applied. For example, you can have Excel apply more than one conditional format to a cell, so if you want to display a value of more than 1,000 in bold text and values that exceed a sales target with a yellow background, you can define those conditions separately and have Excel apply them both.

You can also decide whether Excel should stop after it finds a rule that applies to your data or continue to check other rules. Finally, you can change the order in which Excel checks your conditions to control how Excel applies the rules. Rule order matters only if you choose to have Excel stop after it applies a rule.

Stop when a condition is met

1 Select the cells that contain the rule that you want to edit.

2 Click the Home tab.

3 In the Styles group, click Conditional Formatting.

4 Click Manage Rules.

5 Click the rule that you want to change.

6 Select the Stop If True check box.

7 Click OK.

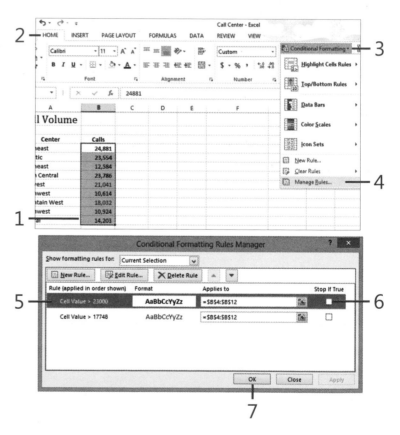

Change the order of conditions

1 Select the cells that contain the rules that you want to edit.

2 Click the Home tab.

3 In the Styles group, click Conditional Formatting.

4 Click Manage Rules.

5 Click the rule that you want to change.

6 Follow either of these steps:

   a Click the Move Up button to move the rule one place higher in the order.

   b Click the Move Down button to move the rule one place lower in the order.

7 Click OK.

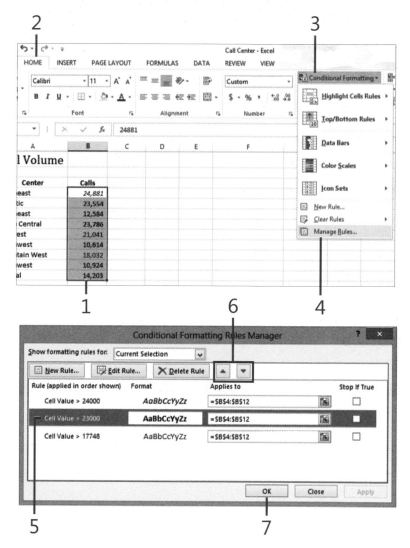

Displaying data bar and icon set formats

Organizations of all kinds track their performance data in Microsoft Excel. The specific numbers are important, of course, but it's also important that you be able to tell how the numbers relate to each other and whether your department is meeting its performance goals. Data bars show how the data in a cell compares to other data in a selected range. The higher a value is in relation to the other values in the range, the longer the data bar. Icon sets, by contrast, test a value to see whether it is in the top, middle, or bottom third of the values in the range. You can change the tests to determine which icon or color is shown when.

Display data bars

1 Select the cells that contain your data.

2 Click the Home tab.

3 In the Styles group on the ribbon, click Conditional Formatting.

4 Point to Data Bars.

5 Click the data bar option that you want to apply.

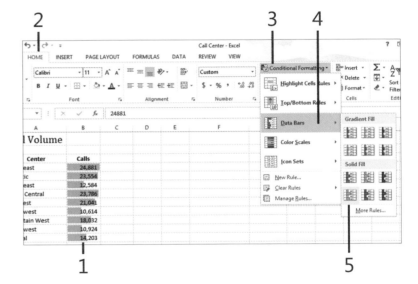

Display icon sets

1 Select the cells that contain your data.

2 Click the Home tab.

3 In the Styles group on the ribbon, click Conditional Formatting.

4 Point to Icon Sets.

5 Click the icon set that you want to apply.

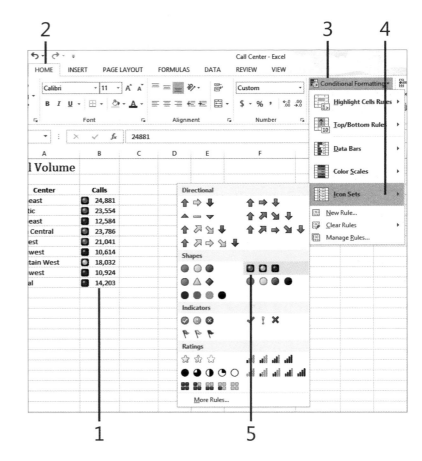

Displaying color scales based on cell values

Color scales compare the relative magnitude of values in a cell range by applying colors from a two-color or three-color set to your cells. The intensity of a cell's color reflects the value's tendency toward the top or bottom of the values in the range.

Applying two-color color scales, using colors such as white and red, to a cell range is a terrific way to create an easy-to-interpret visual map of your data.

Display color scales

1 Select the cells that contain your data.

2 Click the Home tab.

3 In the Styles group on the ribbon, click Conditional Formatting.

4 Point to Color Scales.

5 Click the color scale pattern that you want to apply.

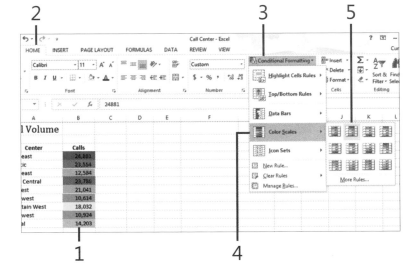

TIP When you click Data Bars, Icon Sets, or Color Scales, you see an item named More Rules at the bottom of the gallery of built-in formats. Clicking More Rules displays a dialog box that you can use to control a format's details.

Deleting conditional formats

If you no longer want to use conditional formats to summarize the data in your workbook, you can delete the formats without affecting the underlying data. When you delete a conditional format, you can select whether to do so for the selected cells, the entire sheet, the active PivotTable, or the active Excel table.

Delete conditional formats

1 Select the cells with the conditional formatting that you want to delete.

2 Click the Home tab.

3 In the Styles group on the ribbon, click Conditional Formatting.

4 Point to Clear Rules.

5 Click the set of rules that you want to delete.

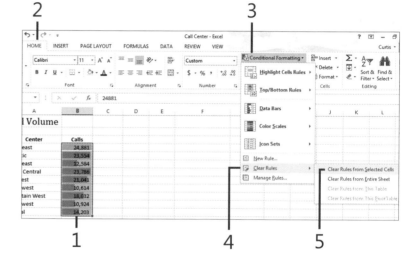

Merging or splitting cells or data

You can change a row's height or a column's width, but this might not be the best way to improve your worksheet's usability. For example, a label might not fit within a single cell, and increasing that cell's width—or every cell's width—might throw off the worksheet's design. One solution to this problem is to merge two or more cells. Merging cells allows you to treat a group of cells as a single cell as far as content and formatting go.

Merge several cells into one

1 Select the cells that you want to merge.

2 Click the Home tab.

3 In the Alignment group, click the Merge & Center button.

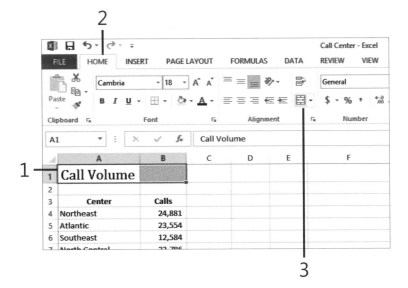

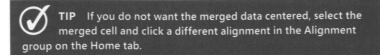

> ⚠ **CAUTION** If the cells you select have data in more than one cell, only the data in the upper-left cell remains after you merge the cells.

> ✓ **TIP** If you do not want the merged data centered, select the merged cell and click a different alignment in the Alignment group on the Home tab.

Split a merged cell

1 Click the merged cell.

2 Click the Home tab.

3 Click the down arrow at the right edge of the Merge & Center button.

4 Click Unmerge Cells.

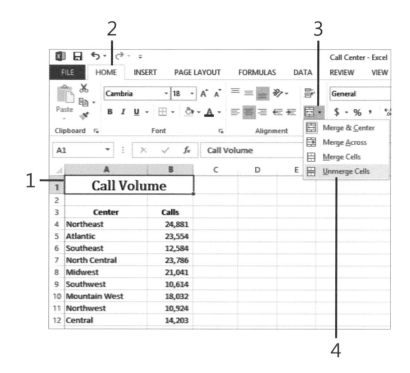

Copying formats with Format Painter

After you create a format for a cell or group of cells, you can copy the format to another group of cells using Format Painter. Format Painter lets you copy the format quickly, saving you the time and effort it takes to copy the contents of another cell with the formats that you want and then changing the data or formula.

Copy styles with Format Painter

1 Select the cells with the formatting that you want to copy.

2 Click the Home tab.

3 In the Clipboard group, click the Format Painter button.

4 Select the cells where you want the formatting applied.

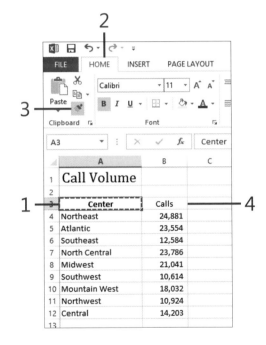

TIP You can apply cell's style multiple times by double-clicking the Format Painter button. Clicking additional cells applies the copied format until you press the Esc key.

Formatting
the worksheet

8

Microsoft Excel 2013 enables you to change your worksheets' appearance and structure to display your data effectively. For example, you can make rows and columns surrounding your data wider or taller to separate your figures from the worksheet's other contents. You can also move entire rows or columns to different locations in the workbook, such as when a worksheet's data columns are in a different order from those of a related paper form. If you want to call attention to one of your worksheets, perhaps one that contains new data that your boss should review, you can change the color of that worksheet's sheet tab so that it stands out within the workbook.

In this section:

- Applying workbook themes
- Coloring sheet tabs
- Changing a worksheet's gridlines
- Changing row heights and column widths
- Inserting, moving, and deleting rows and columns
- Hiding and showing rows and columns
- Protecting worksheets from changes

Applying workbook themes

Designing attractive Excel worksheets challenges even the most advanced users. Excel 2013 comes with a wide variety of attractive themes that you can apply to your worksheets. But you're not limited to the themes included when you install Excel! You can also change the colors used within a theme to customize your worksheet's appearance.

Apply a workbook theme

1 Click the Page Layout tab.

2 In the Themes group on the ribbon, click Themes.

3 Click the theme that you want to apply.

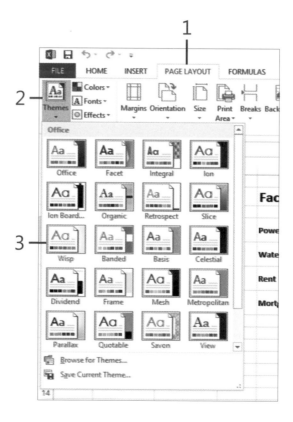

Change colors within a theme

1 Click the Page Layout tab.

2 In the Themes group on the ribbon, click Colors.

3 Click the color scheme that you want to apply.

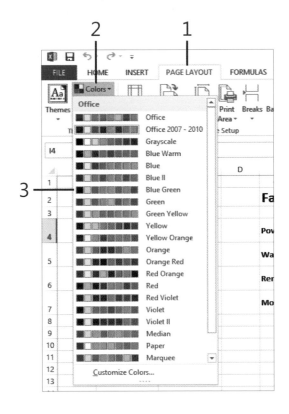

Changing theme fonts and effects

The Office themes that are included with the Microsoft Office program suite give you a wide range of formats that work well together. However, if you want to change the fonts or effects applied to your worksheet's contents, you can always modify either of those aspects of your theme.

Change fonts within a theme

1 Click the Page Layout tab.

2 In the Themes group on the ribbon, click Fonts.

3 Click the font scheme that you want to apply.

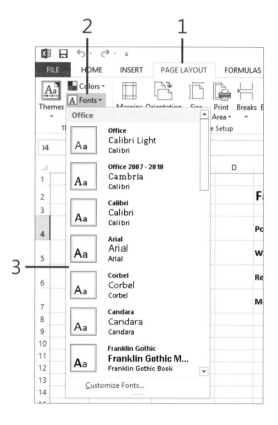

Change effects within a theme

1 Click the Page Layout tab.

2 In the Themes group on the ribbon, click Effects.

3 Click the effects scheme that you want to apply.

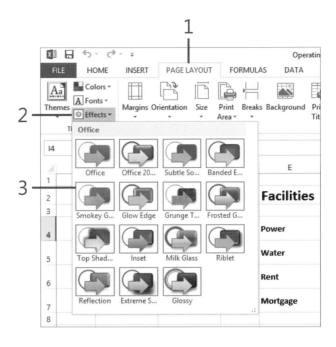

Creating new workbook themes

You can change any aspect of a theme to define exactly how you want your worksheet's contents to appear when you apply it. After you've modified the color, font, and effects settings for your workbook, you can save them as a custom theme.

Create a new workbook theme

1 Format your worksheet with the colors, fonts, and effects that you want to include in your theme.

2 Click the Page Layout tab.

3 In the Themes group on the ribbon, click Themes.

4 Click Save Current Theme.

5 Type a name for your theme.

6 Click Save.

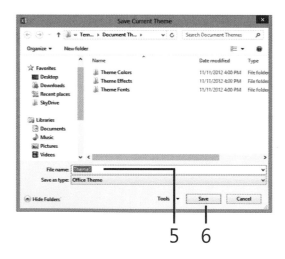

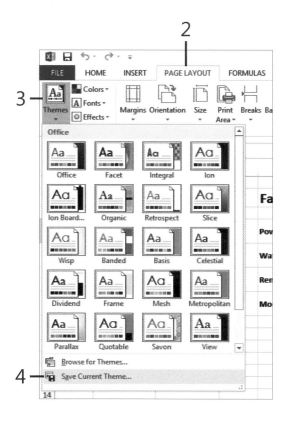

Coloring sheet tabs

A great way to make any worksheet element stand out is to change it to a color that contrasts with the other colors used in the worksheet. In Excel 2013, you can change the color of sheet tabs. For example, you can change the color of a sheet tab in a workbook in which you track sales for a year with a worksheet for each month. Rather than move the current worksheet to the front of the list, which would put the worksheets out of order, you can change the color of the sheet tab to make it stand out. When the month ends, you can remove the color from that sheet tab and apply it to the next month's sheet tab.

Color a sheet tab

1 Click the sheet tab that you want to color.

2 Right-click the selection, and point to Tab Color on the shortcut menu.

3 Click the color that you want.

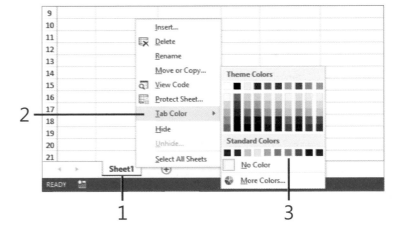

TIP If you select a sheet tab color from the Theme Colors section of the color palette, changing your workbook's theme will change your sheet tabs' colors.

Changing a worksheet's gridlines

Gridlines are the lines on your worksheets that define the cells formed by the intersections of rows and columns. The default gridline color is gray, but not all worksheets work well with this standard setting. Sometimes you'll want to change the color of the cell gridlines or even turn them off. Excel 2013 also makes it easier than previous editions to control whether your gridlines appear when you print a worksheet.

Change the color of cell gridlines

1 Click the File tab.

2 Click Options.

3 Click Advanced.

4 Click the Display Options For This Worksheet down arrow.

5 Select the worksheet, or workbook, to which you want to apply the change.

6 Click the Gridline Color button.

7 Select the color that you want to use for the gridlines.

8 Click OK.

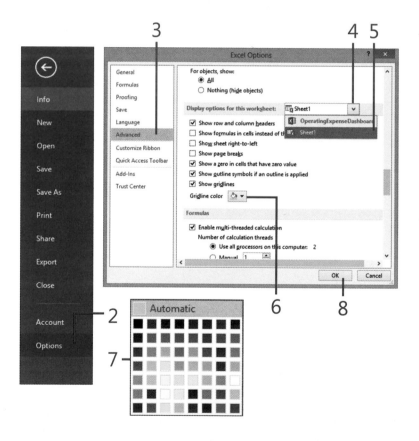

Show or hide cell gridlines

1 Click the Page Layout tab.

2 Using the controls in the Sheet Options group on the ribbon, follow either or both of these steps by using the check boxes in the Gridlines section of the group:

a Select the View check box to show the gridlines as you work in Excel, or clear the View check box to hide the gridlines as you work.

b Select the Print check box to show the gridlines when you print the worksheet, or clear the Print check box to hide the gridlines when you print.

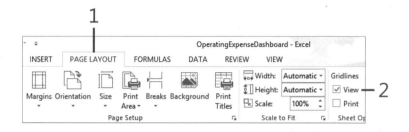

Changing row heights and column widths

When you create an Excel workbook, the default worksheet rows are tall enough to accommodate text and numbers entered in the standard character format (Calibri, 11 point) and wide enough to display about eight characters. If your text takes up too much space to fit in the cell (for example, because you've changed the font size for a column label), you can widen the column so that the contents of every cell can be seen. You can also increase the height of rows in your worksheet to put some space between values, which makes your data easier to read. If a column is too wide or a row is too high, you can make it narrower or shorter as needed.

Resize a row

1 Hover the mouse pointer over the lower boundary of the row that you want to resize until the mouse pointer turns into a two-headed arrow.

2 Drag the boundary until the row is the height you want.

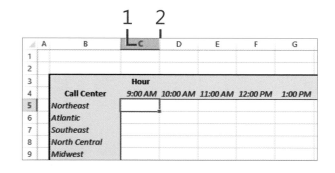

Resize a column

1 Hover the mouse pointer over the right boundary of the column that you want to resize until the mouse pointer turns into a two-headed arrow.

2 Drag the boundary until the column is the width you want.

 TIP You can resize a column to fit the text of its widest cell by double-clicking the right boundary of the column.

Resizing multiple rows or columns

In most worksheets, your data will tend to come in groups. For example, you might have column and row headers in some cells and the main body of your data collection in others. If you find that your header cells are too wide or too short to display your data correctly, you can resize multiple rows or columns at the same time.

Resize multiple rows or columns

1 Select the rows or columns that you want to resize.

2 Drag the border of any selected column or row to the width or height that you want.

Inserting rows or columns

After you create a worksheet and begin filling in your data, you might decide to insert a row or column to add data that you didn't think to include when you started. For example, a customer might want to add a product to an order. To accommodate this, you can insert a blank row below the last row in the existing order and add the new item there. If you want to add a row in the middle of the existing order data, you can insert a blank row above an existing row. You can perform similar actions with columns, For example, if you want to begin recording a new piece of information about your customers, such as a website or email address, you can add a column to store that information.

Insert a row in a worksheet

1 Right-click the row header below where you want the new row to appear.

2 Choose Insert from the shortcut menu.

Insert a column in a worksheet

1 Right-click the column header to the right of where you want the new column to appear.

2 Choose Insert from the shortcut menu.

> **TIP** If you want to insert more than one row or column at a time, select the number of existing rows or columns equal to the number that you want to insert and then choose the Insert command from the shortcut menu.

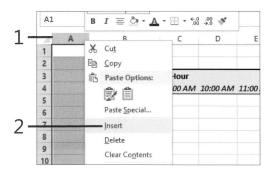

Setting insert options

When you insert a row or column into a worksheet, Excel examines the rows and columns surrounding the inserted element to determine whether there is any formatting applied to those rows or columns. If there is, you can use the controls made available by clicking the Insert Options button to determine what, if any, formatting is applied to your new rows or columns.

Set insert options

1 After inserting rows or columns, open the Insert Options menu.

2 Select the type of formatting that you want the new cells to have.

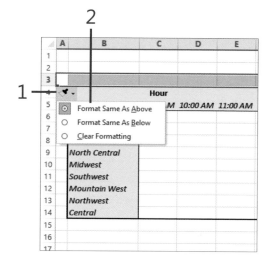

✓ **TIP** The Insert Options indicator appears only if the cells above or below the insertion point have special formatting.

Moving rows and columns

In many cases, the data in your worksheets is first recorded on paper—for example, when you record times for a race or collect customer responses on survey forms. Sometimes it's easier to type the information into your worksheet so that it looks the same way as it looks on paper. To present the information the way you want it to look, you can move rows and columns to new positions on the worksheet.

Move one or more rows

1 Select the rows that you want to move.

2 Click the Home tab.

3 In the Clipboard group, click the Cut button.

4 Click the first cell in the row where you want to move the rows.

5 In the Clipboard group, click Paste.

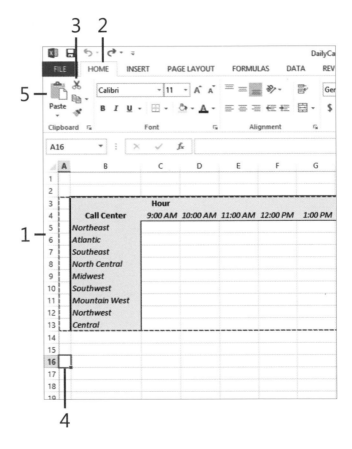

Move one or more columns

1 Select the columns that you want to move.

2 Click the Home tab.

3 In the Clipboard group, click the Cut button.

4 Click the first cell in the column where you want to move the columns.

5 In the Clipboard group, click Paste.

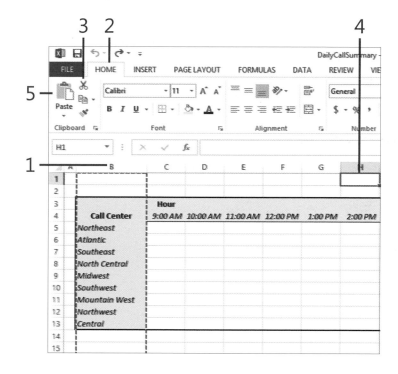

Deleting rows and columns

Excel workbooks are a great place to store and manipulate your data, but there might be times when you no longer need to use a particular row or column. Whether you placed an extra column to add some white space between the main body of data and a summary calculation or a row holds the contact information of a customer who asked to be removed from your list, you can delete a row or column quickly and easily.

Delete a row or column

1 Select the row or column that you want to delete.

2 Right-click the selection, and choose Delete from the shortcut menu.

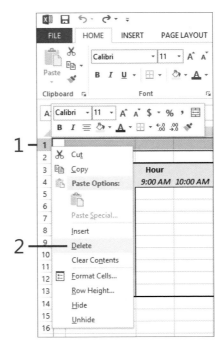

Grouping and ungrouping worksheet rows

As you develop worksheets, you'll probably try to keep similar entries together. For example, if you create a worksheet that lists all the products you sell, you can group the products by category. In the case of a garden supply store, all the tools can be together, then the furniture, and then a new category for each type of plant. You can always remove a group, or the entire outline, when you no longer need it.

Group worksheet rows

1 Select the rows or columns that you want to group.

2 Click the Data tab.

3 In the Outline group on the ribbon, click Group.

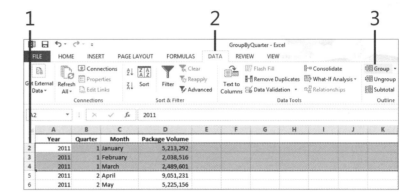

Ungroup worksheet rows

1 Select the rows or columns that you want to ungroup.

2 Click the Data tab.

3 In the Outline group on the ribbon, click Ungroup.

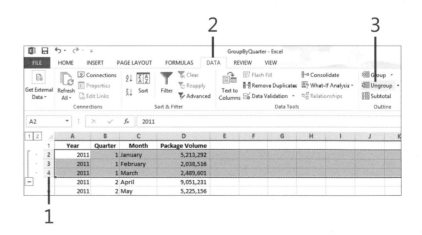

Hiding rows and columns

If you're working with a worksheet that contains lots of data, you might need to refer to the contents of rows or columns that aren't close enough on the worksheet to appear on the same screen. Rather than scroll back and forth to access the data you need, you can hide any intervening rows or columns so that everything you need to see is displayed on the screen at the same time. The rows that you hide are gone only temporarily. The data isn't deleted, it's just moved out of your way while you don't need it.

Hide rows or columns

1 Select the rows or columns that you want to hide.

2 Right-click the selection, and choose Hide from the shortcut menu.

Unhide rows or columns

1 Select the rows or columns that surround the rows or columns that you want to unhide.

2 Right-click any of the selected row or column headers, and choose Unhide from the shortcut menu.

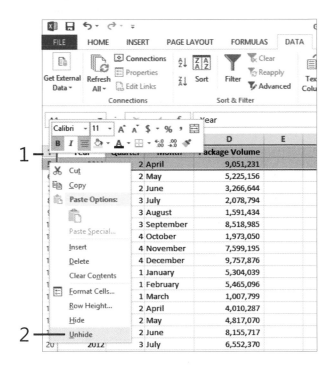

Outlining to hide and show rows and columns

Outlining the rows in a worksheet lets you determine which rows are displayed, making it easier to focus on the data that's important to you. If you want to hide the rows for one set of products, you can define the rows as a group. You then have the option to choose which rows that you want to display. The rows that you hide are gone only temporarily. The data isn't deleted, it's just moved out of your way while you don't need it. You can bring it back with a single click.

Hide grouped rows and columns

1 Click the Hide Detail button next to the group that you want to hide.

	1	2		A	B	C	D	E
			1	Year	Quarter	Month	Package Volume	
			2	2011	1	January	5,213,292	
			3	2011	1	February	2,038,516	
			4	2011	1	March	2,489,601	
			5	2011	2	April	9,051,231	
			6	2011	2	May	5,225,156	
			7	2011	2	June	3,266,644	
			8	2011	3	July	2,078,794	
			9	2011	3	August	1,591,434	
			10	2011	3	September	8,518,985	

Show grouped rows and columns

1 Click the Show Detail button next to the group that you want to show.

	1	2		A	B	C	D	E
			1	Year	Quarter	Month	Package Volume	
			5	2011	2	April	9,051,231	
			6	2011	2	May	5,225,156	
			7	2011	2	June	3,266,644	
			8	2011	3	July	2,078,794	

> **SEE ALSO** For information about calculating subtotals for groups of rows, see "Summing with subtotals and grand totals" on page 110.

Protecting worksheets from changes

When you create a worksheet that contains sensitive data or data that you don't want anyone other than yourself to change, you can protect the worksheet from unauthorized changes. In the Protect Sheet dialog box, you can choose the actions that you want all users to be able to perform on the worksheet. The options selected by default allow anyone to select a cell but prevent them from deleting rows or columns, changing any formatting, or editing scenarios attached to the worksheet.

Protect a worksheet

1 Click the Review tab.

2 Click Protect Sheet.

3 Select the protection options that you want.

4 Click OK.

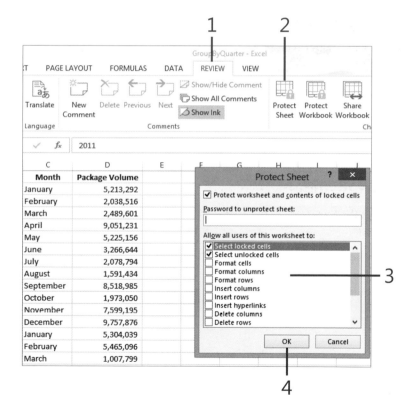

Locking cells to prevent changes

When you protect a worksheet, locking an individual cell prevents it from being changed. This level of protection goes beyond simply protecting a worksheet; it prevents anyone who uses the worksheet from changing the contents or the formatting of the cell. Excel 2013 enables this option by default.

Lock cells

1 Select the cells that you want to lock.

2 Right-click the selection, and click Format Cells on the shortcut menu.

3 Click the Protection tab.

4 Select the Locked check box.

5 Click OK.

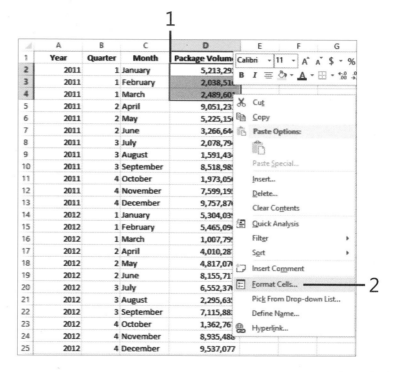

Printing worksheets

9

After you create your worksheet, you can print a copy for reference, for backup, or to distribute to your colleagues. Although you might be tempted to print your worksheet as soon as you complete it, it's usually a good idea to check your work first. All you need to do to see how your worksheet will look when it's printed is to display the worksheet in Backstage view. If you want to change how your worksheet will appear on the printed page, you can do anything from changing the orientation of the printout (that is, printing in a vertical format, called portrait mode, or a horizontal format, called landscape mode) to scaling the worksheet to fit within a specific number of pages. It's easy to fine-tune margins, adjust headers and footers, and customize a variety of other print options as well.

In this section:

- Previewing worksheets before printing
- Choosing a printer and page size
- Printing part of a worksheet
- Printing row and column headings on each page
- Setting and changing print margins
- Setting page orientation and scale
- Creating headers and footers
- Adding graphics to a header or footer
- Setting and viewing page breaks

Previewing worksheets before printing

Before you print a worksheet, it's helpful to take a step back and look at how your data will appear on the printed page. To do that in Microsoft Excel 2013, you display your worksheet in Backstage view. While you have your workbook open in Backstage view, you can zoom in to see cell contents clearly without altering printing size. Excel 2013 also enables you to view your workbook in Page Layout view, which displays your workbook as it will be printed while still enabling you to edit the workbook's contents easily. You can adjust the widths of any columns or rows in Page Layout view, saving you the trouble of switching between Backstage view and the standard Excel window.

Display a worksheet in Page Layout view

1   Click the View tab.

2   In the Workbook Views group, click Page Layout.

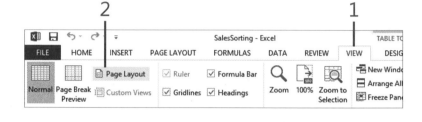

View and zoom worksheets in Backstage view

1   Click the File tab.

2   Click Print.

3   Click the Zoom To Page button.

4   Click the Return To Workbook button to exit Backstage view.

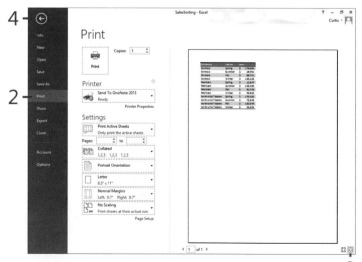

Change column widths and row heights in Page Layout view

1 Click the View tab.

2 Click Page Layout.

3 Hover the mouse pointer over the edge of a column or row header until the mouse pointer becomes a two-headed arrow. Drag the edge until the column or row is the size that you want.

4 Click Normal to return to Normal view.

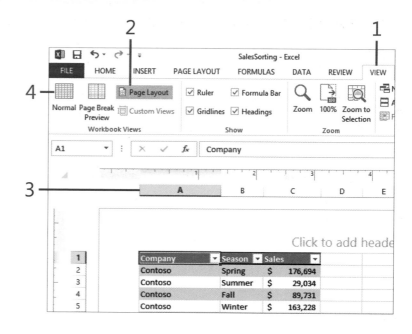

Printing worksheets with current options

After you enter all your data and format your worksheets so that the data is easy to read, you can print your worksheets. Clicking the File tab, clicking Print, and clicking the Print button prints only the worksheet displayed on the screen. However, if you want to print more than one worksheet at a time, such as when you want to print several months of sales results and each month is recorded on a separate worksheet, you can do that as well.

Print multiple worksheets from the same workbook

1 Hold down the Ctrl key, and click the sheet tabs of the worksheets that you want to print.

2 Click the File tab.

3 Click Print.

4 Click the Print button.

5 Click the Return To Workbook button to exit Backstage view.

TIP If all the worksheets in a workbook are adjacent, click the sheet tab for the first worksheet, hold down the Shift key, and click the sheet tab for the last worksheet. Click the Quick Print button on the Quick Access toolbar to print the selected worksheets.

Choosing whether to print gridlines and headings

Excel is a spreadsheet program, which means that it generally expects the data that you enter in it to be organized into rows and columns. However, you're not limited to entering just rows and columns of dry figures; you can add images, place text in cells outside your tables, and format your worksheet so that your data looks exactly the way that you want it to.

In the spirit of offering you as much control as possible, Excel enables you to choose whether to print your worksheets'

gridlines, column headings, and row headings. If you've printed any Microsoft Office document, you've probably noticed that some elements that work very well on your computer screen don't translate well to the printed page. Gridlines, column headings, and row headings are like that. When you're looking at data on a computer screen, those three elements usually help you make sense of your data, but those same elements can clutter your printouts. Excel leaves it up to you; you can choose to print your headings and gridlines or not.

Choose to print gridlines

1 Click the Page Layout tab.

2 In the Sheet Options group, under Gridlines, select the Print check box.

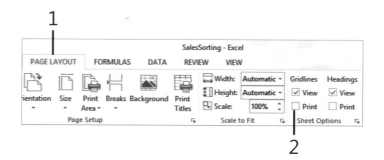

Choose to print headings

1 Click the Page Layout tab.

2 In the Sheet Options group, under Headings, select the Print check box.

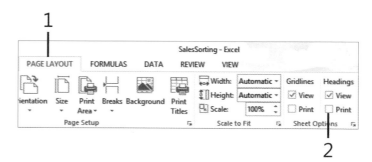

Choosing printers and paper options

You might not want to use the same printer and paper type for everything you print. Standard 8.5-by-11-inch letter size paper is fine for printing some of your worksheets, but from time to time, you'll probably need to use 8.5-by-14-inch legal size paper. In Excel 2013, you can display a list of every paper size available for your use. You can also select which printer you want to use. Depending on the software available on your computer, you might be able to print your worksheet to a file in another program's format.

Choose a printer

1 Click the File tab.

2 Click Print.

3 Click the Printer button.

4 Click the printer you want to use.

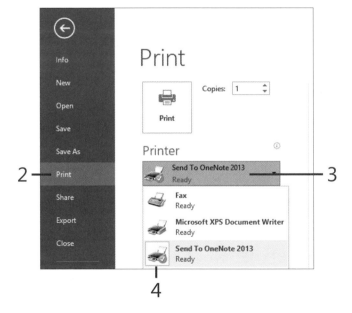

> ⚠ **CAUTION**   Depending on your printer and network configuration, you might not see all of the options described in these procedures.

Choose the paper

1 Click the File tab.

2 Click Print.

3 Click the Paper button.

4 Select the paper size.

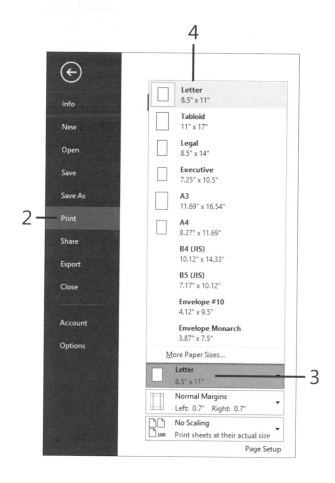

 CAUTION If you change the paper size for one worksheet, the change is effective only for that worksheet.

Printing part of a worksheet

When you create a worksheet containing lots of data, you might want to print just the section of the worksheet with the data relevant to the point that you're trying to illustrate. The good news is that you can set a print area so that Excel prints as much or as little of your worksheet as you like. The print area is outlined

with a dashed line, which lets you see which cells will be printed and which won't. When you set a print area, you can select cells in a single rectangle or select cells located in various areas of your worksheet.

Set a print area

1 Select cells that you want to print.

2 Click the Page Layout tab.

3 Click Print Area.

4 Click Set Print Area.

> **TIP** Try to arrange your data so that the content to be printed looks the same on the screen as it will on the printed page. You can define print areas composed of multiple parts of the same worksheet, but you should keep that technique in reserve for when your worksheet data appears on more than one page.

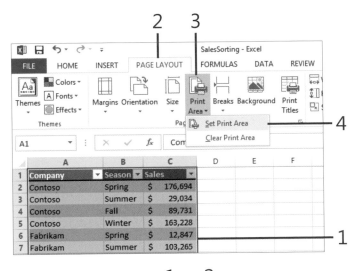

Remove a print area

1 Click the Page Layout tab.

2 Click Print Area.

3 Click Clear Print Area.

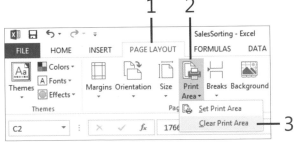

Printing row and column headings on each page

When you print a worksheet in which the data doesn't fit on a single screen, you might have trouble remembering which data is stored in which column. Rather than having to look back to the top of the worksheet—or even type your headings where you guess that the screen transitions occur—you can have Excel print your column and row headings at the top and left of every page. By printing the column and row headings on each page, you save time, improve comprehension, and reduce frustration when dealing with large worksheets.

Identify the rows and columns to repeat

1 Click the Page Layout tab.

2 Click Print Titles.

3 Click the Sheet tab.

4 Click in the Rows To Repeat At Top box.

5 On your worksheet, select the row headings that you want to repeat.

6 Click the Columns To Repeat At Left box.

7 On your worksheet, select the column headings that you want to repeat.

8 Click OK.

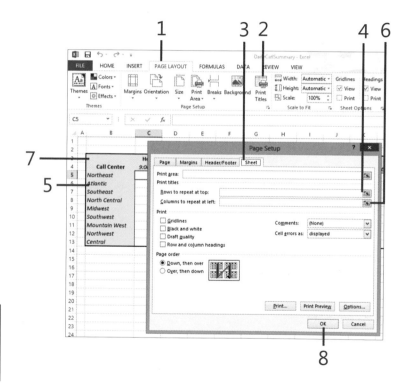

 TIP Repeating rows and columns on every page is useful when your worksheet contains frozen panes and you want to have the frozen panes appear on every page of the printout, just as they appear on the screen.

SEE ALSO For more information about frozen panes, see "View multiple parts of a worksheet by freezing panes" on page 93.

Setting and changing print margins

Margins define the boundary areas of the page, which provide a visual border around your printed data. Changing a worksheet's margins increases or decreases the amount of data that can fit on a printed page, which allows you to make room for one last column of data, divide your columns evenly between two pages, or provide for enough room at one edge for the page to be bound in a report or three-ring binder. In Backstage view, margins appear as dark gray lines that you can drag to the positions where you want them.

Set page margins

1 Click the Page Layout tab.

2 Click Margins, and either click the margin settings that you want to use or click Custom Margins.

3 If you selected Custom Margins, type new values for the worksheet's margins in the Top, Bottom, Left, and Right boxes.

4 Click OK.

TRY THIS Select multiple worksheets by holding down the Ctrl key and clicking the sheet tabs, click the Page Layout tab, click Margins, and then click Custom Margins. Type **0.75** in the Top, Bottom, Left, and Right boxes, and then click OK. All the selected worksheets' margins are changed to three-quarters of an inch.

Adjust page margins in Backstage view

1 Click the File tab.

2 Click Print.

3 If necessary, click the Show Margins button to display the margin lines.

4 Hover the mouse pointer over one of the gray lines until the mouse pointer becomes a two-headed arrow. Drag the line until the margin is set the way that you want.

5 Click the Return To Workbook button to exit Backstage view.

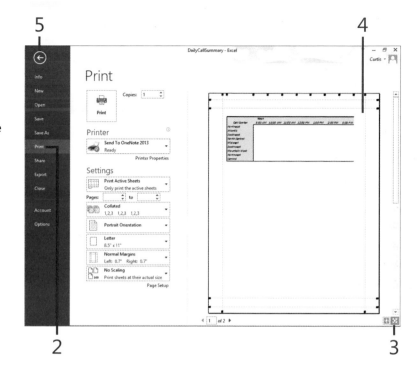

⚠ **CAUTION** In Backstage view, it's sometimes difficult to distinguish between margins and header or footer lines. Be sure to keep track of which is which.

Setting page orientation and scale

As you look at your worksheet and think about how you want it to appear on the printed page, be aware that you have the choice of printing in a vertical format (portrait mode) or a horizontal format (landscape mode). Landscape mode is particularly useful when you have a lot of columns in your worksheet, such as in a worksheet storing customer contact or product sales information. You can fit your worksheet onto a specific number of printed pages, which helps if you have been allotted a fixed number of pages in which to present your data in a typeset report.

Set page orientation

1 Click the Page Layout tab.

2 Click Orientation.

3 Select either the Portrait or Landscape option.

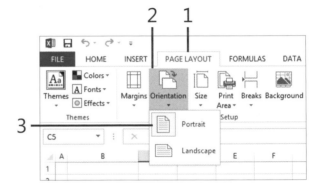

TIP Select Portrait orientation for long worksheets that are not very wide, or select Landscape orientation for worksheets with many columns.

Scale the printout to a fixed number of pages

1 Click the Page Layout tab.

2 In the Scale To Fit group, click the Width down arrow and select the number of horizontal pages that your worksheet should take up when printed.

3 In the Scale To Fit group, click the Height down arrow and select the number of vertical pages that your worksheet should take up when printed.

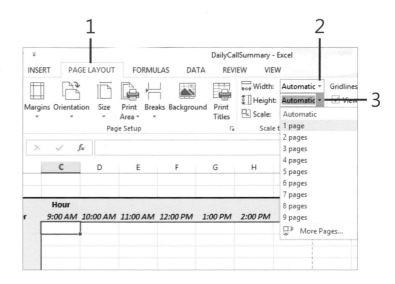

TIP If you want to force your worksheet to print on 10 or more pages in either dimension, click the Width or Height control's down arrow, and click More Pages. Then, using the controls on the Page tab of the Page Setup dialog box, select the Fit To option and type the number of pages the rows (pages wide) and columns (tall) of your worksheet should be forced to fit on. Click OK.

TRY THIS Click the Page Layout tab, and then click the Page Setup group's dialog box launcher. In the Page Setup dialog box, click the Page tab, and then select the Fit To option. Type 1 in the Page(s) Wide box, and delete the contents of the Tall box. The worksheet now fits on a single page wide but prints on additional vertical pages if necessary.

Creating headers and footers

Headers and footers contain information that appears at the top and bottom of each page of your printed worksheet. You can select a premade header or footer that contains information about your file, or you can create custom headers and footers using predefined text. Excel 2013 comes with a list of expressions that you can insert into your headers and footers to display certain information about your worksheet, such as page numbers or file names. Headers might include helpful information such as a workbook name, and footers can include page numbers, file names, or dates.

Add a premade header and footer

1 Click the Insert tab.

2 Click Text.

3 Click Header & Footer.

4 Click Header.

5 Click the premade header that you want to use.

6 If you want to, click Footer, and then click the premade footer to use.

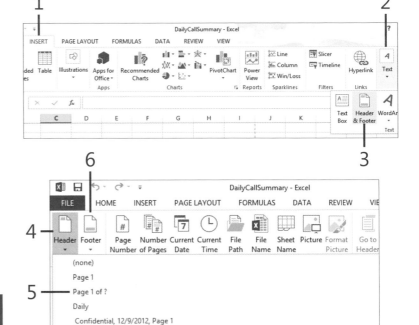

 TIP Click the File tab and then click Print to preview your headers and footers before you print.

 SEE ALSO For more information about how to change the size of your headers, see "Adjust header and footer height" on the following page.

Add predefined text to the header or footer

1 Click the Insert tab.

2 Click Text.

3 Click Header & Footer.

4 Click the section of the header or footer where you want your text to appear, and type the text that you want.

5 If you want to use predefined text, position the insertion point where you want the text to appear.

6 Click a button to insert the predefined text.

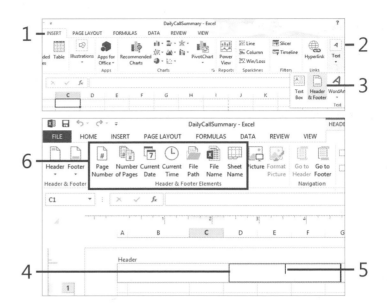

> ✓ **TIP** You can change the appearance of your header and footer text by selecting the text or the code representing the value to be printed (for example, the current time) and then using the controls on the Home tab on the ribbon.

Adjust header and footer height

1 Click the Page Layout tab.

2 Click the Page Setup group's dialog box expander.

3 On the Page Setup dialog box, if necessary, click the Margins tab.

4 Type a new height for the header in the Header box.

5 Type a new height for the footer in the Footer box.

6 Click OK.

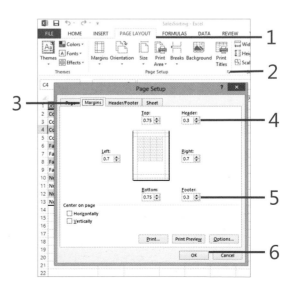

> ✓ **TIP** The directions of the arrowheads show you in which direction you can move the line.

Adding graphics to a header or a footer

Creating attractive and professional-looking printouts helps you communicate your message better. Often, the addition of a simple graphic to a header or footer gives your worksheet a truly professional appearance. You might want to create printouts that include your company's letterhead or logo or a graphic related to the information on your worksheet. An excellent way to include graphics on every printed page is to place them into the header and footer of your worksheet.

Include a graphic in a header or footer

1 Click the Insert tab.

2 Click Text.

3 Click Header & Footer.

4 Click in the section of the header or footer where you want your graphic to appear.

5 Click the Picture button.

6 In the From a File section, click Browse.

7 Navigate to the folder that contains the picture that you want to insert.

8 Double-click the image.

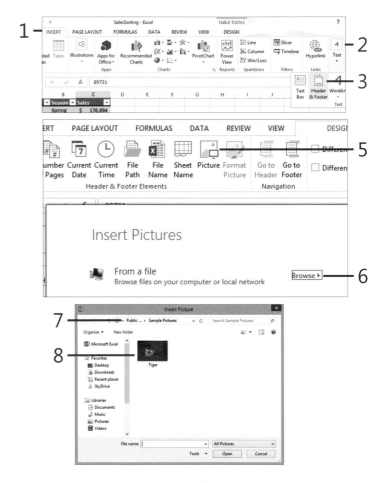

 CAUTION If the graphic is larger than the area allotted for the header or footer, the image will cover up some of the worksheet data.

Format a graphic in a header or footer

1 Click the Insert tab.

2 Click Text.

3 Click Header & Footer.

4 Select the text &[Picture].

5 Click the Format Picture button.

6 Click the Size and Picture tabs, and specify the options that you want.

7 Click OK.

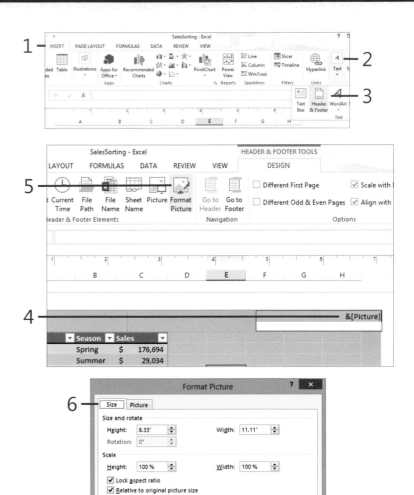

CAUTION When using Format Picture, you cannot use the Undo button to reverse your actions after they are complete.

Setting and viewing page breaks

Excel determines where one printed page ends and the next begins based on the page size, margins, and orientation; however, the page breaks Excel sets might not work for a particular worksheet. You might want to place a chart or table on its own sheet, or you might want to force two separate tables onto one printed page. You can display all existing page breaks by opening your worksheet in Page Break Preview mode, which displays the page breaks as blue lines. If the blue lines are dashed, they represent an automatic page break; if the blue lines are solid, they represent a manually set page break. While in Page Break Preview mode, you can change the location of any existing page breaks to ensure that your worksheets print exactly the way that you want.

View current page breaks

1 Click the View tab.

2 Click Page Break Preview.

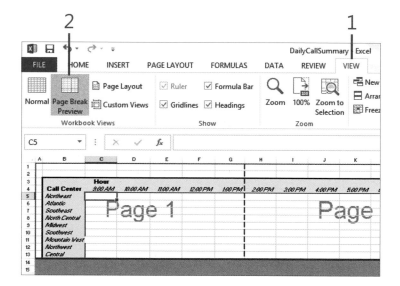

Set manual page breaks

1 Click the cell below and to the right of where you want to insert a page break.

2 Click the Page Layout tab.

3 Click Breaks.

4 Click Insert Page Break.

Change manual page breaks

1 Click the View tab.

2 Click Page Break Preview.

3 Hover the mouse pointer over one of the blue lines until the mouse pointer becomes a two-headed arrow. Drag the line until the page break is where you want it.

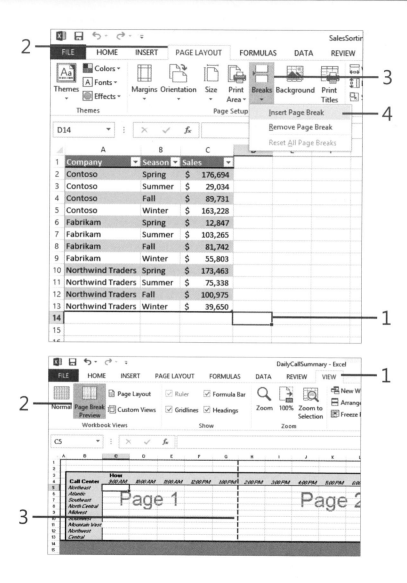

Customizing Excel to the way you work

10

Another way to make your life easier is to create templates. A template is a workbook that you use as a pattern for other workbooks. When you open a template, which is a separate Excel file type, you have the outline you need to create frequently used workbooks quickly.

You also have a great deal of control over how Excel handles the data that you enter in your worksheets. Excel tries to be helpful by identifying formulas that it thinks are mistakes, probably because the formula isn't consistent with other formulas near it or because it leaves out cells in a range. Sometimes those mistakes are exactly what you intended. The same is true for potential misspellings. Excel identifies and corrects the most common misspellings, but if a word Excel identifies as misspelled is actually correct, you can prevent Excel from making that change without turning off the corrective behavior entirely.

Microsoft Excel 2013 gives you lots of ways to work with your data, with literally hundreds of commands at your disposal. If you find that it takes several mouse clicks to reveal a command that you use all the time, you can add that command to the Quick Access toolbar so that you can activate it with a single click. Excel 2013 also enables you to create custom tabs on the ribbon.

In this section:

- Opening ready-to-use workbook templates
- Saving a workbook as a template
- Adding commands to and moving the Quick Access toolbar
- Adding, reordering, and removing ribbon elements
- Creating new ribbon tabs and groups
- Renaming a ribbon element
- Hiding and displaying ribbon tabs
- Controlling which error messages appear
- Choosing the color Excel uses to display errors
- Defining AutoCorrect entries
- Controlling AutoFormat rules

Opening ready-to-use workbook templates

Excel 2013 comes with a wide variety of templates that you can use to create workbooks to manage your data with a few clicks of the mouse. You can select from built-in templates for both business and personal use, or you can search the online template collection that includes workbooks for managing budgets, creating invoices, printing calendars, managing your expenses, creating lists, projecting loan payments, and keeping a schedule. After you create a workbook based on a template, you can modify it to meet your specific needs.

Create a workbook from a template

1 Click the File tab.

2 Click New.

3 If necessary, click a template category.

4 Double-click the template that you want to use to create your workbook.

(continued on next page)

TIP If you have an active Internet connection, you can type one or more keywords in the Search Office.com For Templates box and click the Start Searching button (it looks like a right-pointing arrow) to look for templates on the Office.com website.

Create a workbook from a template *(continued)*

5 Press Ctrl+S to display the Save As page of the Backstage view.

6 Click Computer.

7 Click Browse.

8 Navigate to the folder where you want to save the file.

9 Type a name for the file.

10 Click Save.

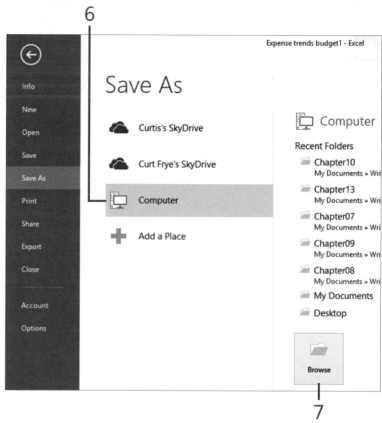

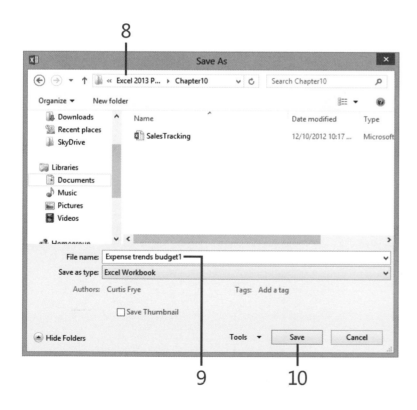

Saving a workbook as a template

When you decide which type of data that you want to store in a workbook and what that workbook should look like, you will probably want to create similar workbooks without adding all the formatting and formulas again. For example, you might have settled on a design for your monthly sales-tracking workbook. When you settle on a design for your workbooks, you can save one of the workbooks as a pattern, or template, for similar workbooks that you create in the future.

Save a workbook as a template

1 Click the File tab.

2 Click Export.

3 Click Change File Type.

4 Click Template.

5 Click the Save As button.

6 Type a name for the template.

7 Click Save.

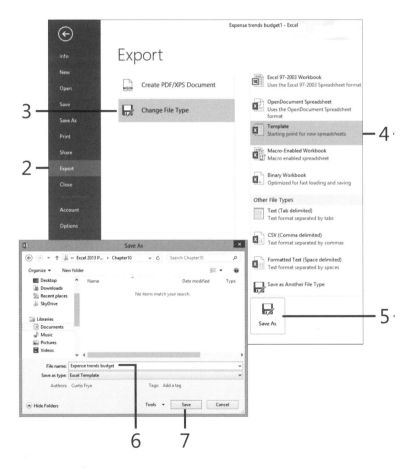

> ⚠️ **CAUTION** Be sure that you don't change the directory where Excel offers to save your template. If you do change it, your template won't show up in the list of available templates, but you can still open it by navigating to the folder in which you save it.

> ✓ **TIP** You should remove any existing data from a workbook that you save as a template, both to avoid data entry errors and to remove any confusion as to whether the workbook is a template. The one exception to this rule is when your template contains formulas that result in an error if you delete all data from the worksheet. In that case, you should enter some obviously incorrect data that future users know to replace.

Modify a template

1 Click the File tab.

2 Click Open.

3 Click Computer.

4 Click Browse.

5 Click the template that you want to modify.

6 Click Open.

7 Make the changes that you want.

8 Click the Save button.

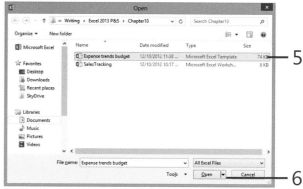

TIP You can always change a workbook's file type to Excel Template, so don't worry if you accidentally try to create a regular workbook instead of saving your changes to the template.

Adding commands to the Quick Access toolbar

The majority of commands you use in Excel 2013 appear on the ribbon, but some of the commands require you to move through one or two levels of the user interface (for example, click the correct ribbon tab and then click a button to open a dialog box). If there's a specific command that you use all the time, you can make that command easier to find by adding it to the Quick Access toolbar. If you later find that you don't use the command as much as you used to, you can always remove the command and make room for the commands that you do use.

Add a command to the Quick Access toolbar

1 Right-click any command on the Quick Access toolbar.

2 Click Customize Quick Access Toolbar.

3 Click the Choose Commands From down arrow.

4 Click the category from which you want to choose the command.

5 Click the command that you want to add.

6 Click Add.

7 Click OK.

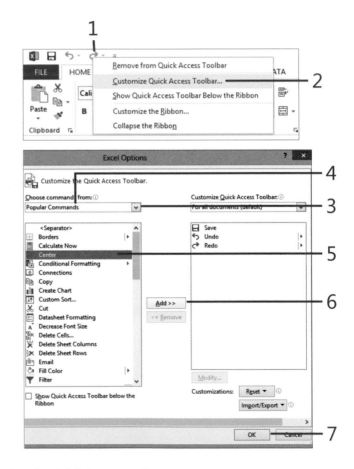

Remove a command from the Quick Access toolbar

1 Right-click the command that you want to remove from the Quick Access toolbar.

2 Click Remove From Quick Access Toolbar.

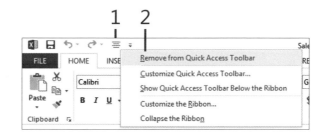

Moving the Quick Access toolbar

When you install Excel 2013, the Quick Access toolbar appears at the top of the Excel program window, above the ribbon. To get to that area of the screen by using your mouse, you move the mouse pointer toward the top of the screen. When your mouse pointer stops going up, move to the left or right to click the Quick Access toolbar button that you want to use.

If you want to add a large number of commands to the Quick Access Toolbar or if you'd prefer to have its buttons closer to the body of a worksheet, you can display the Quick Access toolbar below the ribbon instead of above it. As with all other interface changes, you can always put it back on top if you think that position better fits your workflow.

Move the Quick Access toolbar

1 Right-click any command on the Quick Access toolbar.

2 Click Show Quick Access Toolbar Below The Ribbon.

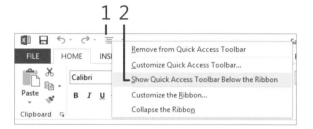

TIP You can change the order of the buttons on the Quick Access Toolbar by displaying the Quick Access Toolbar page of the Excel Options dialog box, clicking the command that you want to move, and then clicking the Move Up or Move Down button.

TRY THIS Select a button on the ribbon, and add it to the Quick Access toolbar by right-clicking the button and choosing Add To Quick Access Toolbar.

Removing a ribbon element

If you add elements to one or more ribbon tabs, you might find that those tabs start to become a bit crowded. Even if you bring all of your favorite commands onto a single tab, you might need to remove a few of them to make your tab easier to use.

To remove a ribbon element, you display the Customize The Ribbon page of the Excel Options dialog box and use its controls to get rid of the element that you no longer want.

Remove a ribbon element

1 Right-click any ribbon tab.

2 Click Customize The Ribbon.

3 Click the command, group, or tab that you want to remove.

4 Click Remove.

5 Click OK.

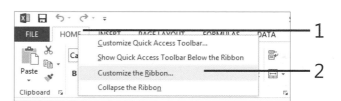

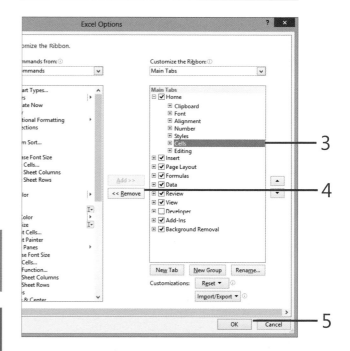

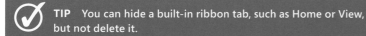

⚠ **CAUTION** Removing a custom tab or group deletes that element. If you want the element to remain available for use, hide it instead of removing it.

✓ **TIP** You can hide a built-in ribbon tab, such as Home or View, but not delete it.

Adding and reordering ribbon elements

Excel 2013 enhances your ability to customize the entire ribbon user interface. The ribbon consists of several elements: tabs, which are designated by the clickable words at the top of the ribbon (for example, Home, Insert, and Page Layout); groups, which are named collections of commands (such as the Font group on the Home tab); and commands, which are individual items within a group (such as the Bold button in the Home tab's Font group). In Excel 2013, you can add and reorder ribbon elements to best suit your workflow. The only limitation is that you can add commands only to custom groups, not built-in groups.

Add a command to a ribbon tab

1 Right-click any ribbon tab.

2 Click Customize The Ribbon.

3 Click the Choose Commands From down arrow.

4 Click the category from which you want to choose the command.

5 Click the command that you want to add.

6 Click the tab to which you want to add the command.

7 Click the group or command that you want the new command to appear to the right of on the ribbon.

8 Click Add.

9 Click OK.

> ✓ **TIP** To restore the ribbon to the same configuration it had when you installed Excel 2013, right-click anywhere on the ribbon, click Customize The Ribbon, click Reset, click Reset All Customizations, and then click OK. If you want to remove the changes from a specific ribbon tab, click that tab in the Main Tabs pane, click Reset, click Reset Only Selected Ribbon Tab, and then click OK.

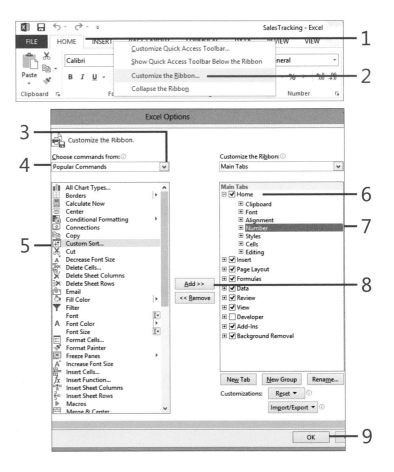

Reorder commands on a ribbon tab

1 Right-click any ribbon tab.

2 Click Customize The Ribbon.

3 Click the command, group, or tab that you want to move.

4 Click the Move Up or Move Down button.

5 Click OK.

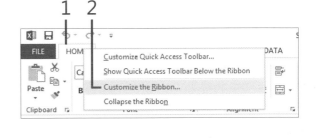

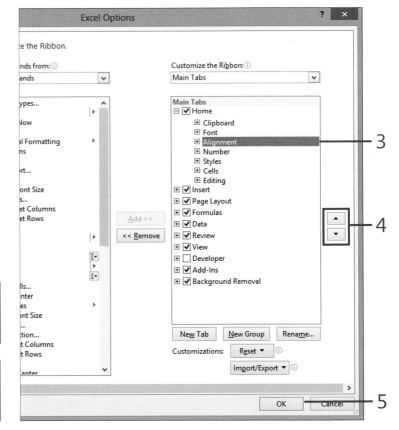

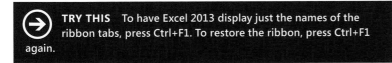

TRY THIS To have Excel 2013 display just the names of the ribbon tabs, press Ctrl+F1. To restore the ribbon, press Ctrl+F1 again.

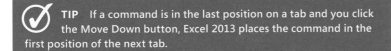

TIP If a command is in the last position on a tab and you click the Move Down button, Excel 2013 places the command in the first position of the next tab.

Creating new ribbon tabs and groups

The Excel 2013 ribbon interface contains all of the commands that you'll use on a regular basis, organized to meet the needs of most users. If you want to create a custom ribbon tab that includes the commands that you use most frequently, you can do so by using the controls on the Customize Ribbon page of

the Excel Options dialog box. After you create the custom tab, you can add existing commands without removing them from their original places on the ribbon. If you want to bring individual commands into their own group, you can create a custom group on a ribbon tab to hold them.

Create a custom ribbon tab

1 Right-click any ribbon tab.

2 Click Customize The Ribbon.

3 Click the tab above where you want the new tab to appear.

4 Click New Tab.

5 Click OK.

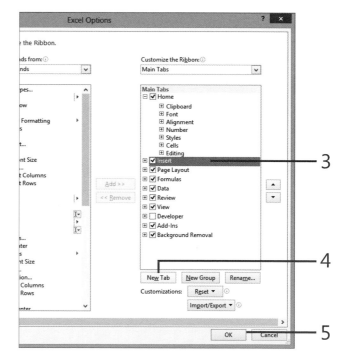

> **TRY THIS** Right-click anywhere on the ribbon and then click Customize The Ribbon. In the Main Tabs pane, click the Insert tab and then click New Tab. Then, in the command list in the left pane, click Font and then click Add. When you click OK to close the Excel Options dialog box, a tab named New Tab appears on the ribbon. When you click the New Tab tab, you'll see that it contains a group named New Group, which in turn contains the Font command.

Add a new group to a ribbon tab

1 Right-click any ribbon tab.

2 Click Customize The Ribbon.

3 Click the group or tab name above where you want the new group to appear.

4 Click New Group.

5 Click OK.

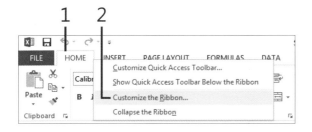

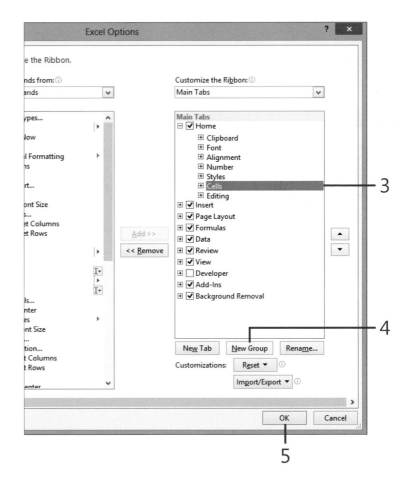

✓ **TIP** Don't feel the need to fill up your custom ribbon tab. If you use five groups of commands and they fit in the left half of the tab, you should leave the rest of the custom tab empty.

Renaming a ribbon element

The Excel user interface design team spends a great deal of time determining the best names and labels for each element. If you want to rename an item or if you create your own custom ribbon elements and want to change the name that you assigned to them, you can do so from within the Excel Options dialog box. The controls you need appear on the Customize Ribbon page of the dialog box.

Rename a ribbon element

1 Right-click any ribbon tab.

2 Click Customize The Ribbon.

3 Click the element that you want to rename.

4 Click Rename.

5 Type a new name for the element.

6 Click OK in the Rename dialog box.

7 Click OK.

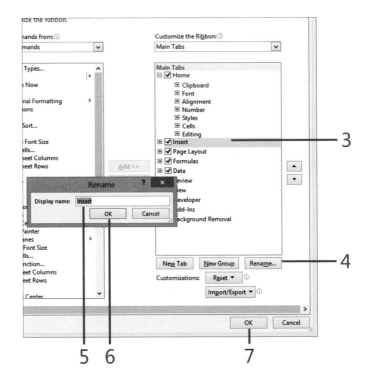

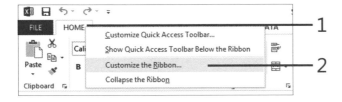

> **✓ TIP** When you rename a custom ribbon command, the Rename dialog box displays a set of icons. Selecting one of the icons helps you identify the element visually.

Choosing the color Excel uses to display errors

Excel 2013 uses a variety of colored flags to convey information about the contents of individual cells. For example, cells with comments have a red flag at the top-right corner. Excel highlights cells that contain formulas with errors by displaying a green flag at the top-left corner of the cell. If you prefer to highlight those cells by using a flag with a color other than green, you can use the controls on the Formulas page of the Excel Options dialog box to select a new color for the flags.

Select the color that Excel uses to display errors

1 Click the File tab.

2 Click Options.

3 Click Formulas.

4 Click Indicate Errors Using This Color.

5 Click the color that you want to use.

6 Click OK.

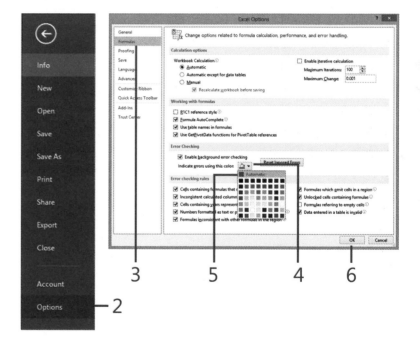

Hiding and displaying ribbon tabs

Every ribbon tab, with the exception of the File tab, can be hidden without removing it from the ribbon's underlying structure. To hide a ribbon tab, open the Excel Options dialog box and display the Customize Ribbon page. On the right side of this page is a list of all tabs that currently appear on the ribbon. Each tab has a check box to the left of its name. Selecting a tab's check box displays the tab on the ribbon, while clearing the check box hides it.

Hide a ribbon tab

1 Right-click any ribbon tab.

2 Click Customize The Ribbon.

3 Clear the check box next to the tab that you want to hide.

4 Click OK.

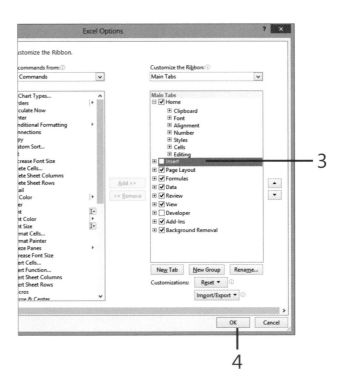

Redisplay a hidden ribbon element

1 Right-click any ribbon tab.

2 Click Customize The Ribbon.

3 Select the check box next to the item that you want to display.

4 Click OK.

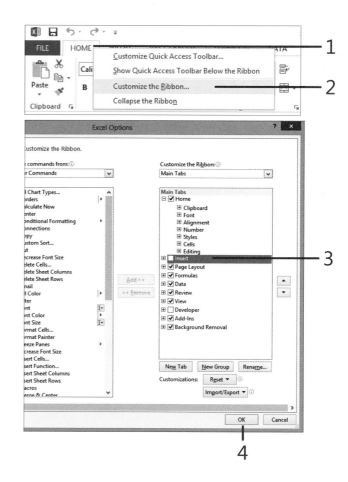

Controlling which error messages appear

We all make mistakes, but some of those mistakes are easier to recover from than others. If you create a formula that tries to have Excel divide a value by zero or use a value from a cell that's currently blank, Excel displays an error flag indicating that it thinks you made a mistake. If the error is that no value is in a cell that you refer to in a formula, you can fix the problem by putting a value in that cell.

However, sometimes Excel identifies a formula as an error when it's exactly what you intended. For example, if you create

a worksheet that contains five columns of data and you find the sum of each of those columns, Excel identifies the pattern inherent in those formulas. If you put a different type of formula (such as a formula that finds the maximum value in all five rows) in the cell next to those five consistent formulas, Excel displays an error indicating that the formula is inconsistent. Fortunately, you can choose to turn several types of error indicators on or off, saving you and your colleagues from worrying about errors that don't exist.

Choose which error messages appear

1 Click the File tab.

2 Click Options.

3 Click Formulas.

4 Clear the check boxes next to the errors that you want Excel to ignore.

5 Click OK.

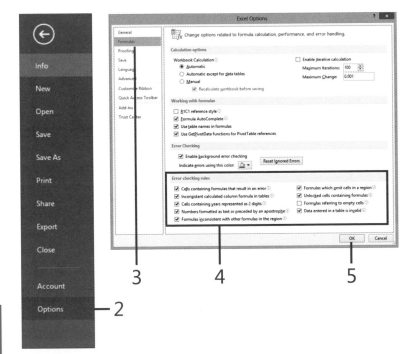

> **TIP** The most common errors that you'll want to ignore are formulas that are inconsistent with other formulas in the region and formulas that omit cells in a region.

Reset ignored errors

1 Click the File tab.

2 Click Options.

3 Click Formulas.

4 Click Reset Ignored Errors.

5 Click OK.

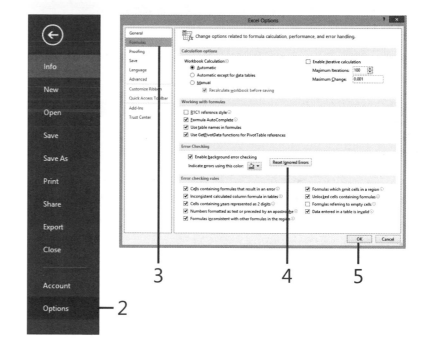

Defining AutoCorrect entries

You're bound to make typing mistakes when you spend a lot of time at the keyboard. In fact, slowing down doesn't help; the more slowly you go, the more likely you are to hit the wrong keys.

Over the years, many Excel users have allowed the programming team to monitor their typing, which means that the Excel team has identified the most common mistakes resulting from popular misspellings, letter transpositions, and errors that are the result of not pressing the Spacebar fast enough to put a space between words. If one of the words that Excel identifies as an error is actually correct (for example, you work with a client corporation named Idae, a popular misspelling of the word idea), you can delete that entry from the AutoCorrect list.

Create an AutoCorrect entry

1 Click the File tab.

2 Click Options.

3 Click Proofing.

4 Click AutoCorrect Options.

5 Type the text to be replaced.

6 Type the text with which to replace the previous entry.

7 Click Add.

8 Click OK in the AutoCorrect dialog box.

9 Click OK.

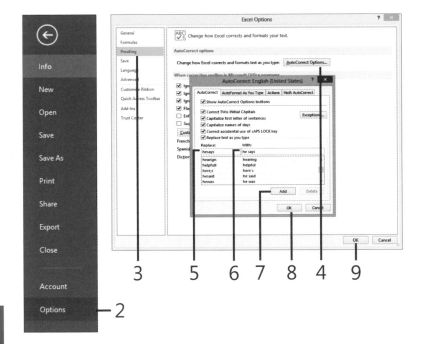

> **TIP**   Many users type the same text frequently, such as "Payment is due within 30 days. If payment is made within 10 days, you may deduct 2% from the total amount due." If you often type this text, you could create an AutoCorrect entry that replaces the phrase *Net30/2* with the text describing the payment terms already listed.

Delete an AutoCorrect entry

1 Click the File tab.

2 Click Options.

3 Click Proofing.

4 Click AutoCorrect Options.

5 Click the entry to be removed.

6 Click Delete.

7 Click OK in the AutoCorrect dialog box.

8 Click OK.

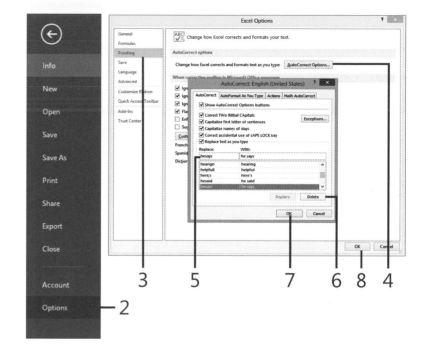

✓ TIP   To undo an AutoCorrect correction, press Ctrl-Z.

Controlling AutoFormat rules

When you enter data into an Excel worksheet, the program examines the data to determine whether it fits specific patterns. For example, if you enter an Internet address for a website, the program changes the address's formatting from plain text to a hyperlink. Users can then click the hyperlink to display the site referred to by the link. Other rules cause Excel to include new rows of data in nearby Excel tables and fill formulas throughout an Excel table column. You can control these behaviors by using the tools on the AutoFormat As You Type tab of the AutoCorrect dialog box.

Control AutoFormat rules

1 Click the File tab.

2 Click Options.

3 Click Proofing.

4 Click AutoCorrect Options.

5 Click the AutoFormat As You Type tab.

6 Clear the check boxes next to the rules that you want to turn off, or select the check boxes next to the rules that you want to turn on.

7 Click OK in the AutoCorrect dialog box.

8 Click OK.

Sorting and filtering worksheet data

11

After you add data to your worksheets, you might want to change the order in which the worksheet rows are displayed. For example, if you have a worksheet listing orders for a week, you might want to list the orders for each customer or perhaps reorder the rows in your worksheet so that the most expensive orders are at the top of the list and the least expensive at the bottom. You can also hide any rows that don't meet your criteria, which is particularly useful if you work with a large data set.

Just as you can change or limit how your worksheet data is displayed, you can control what data is entered in your worksheets. By setting validation rules for groups of cells, you can check each value, and if the value you or your colleague enters falls outside the accepted range, you can display an error message informing you or your colleague what went wrong and what sort of value should be entered.

In this section:

- Sorting worksheet data
- Creating a custom sort list
- Filtering data quickly with AutoFilter
- Filtering data with a search filter
- Clearing a filter
- Creating an advanced filter
- Filtering Excel tables visually by using slicers
- Clearing and removing slicers
- Validating data for correctness during entry
- Creating a recommended PivotTable
- Analyzing data using PowerPivot
- Presenting data using Power View

Sorting worksheet data

You can sort a group of rows in a worksheet in a number of ways, but the first step is to identify the column that includes the values by which to sort the rows. After you select the column by which you want to sort the worksheet, you can choose whether to display the sorted values in ascending or descending order. For example, if you have a list of products that your company sells with each product's sales in the same row, you could sort the worksheet by the contents of the sales column in descending order to discover which products generated the most revenue for your company. You could sort the worksheet rows in ascending order to put the lowest-revenue products at the top of the list. If you want to sort by the contents of more than one column, you can create a multicolumn sort. One handy use for a multicolumn sort is to sort your products by category and then by total sales.

Sort data in ascending or descending order

1   Click any cell in the column by which you want to sort your data.

2   Click the Data tab.

3   Follow either of these steps:

   a   Click the Sort Ascending button in the Sort & Filter group on the ribbon.

   b   Click the Sort Descending button in the Sort & Filter group on the ribbon.

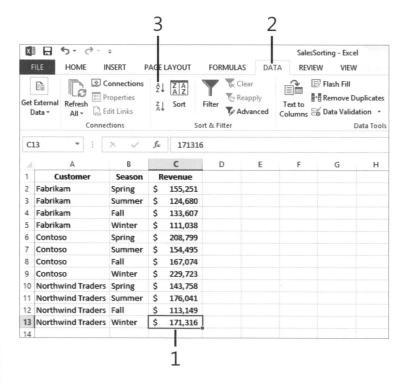

> ✓ **TIP** The names of the sorting buttons in the Data tab's Sort & Filter group change to reflect the type of data in the column to be sorted. If the column contains numbers, the buttons are named Sort Smallest To Largest and Sort Largest To Smallest; for text, the buttons are named Sort A To Z and Sort Z To A; for dates, they are named Sort Oldest To Newest and Sort Newest To Oldest.

Create a multicolumn sort

1 Select a cell in the data list or Excel table you want to sort.

2 Click the Data tab.

3 Click Sort.

4 Click the Sort By down arrow and then click the first column by which you want to sort.

5 Click the Sort On down arrow and then click the criteria by which you want to sort.

6 Click the Order down arrow.

7 Select the A to Z item or the Z to A item to indicate the order in which the column's values should be sorted.

8 Click Add Level.

9 If necessary, repeat steps 4–8 to set the columns and order for additional sorting rules.

10 Click OK.

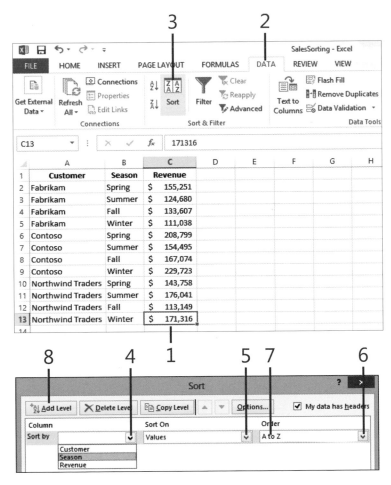

TIP Be sure there are no blank rows or columns in the data you want to sort. Gaps in your worksheet can cause Excel to sort a subset of your data.

CAUTION If you don't have a column with a unique value in each cell, such as a product number or customer identification number, you might not be able to put your worksheet back to its original order.

Creating a custom sort list

When you sort column data, Excel sorts numbers according to their values and words in alphabetical order, but that pattern doesn't work for some sets of values. For example, sorting the months of the year in alphabetical order puts February in front of January. To avoid those errors, Excel comes with four custom lists: days of the week, abbreviations for days of the week, months, and abbreviated month names. You can have Excel sort based on those lists, or if you want to create a custom list of your own, you can do so. Because the day and abbreviated day name lists begin with Sunday, you could create a new list beginning with Monday to reflect your business schedule.

Define a custom list of values

1 Click the File tab.

2 Click Options.

3 Click Advanced.

4 In the General section of the Advanced page, click Edit Custom Lists.

5 Click New List.

6 Type the custom list that you want. Separate each entry by pressing Enter.

7 Click Add.

8 Click OK twice to close the Custom Lists dialog box and the Excel Options dialog box, respectively.

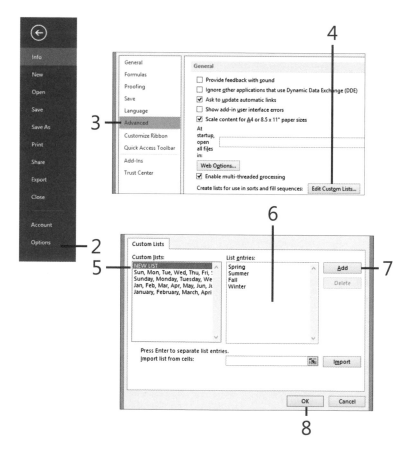

Sort using a custom list

1 Click any cell in the list that you want to sort.

2 Click the Data tab.

3 Click Sort.

4 Click the Sort By down arrow and then click the column that you want to sort by.

5 Click the Sort On down arrow and then click the criteria that you want to sort by.

6 Click the Order down arrow and then click Custom List.

7 Click a custom list.

8 Click OK to close the Custom Lists dialog box.

9 Click OK to sort the data list.

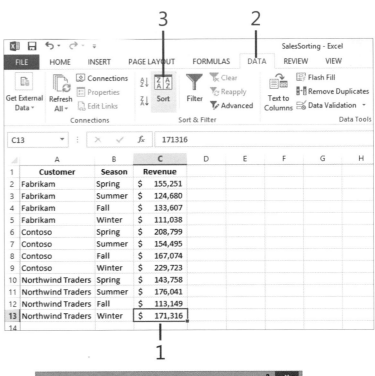

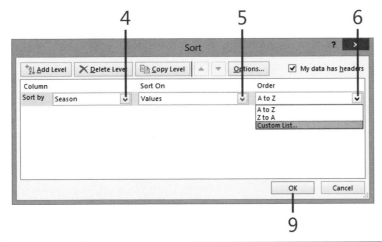

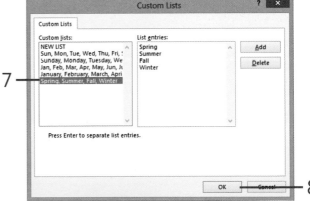

TIP In versions of Excel prior to Excel 2007, you could use a custom list to sort only one column of your worksheet data and that column had to be the first by which you sorted your data. In Excel 2013, you can sort any number of columns according to the values in a custom list.

Filtering data quickly with AutoFilter

An important aspect of working with large amounts of data is the ability focus in on the most important data in a worksheet, whether that data represents the best 10 days of sales in a month or slow-selling product lines that you might need to reevaluate. In Excel 2013, you have a number of powerful, flexible techniques that you can use to limit the data displayed in your worksheet. One of those techniques is to filter the contents of a worksheet. You can filter a data list or Excel table by selecting individual values, creating a rule, or by searching for values within a field.

Create a selection filter

1 Click any cell in the range that you want to filter.

2 Click the Data tab.

3 Click Filter.

4 Click the filter arrow for the column by which you want to filter your worksheet.

5 Select the check boxes next to the values by which you want to filter the list.

6 Click OK.

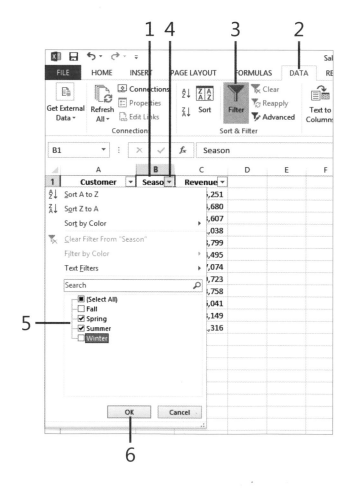

> ✓ **TIP** When you create a custom AutoFilter, the menu item changes to reflect the type of data in the column (date, text, number, and so on).

> → **TRY THIS** To select just a few items, clear the Select All check box and then select the check boxes next to the items that you want to appear in your worksheet.

Create a filtering rule

1 Click any cell in the list that you want to filter.

2 Click the Data tab.

3 If necessary, click Filter to display the filter arrows.

4 Click the filter arrow of the column for which you want to create a custom filter.

5 Point to Text Filters.

6 Click Custom Filter.

7 Click the Comparison Operator down arrow.

8 Click the comparison that you want to use.

9 Type the value with which you want to compare the values in the selected column.

10 Click OK.

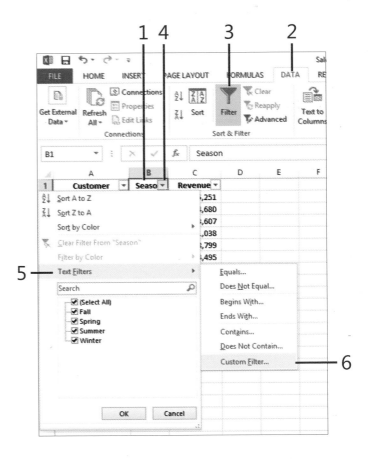

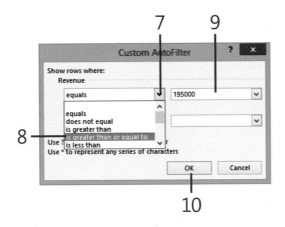

> **TIP**   When a column is filtered, the filter arrow that appears to the right of the filtered list header is replaced by a filter icon.

Filtering data with a search filter

Collections of data often have strings of characters that occur in multiple values. For example, if you maintain a list of sales by region, you might have regions named North Central, Northwest, and Northeast. If you want to display values from the northern regions, you can create a search filter based on the term *north*.

Create a search filter

1 Click any cell in the list that you want to filter.

2 Click the Data tab.

3 If necessary, click Filter to display the filter arrows.

4 Click the filter arrow of the column for which you want to create a search filter.

5 In the Search box, type the character string for which you want to search.

6 Use the check boxes to include or exclude specific values.

7 Click OK.

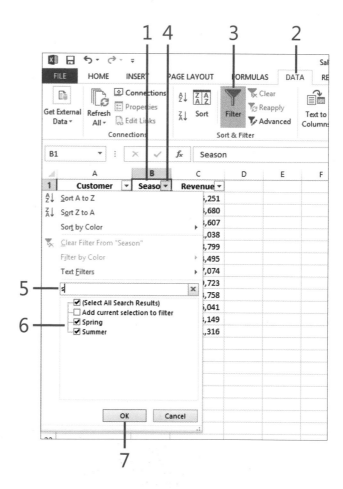

Analyzing data by using PowerPivot

As data collections increase in size, the need to analyze hundreds of thousands or even millions of rows of data grows. Starting in Excel 2007, individual Excel worksheets could store 1,048,576 rows of data. This increased capacity came at a price—worksheets that stored large data collections calculated more slowly, as did PivotTables and other workbook elements based on the large data set.

When Microsoft released Excel 2010, the programming team also released PowerPivot. PowerPivot was made available as an add-in for Excel 2010, but its basic functions have been incorporated into Excel 2013. Using PowerPivot, you can manage data collections that contain many millions of rows without spreading the data across multiple worksheets. Calculations and summaries run quickly regardless of the size of your data collection, you can define relationships among multiple tables to combine the data in meaningful ways, and Excel 2013 greatly compresses the data to reduce the overall size of your workbook file.

You can extend the functionality of PowerPivot in Excel 2013 by installing the PowerPivot add-in. Installing the add-in lets you filter data while you import it, rename tables and columns during import, define relationships among tables, and define Key Performance Indicators for business intelligence applications.

A full discussion of PowerPivot is beyond the scope of this book, but you can find much more information by visiting *www.powerpivot.com.*

As of this writing, PowerPivot is available only for users who have installed Office 2013 Professional Plus, SharePoint 2013 Enterprise Edition, SharePoint Online 2013 Plan 2, and the E3 or E4 editions of Office 365. It is possible that Microsoft will subsequently make both PowerPivot and the related add-in Power View available to all users, as was the case in Excel 2010.

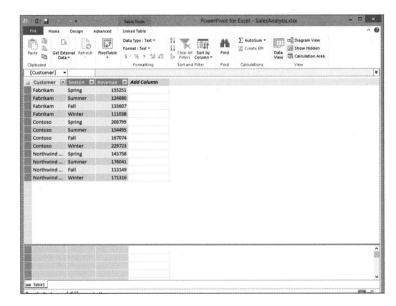

Clearing a filter

Filters limit the data displayed in a worksheet, which helps you focus on the data that means the most to you. When you want to remove a filter from a column of data, you can do so quickly.

Removing a filter from a column doesn't affect filters applied to other columns. You must either remove them individually or clear all filters at the same time.

Clear a filter from a column

1 Click the filter arrow of the filtered column.

2 Click Clear Filter.

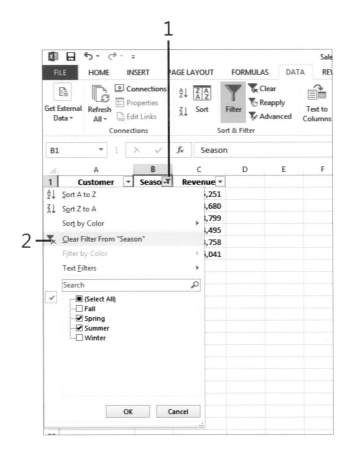

> **TIP** The Clear Filter menu item changes to reflect the name of the filtered column. For example, if you filtered the Season column, the menu item would read Clear Filter From "Season."

Clear all active filters

1 Click a cell in the filtered data range.

2 Click the Data tab.

3 Using the controls in the Sort & Filter group, perform one of the following actions:

a Click the Clear button to clear all filters, and leave the filter arrows displayed.

b Click the Filter button to clear all filters, and remove the filter arrows.

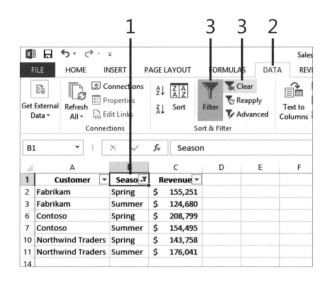

Creating an advanced filter

When you create a filter using AutoFilter, you can create complex rules to filter the contents of the worksheet. The limitation is that the rules used to filter the worksheet aren't readily discernible. If you want the rules used to filter a column's values to be displayed in the body of the worksheet, you can write

each rule in a cell and identify those cells so that Excel knows how to filter the worksheet. If you ever want to change the rules used to filter your data, all you need to do is change a rule and reapply the filter.

Build an advanced filter

1 Copy the column titles of the list that you want to filter.

2 Paste the titles into another spot on your workbook.

3 Under their respective titles, type the criteria that you want the filter to meet.

4 Select a cell in the list that you want to filter.

5 Click the Data tab.

6 In the Sort & Filter group on the ribbon, click Advanced.

7 Click the List Range box.

8 If necessary, select the entire list that you want to filter, including the column headers.

9 Click the Criteria Range box.

10 Select the cells on which you want to base the filter, including the column headers.

11 Click OK.

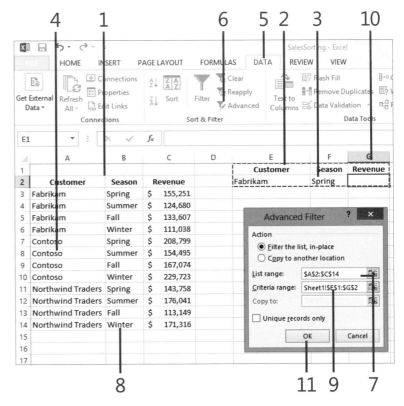

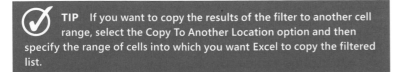

TIP If you want to copy the results of the filter to another cell range, select the Copy To Another Location option and then specify the range of cells into which you want Excel to copy the filtered list.

Remove an advanced filter

1 Select a cell in the range from which you want to remove the filter.

2 Click the Data tab.

3 In the Sort & Filter group on the ribbon, click Clear.

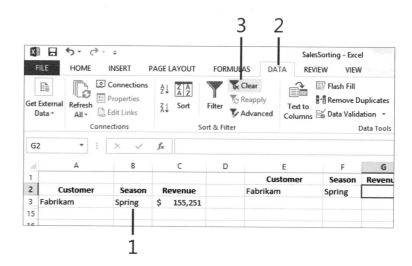

Filtering Excel tables visually by using slicers

In versions of Excel prior to Excel 2013, the only visual indication that you had applied a filter to Excel table column was the indicator added to the column's filter arrow. The indicator told users that there was an active filter applied to that column but provided no information about which values were displayed and which were hidden. In Excel 2013, Slicers provide a visual indication of which items are currently displayed or hidden in an Excel table field.

Add a slicer

1 Click any cell in the Excel table that you want to filter.

2 Click the Insert tab.

3 Click Slicer.

4 Select the check box next to each column by which you want to filter the table.

5 Click OK.

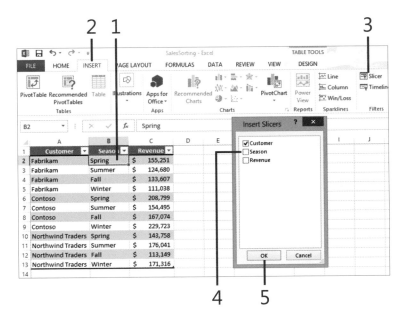

Define a filter using a slicer

1 In the slicer, do any of the following:

    a Click an item to display just its related values.

    b While pressing the Ctrl key, select multiple items to display those items' related values.

    c While pressing the Shift key, click two items to display related values for every value from the first selected item to the second selected item in the slicer's list.

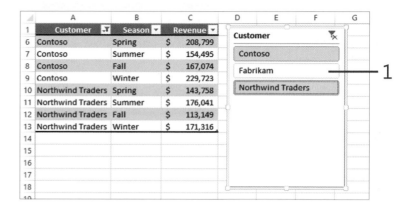

Clearing and removing slicers

Slicers provide a useful and highly visual interface for filtering your Excel tables. As with other filters, you can clear a slicer filter to display all of the data in your worksheet. Switching between the filtered and unfiltered views is a straightforward process, one that you might use when describing your data. The main

disadvantage of slicers is that they take up a lot of room on your screen and can potentially obscure important data. If you find that a slicer does take up too much space, you can always remove it.

Clear a slicer filter

1   Click the slicer.

2   Click the Clear Filter button on the slicer.

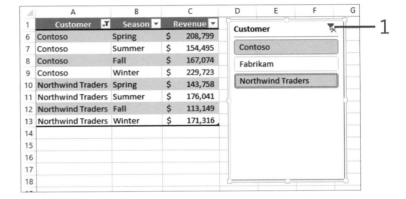

TIP   You can also clear a slicer's filter by clicking the slicer and then pressing Alt+C.

Remove a slicer

1 Right-click the slicer.

2 Click the Remove item in the shortcut menu.

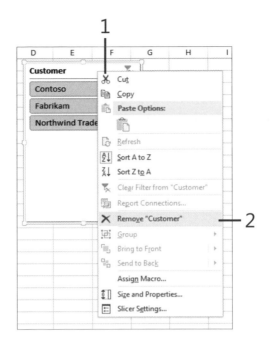

Validating data for correctness during entry

Just as you can limit the data displayed by your worksheets, you can limit the data entered into them. Setting validation rules for data entered into cells lets you catch many of the most common data-entry errors, such as entering values that are too small or too large or attempting to enter a word in a cell that requires a number. When you create a validation rule, you can also create a message to inform you and your colleagues what sort of data is expected for the cell.

Create a validation rule

1 Select the cells that you want to validate.

2 On the Data tab, click the Data Validation button's down arrow.

3 Click Data Validation.

4 Click the Allow down arrow.

5 Click the type of data that you want to allow.

(continued on next page)

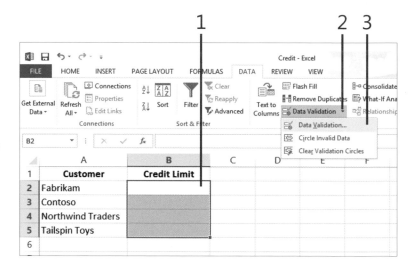

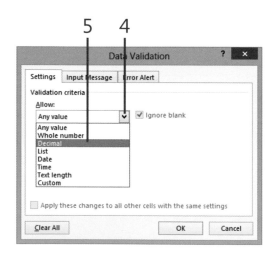

> **TIP** If you want to highlight all of the cells in your worksheet that have validation criteria, click the Home tab on the ribbon, click Find & Select, and then click Data Validation.

Create a validation rule *(continued)*

6 Click the Data down arrow and then click the condition that you want to validate.

7 Type the appropriate values in the boxes.

8 Click the Input Message tab.

9 Select the Show Input Message When Cell Is Selected check box.

10 Type a title for the Input Message box.

11 Type the message that you want Excel to display when the cell is clicked.

12 Click the Error Alert tab.

13 Select the Show Error Alert After Invalid Data Is Entered check box.

14 Click the Style down arrow.

15 Click the style of alert that you want for your message.

16 Type a title for the error message box.

17 Type the error message that you want.

18 Click OK.

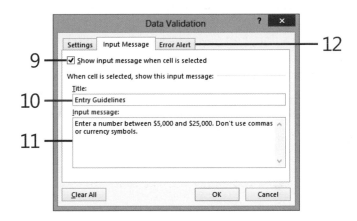

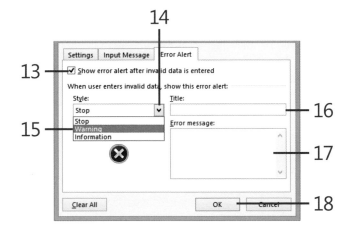

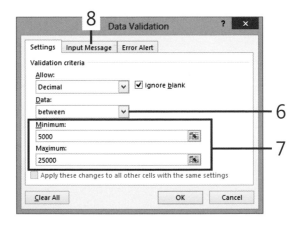

Validating data using a list

When a user enters data into a worksheet cell, you can limit the type of data they enter and constrain numbers to certain ranges. You can also limit text entries to a list of values entered elsewhere in your workbook.

Validate data according to a list in a worksheet range

1 Select the cells that you want to validate.

2 On the Data tab, click the Data Validation button's down arrow.

3 Click Data Validation.

4 Click the Settings tab.

5 Click the Allow down arrow.

6 Click List.

7 Click the Source box.

8 Select the cells that contain the values that you want in your list.

9 Click OK.

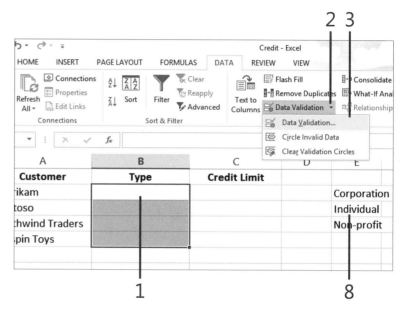

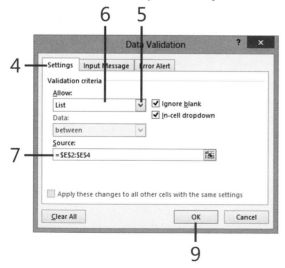

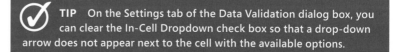

> **TIP** On the Settings tab of the Data Validation dialog box, you can clear the In-Cell Dropdown check box so that a drop-down arrow does not appear next to the cell with the available options.

Presenting data by using Power View

Summarizing data visually helps transform huge collections of individual data points into actionable information. Excel 2013 enhances your ability to visualize your data with Power View, a data visualization tool that originated as part of SharePoint 2010. You will need to have Microsoft Silverlight installed on your computer to take advantage of Power View.

Power View analyzes data that you have included in the Excel 2013 data model. Using the data in the data model, you can summarize your data by using pie charts, maps, Key Performance Indicators, and reports. You have a wide range of formatting and analytical capabilities available to you, so you can change the report style, theme, or text sizing; add and edit background images; and view your data at higher and lower levels of granularity by drilling up, drilling down, and creating analytical hierarchies.

One of the most interesting and useful Power View capabilities is visualizing data in coordination with Bing maps. If your data includes geographical information, combining your data with a Power View map sheet can generate valuable insights.

A full discussion of Power View is beyond the scope of this book, but you can find much more information by visiting *www.office.com/excel* and searching for articles by using the search phrase *power view*.

As of this writing, PowerPivot and Power View are available only for users who have installed Office 2013 Professional Plus, SharePoint 2013 Enterprise Edition, SharePoint Online 2013 Plan 2, and the E3 or E4 editions of Office 365. It is possible that Microsoft will subsequently make both PowerPivot and Power View available to all users.

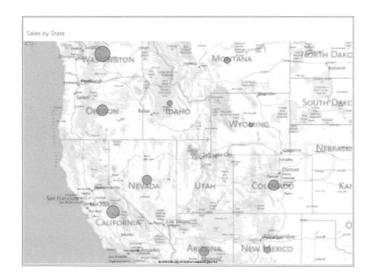

Creating a recommended PivotTable

Excel workbooks enable you to store and summarize large data collections effectively. As versatile as Excel tables and formulas are, they are static. After you create a data arrangement or summary in a standard worksheet, you can change it only by copying, pasting, or moving your data and altering your formulas.

You can extend those capabilities by creating PivotTables. PivotTables are powerful and versatile tools that let you rearrange, sort, and filter your data dynamically, without editing your data or changing any formulas.

Create a recommended PivotTable

1 Click any cell in the Excel table or data list that you want to summarize.

2 Click the Insert tab.

3 Click Recommended PivotTables.

4 Click the PivotTable that you want to create.

5 Click OK.

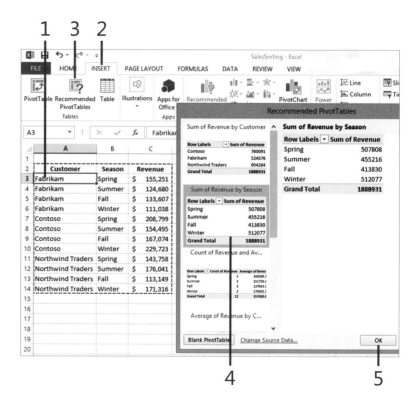

Pivot a PivotTable

1 To change the arrangement of data in a PivotTable, do any of the following:

   a Add a field by dragging it from the Choose Fields To Add To Report area to the columns or rows area.

   b Change the order in which fields are summarized by dragging a field header above or below another header.

   c Remove a field by dragging it from the columns or rows area to the Choose Fields To Add To Report area.

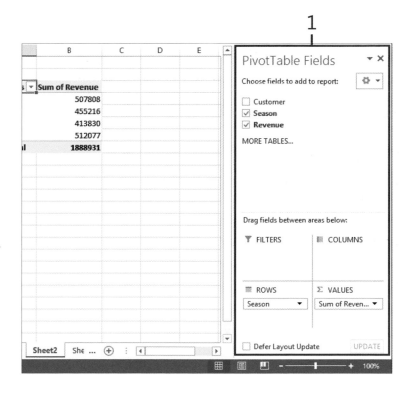

Summarizing data visually using charts

12

Microsoft Excel 2013 gives you lots of ways to change how your numeric data is displayed. You can change the color or font of data you want to emphasize, make your labels bold to set them apart from the body of data in your worksheets, and add graphics to establish your corporate identity. You can use totals and subtotals to summarize your data, making it easier for you and your colleagues to compare values for entire categories of data.

The limitation of working with numbers, even in summary, is that it can be difficult to keep track of several numbers at a time. If you've worked for several years in a package delivery company, you might know that November and December are the busiest months of the year and that February and March show the lowest package volume. If you're presenting results to colleagues or potential investors who are less familiar with your business, you can use charts and graphs to summarize your data visually. By summarizing your data using a chart, you make it much easier for your colleagues to see patterns and relationships.

Creating a chart

To present your Excel data graphically, select the cells you want to summarize, click the Insert tab, and then use the controls in the Chart gallery to select the chart type that's best for your data and the message you want to get across.

The cells with the data to be represented in the chart are part of one or more data series. A series is a collection of related data, such as all sales for a particular product or the sales for each day of a month. A bar chart could contain just one series; a line chart, which might display monthly sales for several years, can have many series.

You can create a chart manually, or you can create a chart that the program recommends. The Recommended Charts gallery, which is new in Excel 2013, displays a set of charts that you can create based on your data. All you need to do is click the chart that you want and confirm your choice. In either case, you can then easily change a chart's appearance to suit your preferences.

Create a chart

1 Click a cell in the data list that you want to summarize.

2 Click the Insert tab.

3 Click the type of chart that you want to create.

4 Click the chart subtype that you want to use.

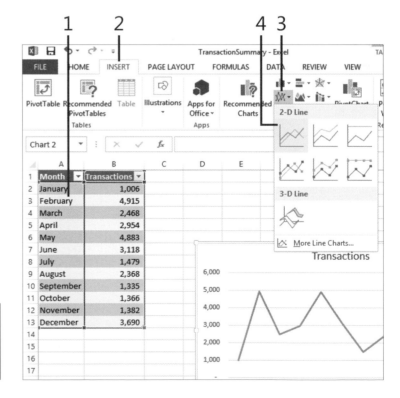

> ✓ **TIP** Pressing F11 creates a chart of the default type (a column chart, unless you've changed it), with the default layout and formatting, on a new workbook sheet. Pressing Alt+F1 creates a similar chart on the same worksheet as your data.

Create a recommended chart

1 Click a cell in the data list that you want to summarize.

2 Click the Insert tab.

3 Click Recommended Charts.

4 Click the chart that you want to create.

5 Click OK.

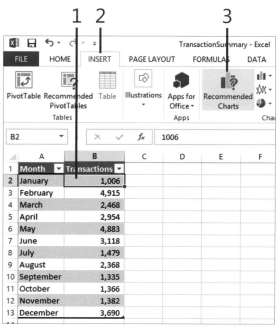

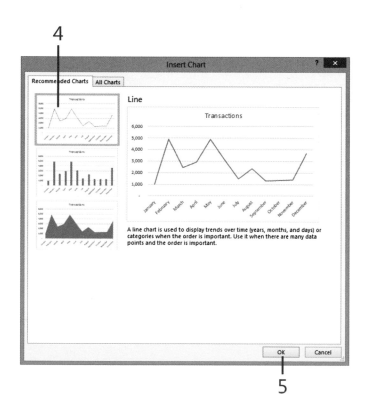

Changing a chart's layout and style

Charts summarize data visually, so every chart has a particular arrangement and presentation of its elements. The overall arrangement of a chart's elements is its *layout*, while the overall appearance of the chart's elements is its *style*. You can apply predefined layouts and styles to your charts. As with any formatting that you apply, you can always fine-tune your choices later.

Change a chart's layout

1   Click the chart that you want to change.

2   Click the Design tab.

3   Click Quick Layout.

4   Click the layout that you want to apply.

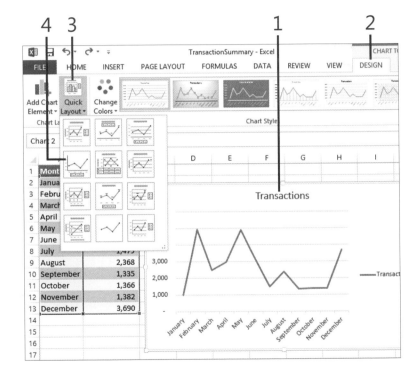

Change a chart's style

1 Click the chart that you want to change.

2 Click the Chart Styles button.

3 In the Chart Styles gallery that appears, click the new style.

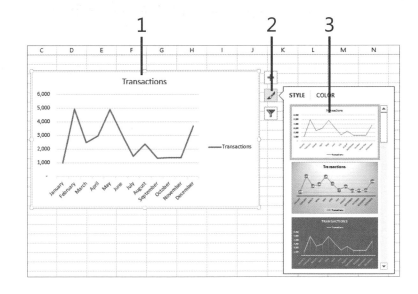

Changing a chart's appearance

After you create a chart, you can change any part of its appearance, including the chart's type! If you display monthly sales data as a series of columns and decide that you want to show the data as a line rising and falling as it moves from month to month, you can change the chart's type at will. You can also change the color, font, and other properties of any chart element. If you want your chart's title to be displayed in your company's official font, you can format the title easily.

Change a chart's type

1 Click the chart that you want to change.

2 Click the Design tab.

3 Click Change Chart Type.

4 Click the type of chart that you want.

5 Click the chart subtype that you want.

6 Click OK.

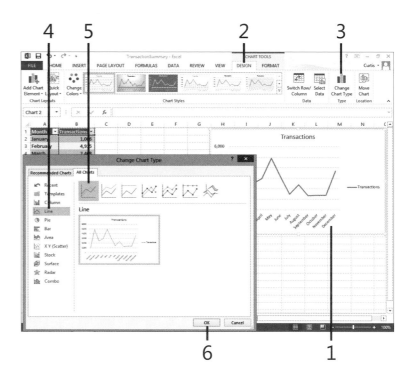

Change the formatting of a chart element

1 Click the chart element that you want to change.

2 Click the Format tab.

3 Use the controls in the Shape Styles group to format the chart element.

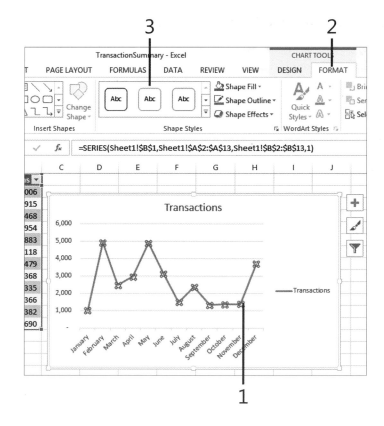

 TIP   To remove the selection from a chart element, press the Esc key.

Formatting chart legends and titles

An important part of creating an informative, easily read chart is to describe the contents of the chart. Two of the chart elements that you can add to describe your Excel charts are legends and titles. A legend is an index of categories in a chart and the color used to describe them. For example, a sales chart comparing monthly sales for several years might display the first year in

yellow, the second year in blue, and the third year in red. The legend identifies those relationships so that you can read the chart accurately. The chart's title provides an overall summary of the chart's contents and can be as simple as a single word, such as *Sales* or *Transactions*.

Show or hide a chart legend

1 Click the chart that you want to format.

2 Click the Chart Elements button.

3 Select or clear the Legend check box.

4 If desired, position the mouse pointer over the Legend item in the Chart Elements list and click the triangle that appears at the right edge of the list.

5 Click any of the items to choose that option, or click More Options for greater control.

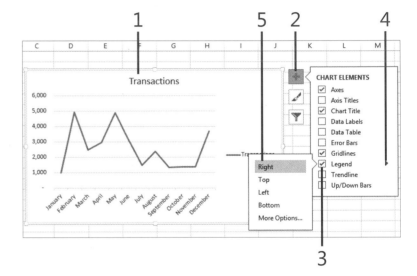

Add titles

1 Click the chart that you want to format.

2 Click the Chart Elements button.

3 Position your mouse pointer over Chart Title.

4 Click the triangle that appears to the right of the Chart Title item.

5 Click the option that you want, or click More Options for greater control.

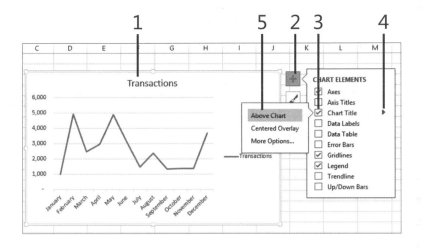

Adding and removing data labels and grid lines

When you summarize numerical data in a chart, you can easily see the relative values of the data points within the chart. If a column is taller than another, you know the first column represents a larger value than the second. Adding grid lines helps you estimate the value represented by a point on a line or a column, but the chart won't display the exact values unless you add data labels. Data labels, as the name implies, display the exact value represented by each chart data point so that the value it represents is unambiguous.

Add and remove data labels

1 Click the chart that you want to format.

2 Click the Chart Elements button.

3 Select or clear the Data Labels check box.

4 If desired, position your mouse pointer over Data Labels and click the triangle that appears.

5 Click an option to apply it, or click More Options for greater control.

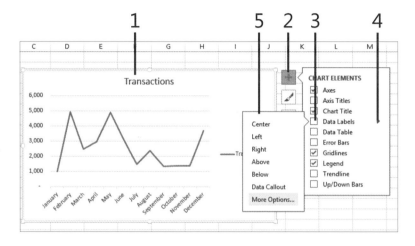

Show or hide chart grid lines

1 Click the chart that you want to format.

2 Click the Chart Elements button.

3 Position your mouse pointer over the Gridlines item.

4 Click the set of gridlines that you want to show or hide.

5 If desired, click More Options for greater control.

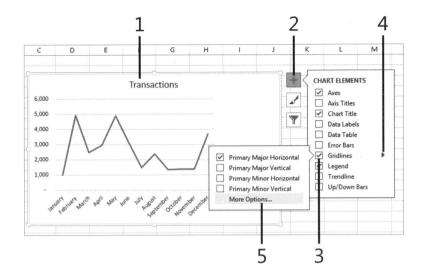

Formatting chart axes

The horizontal and vertical axes help you interpret the values displayed in a chart. For most chart types, including line charts and column charts, the vertical axis summarizes numerical values such as sales or miles driven. The horizontal axis tends to display category data, such as months for which sales data is collected, categories of products, or exhibits at a zoo. You can change the standard formatting of these axes to help viewers understand your data more quickly.

Change the scale on the value axis

1 Click the chart that you want to format.

2 Right-click the vertical axis.

3 Click Format Axis.

4 Under Bounds, in the Minimum box, type a value for the minimum value on the vertical axis.

5 Under Bounds, in the Maximum box, type a value for the maximum value on the vertical axis.

6 Under Units, in the Major box, type a value for the major units to be displayed on the vertical axis.

7 Under Units, in the Minor box, type a value for the minor units to be displayed on the vertical axis.

8 Click Close.

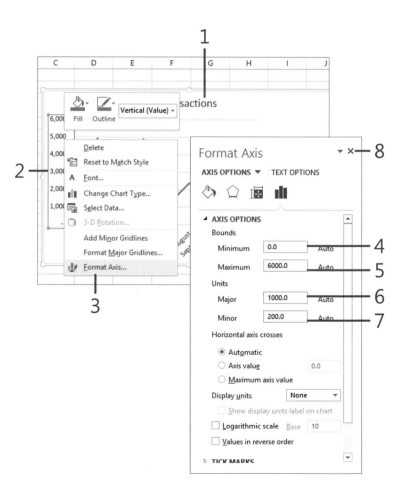

Change the scale on the category (X) axis

1 Click the chart that you want to format.

2 Right-click the horizontal axis.

3 Click Format Axis.

4 Click Tick Marks.

5 Type a number in the Interval Between Marks box.

6 Select an option for the major tick marks.

7 Select an option for the minor tick marks.

8 Select or clear the other options.

9 Click Close.

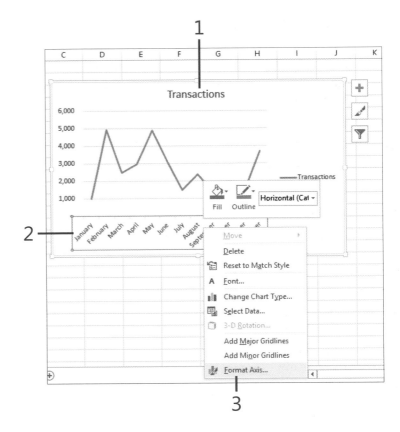

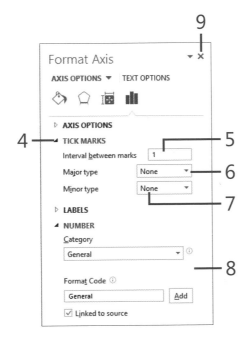

Changing a chart's data source

Whenever you create a chart for a business, there's always the possibility that the data displayed in the chart will change. Whether those changes reflect continuing sales, updated values that account for returns and inventory charges, or investment projections revised to match market conditions, you can update your chart by identifying a new data source. The data can be in any workbook on your computer or network—all you need to do is identify the cells with the data, and Excel does the rest.

Change the source data for your chart

1 Click the chart that you want to change.

2 Click the Design tab.

3 Click Select Data.

4 Click in the Chart Data Range field.

5 Select the cells that you want to provide the new source data.

6 Click OK.

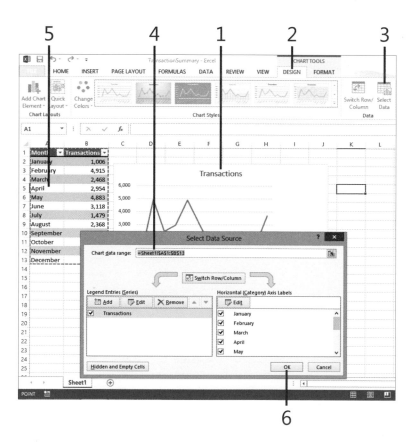

Displaying data graphically

When you enter data into a Microsoft Excel worksheet, you create a record of important events, whether they are individual product sales, sales for an hour of a day, or the price of a product. However, a list of values in cells can't easily communicate the overall trends in your data. The best way to communicate trends in large data collections is through charts and graphs, which summarize data visually.

As an example of how charts and graphs can help present your data more effectively, consider the following Excel table, which lists the number of transactions generated by a small company's website.

When you present the results in a chart or graph, as in a line chart, you can compare the values more readily. The following table explains which types of data each chart type can be used to represent effectively, but feel free to experiment!

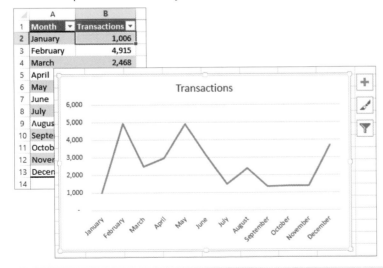

Table 12-1 Standard Excel chart types and uses

Chart type	Use
Column	Compares categories of data in vertical format.
Bar	Compares categories of data in horizontal format.
Line	Displays trends in data over time.
Pie	Compares data as part of a contribution to a whole.
Scatter plot	Compares pairs of values in a dot format.
Area	Compares the trend of values over time or categories.
Doughnut	Compares multiple series of data in a percent format.
Radar	Displays changes in values relative to a center point.
Surface	Displays trends in values across two dimensions.
Bubble	Compares sets of three values.
Stock	Displays a chart to compare stock prices.
Cylinder	Same as a column or bar chart, but a cylinder is used.
Cone	Same as a column or bar chart, but a cone is used.
Pyramid	Same as a column or bar chart, but a pyramid is used.
Combo	Combines two types of charts into a single chart.

Adding and deleting data series

Charts summarize worksheet data and, in many cases, you will include all of the data in a collection. For example, you could have sales data for each month of a year and create a column chart with a column for each month. In other cases, your data collection might have different types of data. One column might contain monthly sales, the next might contain the sales

goal for the month, and the third might display the difference between actual sales and the target. In that case, you might want to limit the data in your chart to just the column summarizing monthly sales. You can add or remove data series from your chart to create exactly the summary you want.

Add a new series

1 Click the chart that you want to change.

2 Click the Design tab.

3 Click Select Data.

4 Click Add.

5 Click the cell that contains the name for the series.

6 Click in the Series Values box.

7 Select the cells that you want to add.

8 Click OK.

9 Click OK.

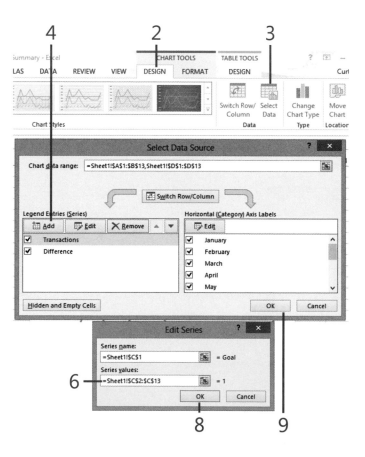

Remove a series

1 Click the chart that you want to change.

2 Click the Design tab.

3 Click Select Data.

4 Click the name of the series that you want to delete.

5 Click Remove.

6 Click OK.

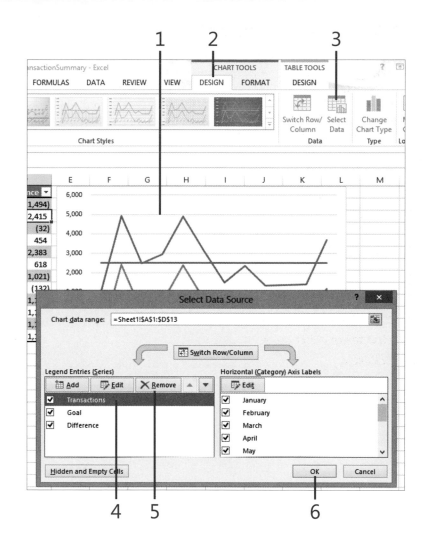

Filtering charts

Limiting the data shown in a chart can help you and your colleagues focus on the facts that are most relevant to your situation. Excel 2013 gives you the ability to select which values appear in your chart by using the Chart Filters button, which the program displays next to the chart. Selecting or clearing the check box next to a category (horizontal) axis value displays or hides that value in the chart. When a filter is applied, the Select All check box contains a gray square to indicate that some values are hidden.

Filter a chart

1 Click the chart that you want to filter.

2 Click the Chart Filters button.

3 Select or clear the check boxes next to items that you want to display or hide.

4 Click Apply.

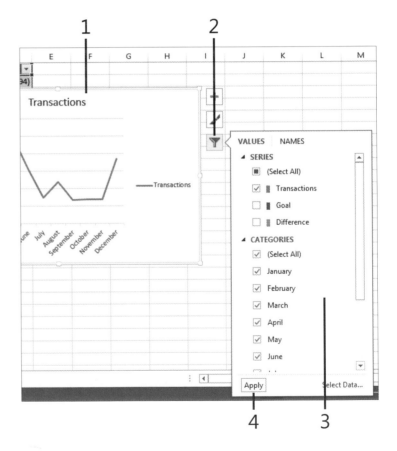

Remove a chart filter

1 Click the chart that you want to filter.

2 Click the Chart Filters button.

3 Select the Select All check box.

4 Click Apply.

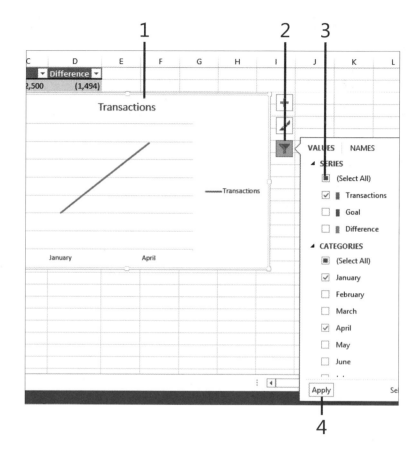

 TIP Clearing the Select All check box hides all of the values in the chart, but you can't apply that filter.

Manipulating pie charts

One chart type that you'll probably work with quite frequently is the pie chart, which displays the contribution of a series of values to the total of those values. Each section represents a category of data, such as a month in a year or a category of product. One way that you can extend the capabilities of a basic pie chart and emphasize part of the data is to pull one section of the pie away from the rest of the chart. You can also change how you look at a three-dimensional chart, moving closer or farther away from the chart and changing your perspective.

Pull a slice out of a pie chart

1 Click the body of the pie chart that you want to change.

2 Click the piece of data that you want to separate.

3 Drag the piece away from the pie.

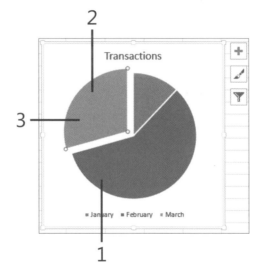

Create a 3-D pie chart

1 Select the cells that you want to summarize in the pie chart.

2 Click the Insert tab.

3 Click the Pie Chart button.

4 Click the 3-D Pie chart.

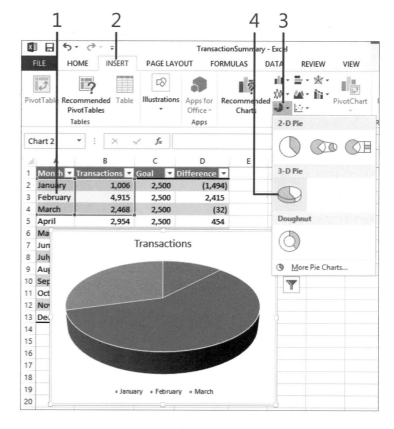

 TIP To change the 3-D shadow effects applied to a chart element, click the chart element, click the Format tab, click Shape Effects, click Shadow, and then click the shadow setting you want.

⚠ **CAUTION** Not all 3-D options are available for all chart types.

Creating a stock chart

When you pick a type of chart or graph to present your data, you'll probably consider pie charts, line graphs, and bar charts. Those chart types are used most often because of their familiarity and their straightforward presentation of the relationships between elements of a data series. However, you can use other types of charts when appropriate. One of those chart types is the stock chart, which you can use to present stock market data.

Create a stock chart

1 Select the stock data that you want to chart. Be sure that the data is formatted as shown in the figure.

2 Click the Insert tab.

3 Click Other Charts.

4 Click a Stock chart subtype.

TIP Several stock chart subtypes are available, each of which requires a different set of data columns. When you hover your mouse pointer over a chart subtype, Excel displays information about the subtype and the data it requires.

Adding a trendline to a chart

You can use the data in your Excel workbooks to analyze past performance, but you can also have Excel make its best guess as to future performance if current trends continue. For example, if you create a chart that represents your company's sales for the past five years, you can have Excel analyze the data and add a trendline to the chart to represent how much sales would increase if the current trend holds true for the next year.

Add a trendline to a data series

1 Click the chart to which you want to add a trendline.

2 Click the data series to which you want to add a trendline.

3 Click the Chart Elements button.

4 Position the mouse pointer over Trendline.

5 Click the gray triangle that appears.

6 Click Linear.

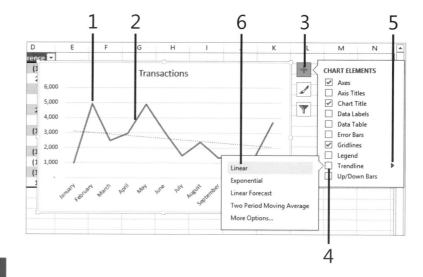

TIP If you want more control over your trendline, such as by choosing a different mathematical procedure to extend the line (although the default Linear option works the majority of the time) or by choosing the number of units by which to extend the line, click the gray triangle next to Trendline and then click More Options to display the Format Trendline task pane.

CAUTION Unless you're working with certain types of scientific data and you know that your trendline requires a logarithmic, exponential, or other regression type, select the Linear Trendline option. If you don't, you won't get meaningful results.

Summarizing data using sparklines

Creating charts in Excel 2013 workbooks enables you to summarize your data visually, using legends, labels, and colors to highlight aspects of your data. It is possible to create very small charts to summarize your data in an overview worksheet, but you can also use sparklines to create compact, informative charts that provide valuable context for your data.

Edward Tufte introduced sparklines in his book *Beautiful Evidence*, with the goal of creating charts that imparted information in

approximately the same space as a word of printed text. In Excel 2013, a sparkline occupies a single cell, which makes it ideal for use in summary worksheets. You can create three types of sparklines: line, column, and win/loss. The line and column sparklines are compact versions of the standard line and column charts. The win/loss sparkline indicates whether a cell value is positive (a win), negative (a loss), or zero (a tie).

Create a line or column sparkline

1 Select the cells that you want to summarize.

2 Click the Insert tab.

3 In the Sparklines group, click Line or Column.

4 Click the Location Range box.

5 Click the cell where you want the sparkline to appear.

6 Click OK.

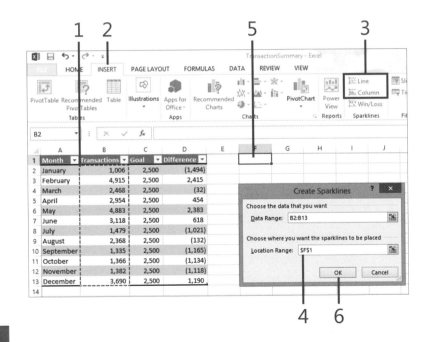

> **TIP** A sparkline fits into a single worksheet cell, which leaves no room for labels. For that reason, you have to select only the data to be summarized, not the category labels.

Create a win/loss sparkline

1 Select the cells that you want to summarize.

2 Click the Insert tab.

3 In the Sparklines group, click Win/Loss.

4 Click the Location Range box.

5 Click the cell where you want the sparkline to appear.

6 Click OK.

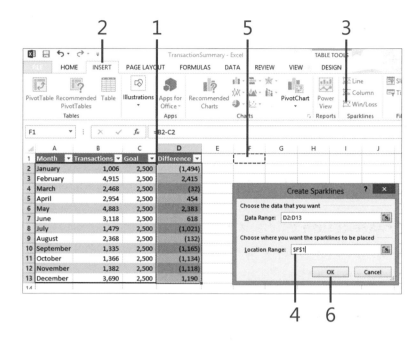

> ⚠ **CAUTION** A win/loss sparkline distinguishes between positive, negative, and zero values. Summarizing a series of monthly sales values using a win/loss sparkline won't provide any useful information. However, comparing the sales figures to each month's goal would be appropriate for a win/loss sparkline.

Formatting and deleting sparklines

After you create sparkline, you can change its appearance to fit your worksheet's style. When you click a cell that contains a sparkline, you can use the controls on the Design tab of the ribbon to change the sparkline's colors, add markers to line sparklines, and even change the sparkline's type. You can also remove the sparkline entirely if you change your vision for the worksheet and the data it summarizes.

Format a sparkline

1 Select the sparkline that you want to change.

2 Click the Design tab.

3 Use the controls in the Sparkline group to change which data the sparkline summarizes.

4 Use the controls in the Type group to change the sparkline's type.

5 Use the controls in the Show group to determine which sparkline elements to show.

6 Use the controls in the Style group to change the sparkline's style, color, and marker color.

7 Use the controls in the Group group to reformat the sparkline's axes.

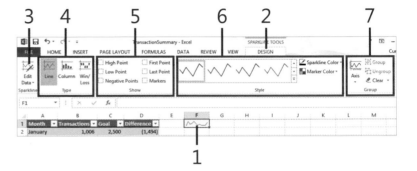

✓ **TIP** You can make a sparkline larger or smaller by changing the cell's column height and row width.

Delete a sparkline

1 Select the cell that contains the sparkline that you want to delete.

2 Click the Design tab.

3 Click the Clear button.

4 Click Clear Selected Sparklines.

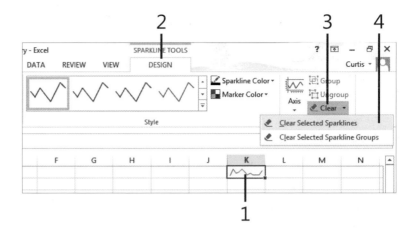

Enhancing your worksheets with graphics

13

W hen you create a worksheet, your first consideration is to ensure that the data is stored in an understandable format and that all the formulas produce the expected results. However, after you take care of the worksheet's structure, you should ensure that you and your colleagues can comprehend the data easily. One way that you can help you and your colleagues understand the data in your worksheet is to add drawing objects—such as boxes, stars, and banners—to make your annotations and labels stand out.

Another way you can present business data in an Excel worksheet is to create a diagram. In Excel, diagrams encompass common business items such as Venn diagrams, which show the intersection of several data sets, and organization charts, which describe the hierarchy of a company or other organization.

In this section:

- Adding an image to a worksheet
- Creating and editing drawing objects
- Adding text to drawing objects
- Changing the appearance of drawing objects
- Aligning and grouping drawing objects
- Adding WordArt to a worksheet
- Inserting clip art into a worksheet
- Creating common business diagrams
- Creating an organization chart

Working with graphics in your worksheets

When you add graphics to your worksheets, you can use the Insert tab on the ribbon. The buttons on the Insert tab let you add lines, shapes of many different types, and images to your worksheets. After you create a drawing object, you can change its line color or, if the object has an interior space, fill that space with a color or pattern of your choosing. Another way you can make your images and drawing objects stand out is to add a shadow so that the objects appear to float above the surface of the worksheet. Hard shadows, which you create with black lines, mark the shadowed object as separate from the surrounding items. A softer shadow, one created with a lighter shade of gray, makes the shadowed object appear as part of the collection of objects on the worksheet. You can also add a reflection to an image, adding depth to the image and implying that the worksheet contains a reflective surface.

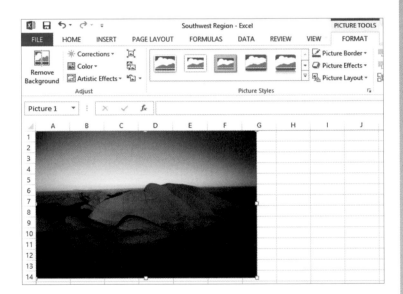

Adding drawing objects to a worksheet

Adding graphics or pictures of items described in your worksheets makes it easier to understand the data in those worksheets, but you're not limited to adding images from other sources. If you want, you can add drawing objects to your worksheets. For example, you can add shapes such as rectangles and lines to your worksheets, both to add visual interest and to convey additional information about your worksheet's contents.

Add a simple shape

1 Click the Insert tab.

2 Click Illustrations.

3 Click Shapes.

4 Click the button representing the shape that you want to add.

5 Drag to where you want your shape to appear.

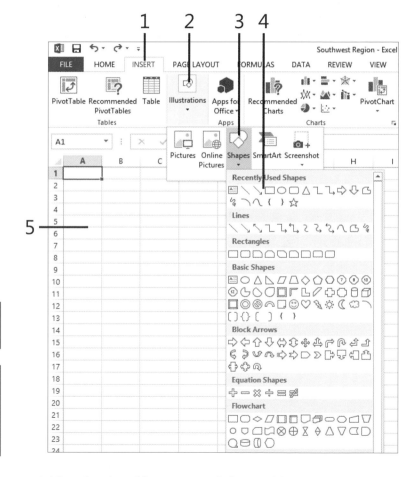

 TIP To create a circle or square instead of an oval or rectangle, hold down the Shift key while you drag the mouse pointer.

 TIP You can display a list of the shapes and other objects on a worksheet by clicking any drawing object and then. on the Format tab, clicking Selection Pane. You can show or hide all objects, or you can click an object's name in the Selection Pane to show or hide just the selected object.

Adding graphics to worksheets

After you create a worksheet, you can add graphics to enhance the data on the worksheet. If your worksheet details the sales of a specific product, you can add a photograph of the product to the worksheet. Adding a visual representation of the item

described in the worksheet makes the results you offer much more memorable. Not only do you and your colleagues have numbers to work with, you also have something solid with which to associate the data, enhancing recall.

Add a picture

1 Click the Insert tab.

2 Click Illustrations.

3 Click Pictures.

4 Navigate to the folder with the picture that you want to insert.

5 Double-click the picture that you want to insert.

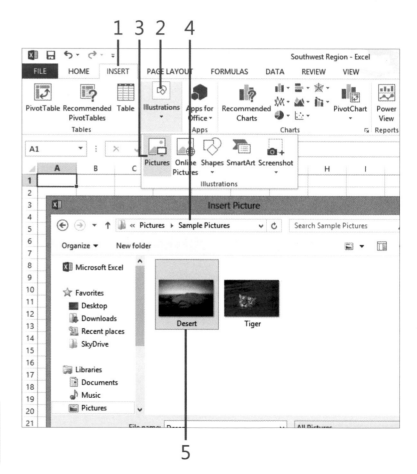

SEE ALSO For information about adding a picture to a worksheet header or footer, see "Include a graphic in a header or footer" on page 188.

Delete a picture

1 Click the picture that you want to delete.

2 Press the Delete key.

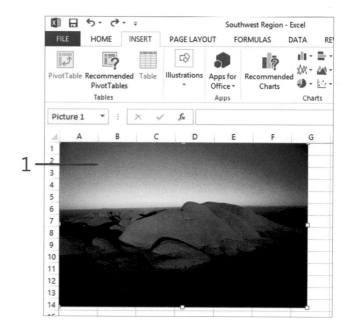

Adding text to a shape

Shapes can represent abstract concepts, such as steps in a procedure, or they can highlight part of a worksheet, but plain shapes don't communicate specific information well. You can add explanatory text, such as one-word or two-word captions describing the contents of a cell, to make your worksheet's contents easier to understand. If the standard formatting of your shape's text doesn't meet your needs, you can always change its appearance by using the controls on the Home tab.

Add text to any shape

1 Click the shape.

2 Type the text that you want, and then click outside the shape.

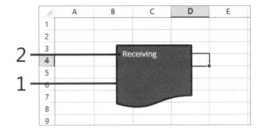

Format text in a shape

1 Click the shape.

2 Click the Home tab.

3 Using the controls in the Font and Alignment groups on the ribbon, follow any of these steps:

a Click the Font down arrow and then click the font that you want to use.

b Click the Font Size down arrow and then click the font size.

c Click the Font Color down arrow and then click a color.

d Use the other controls to assign bold, italic, underline, and other formatting options.

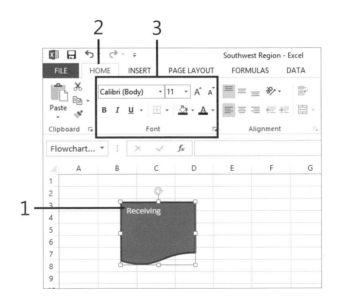

> ⚠ **CAUTION** If your text doesn't fit in the shape, you see only the first part of the text you added. To view the rest of the text, you can enlarge the shape or make the text's font size smaller.

Applying shape styles

When you create a drawing object in Excel, you create a default version of the object, meaning that the object has the program's usual color or pattern filling its interior. If you want to change the object's appearance, you can select from a series of built-in styles that control the image's fill color, outline, and text color.

Apply a shape style

1 Click the object that you want to format.

2 Click the Format tab.

3 In the Shape Styles group on the ribbon, click the style that you want to apply.

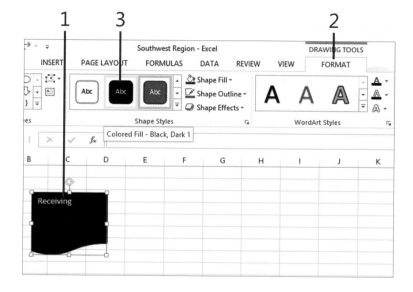

 TIP You can display the entire Shape Styles gallery by clicking the gallery's More button.

Applying shape styles: Apply a shape style   **273**

Changing a shape's fill color or image

Excel 2013 includes a wide range of built-in styles for your shapes. It's likely that you'll find a style that fits your needs. If not, you can change a shape's colors and patterns to bring the object's appearance in line with your company's color scheme or to make an object stand out from its surroundings. You can also fill an object with a picture, adding a further dimension to your control over the shape. Selecting the right image to show within a shape can make your information that much more compelling.

Apply a fill

1 Click the shape that you want to fill.

2 Click the Format tab.

3 Click the Shape Fill down arrow, and use the controls on the menu that appears to pick a fill color, gradient, or texture.

4 Click the color with which you want to fill the object.

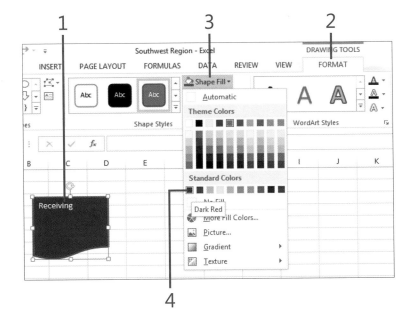

TIP Textures are a great way to apply a gentle, overall pattern to an object without interfering with any text or image already positioned in the object.

Fill an object with a picture

1 Click the object that you want to fill.

2 If necessary, click the Format tab.

3 Click Shape Fill.

4 Click Picture.

5 Click Browse.

6 Navigate to where the picture that you want is located.

7 Double-click the picture that you want.

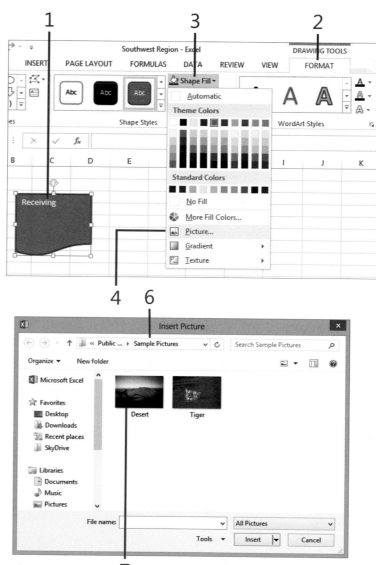

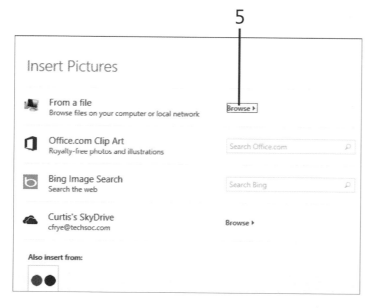

Adding effects to drawing objects

When you add a drawing object to a worksheet, you can add text or color to the object to make it stand out from the rest of the worksheet's contents. Other options that you have to make drawing objects stand out are to add a shadow to the object, which makes it appear that the object is raised off the surface of the worksheet, and to make the object appear as though it is three-dimensional. Excel knows how to make its drawing objects appear three-dimensional—all you need to do is describe how you want the object to look!

Add or edit an object's shadow

1 Click the object that you want to edit.

2 If necessary, click the Format tab.

3 Click Shape Effects.

4 Click Shadow.

5 Click the shadow style that you want for your object.

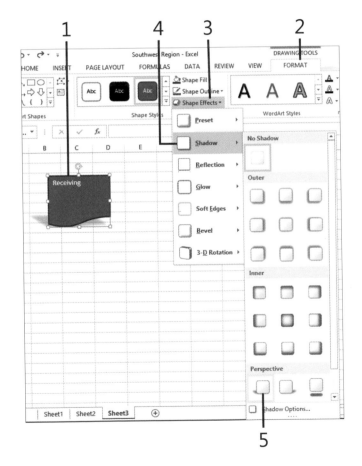

Rotate an object in three dimensions

1 Click the object that you want to edit.

2 If necessary, click the Format tab.

3 Click Shape Effects.

4 Click 3-D Rotation.

5 Click the 3-D rotation that you want for your object.

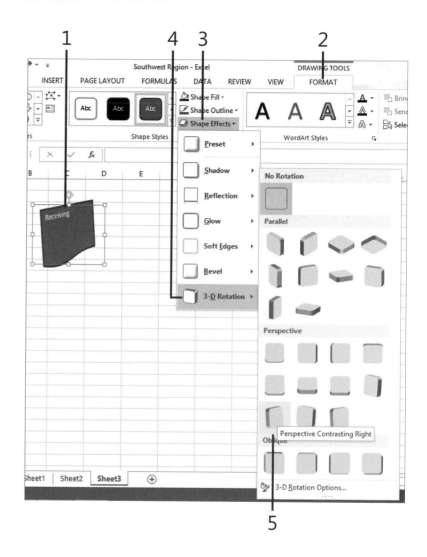

Resizing and rotating pictures and objects

After you add a picture or drawing object to a worksheet, you can change the object's size to have it take up more or less space on the sheet. You can also rotate the object to change its orientation on the page. Rotating an image a little to one side can imply action or fun, while turning an image upside down indicates something a bit more unconventional. Of course, if your image is upside down when you add it to your worksheet, you can rotate it to its "normal" position. Also, if you find that you want to work only with the foreground element of the image, Excel 2013 provides a background removal tool that you can use to edit the image.

Resize a picture or object

1 Click the object that you want to resize.

2 Hover over one of the white handles surrounding the object, and drag the handle to the size that you want.

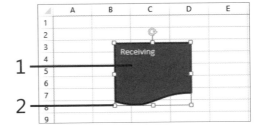

> **TIP** Some shapes, such as trapezoids, have a sizing control shaped like a yellow diamond near one of the shape's sides. You can drag the yellow diamond to control the length of one side of the shape, such as the top of a trapezoid.

Rotate a picture or object

1 Click the object that you want to rotate.

2 If necessary, click the Format tab.

3 Follow either of these steps:

    a In the Arrange group, click Rotate and then select how you want to rotate the object.

    b Hover over the rotation handle (the white circular arrow), and then drag the handle to rotate the object to the angle that you want.

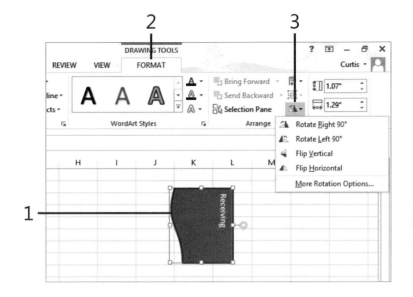

> **TIP** When you select an object, your object's size dimensions appear in the Size group on the Format tab on the ribbon. If you want to resize your object to a specific size, such as 1.53" wide by 1.77" high, you can type those values directly into the group's fields. You can also click the spin control at the right edge of the fields to increase or decrease a dimension by 0.1" per click.

Removing the background from an image

Most photographs have both a foreground image, which is the focus of the picture, and a background. In many cases, the foreground image is in sharp focus while the background is softer and slightly out of focus. It's also likely that the image's background is significantly wider than the foreground and makes the image significantly wider and taller. If you find that you want to work only with the foreground element of the image, Excel 2013 provides a background removal tool that you can use to edit the image.

Remove the background from a picture

1 Click the picture that you want to edit.

2 If necessary, click the Format tab.

3 Click Remove Background.

(continued on next page)

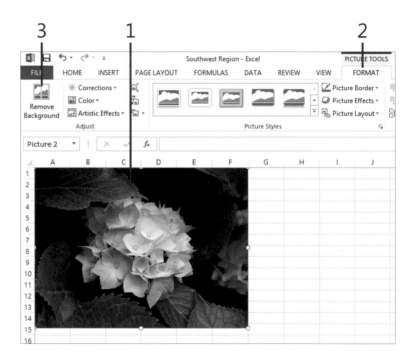

Remove the background from a picture *(continued)*

4   If necessary, drag the handles at the corners and edges of the interior box to identify the image background.

5   Click Keep Changes.

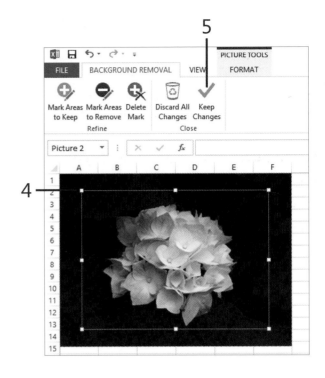

Aligning and grouping drawing objects

One important design element is ensuring that any objects you add to your worksheets are aligned properly, both in relation to the edges of the worksheet and to any other objects. If you want a number of your objects to line up with each other, such as aligning all objects with the left edge of the page, you can

do so. In a similar manner, if you want to work with a set of objects as a single unit, such as three text boxes that you want to appear together regardless of position, you can define the objects as a group and work with them as a single entity.

Align objects

1 Hold down the Ctrl key, and click the objects that you want to align.

2 If necessary, click the Format tab.

3 Click Align.

4 Click how you want to align your objects.

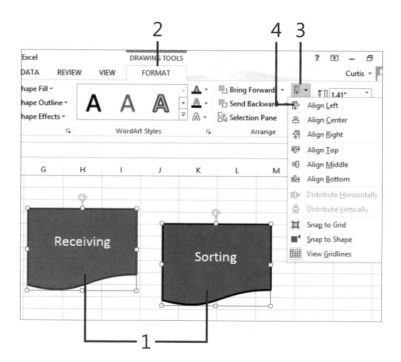

Group or ungroup objects

1 Hold down the Ctrl key, and click the objects that you want to group.

2 If necessary, click the Format tab.

3 Click the Group button.

4 Click the Group menu item.

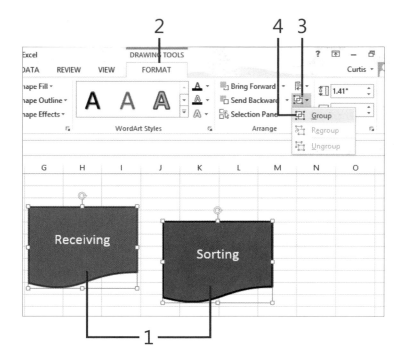

→ TRY THIS Right-click any object in a group that you want to ungroup, and click Group, Ungroup. If you have many objects grouped together and then ungroup them, you might want to regroup them in the same way. You can do this quickly and easily by right-clicking one of the objects that you want to regroup, clicking Group, and then clicking Regroup.

✓ TIP If you want to apply a format to more than one object, you can group the objects and apply the formatting to all objects at once!

Using WordArt to create text effects in Excel

One of the benefits of working with Excel 2013 is that you can take advantage of the capabilities of Microsoft Office 2013 to enhance your worksheets. One of those capabilities is WordArt, which lets you select from a wide range of styles to add exciting two-dimensional and three-dimensional text to your worksheets. Every style comes with a predefined color scheme, but you can change the color, size, and alignment of your WordArt by using the tools on the ribbon's Home tab.

Add WordArt text

1 Click the Insert tab.

2 Click Text.

3 Click WordArt.

4 Click the WordArt style that you want.

5 Type the text that you want to style.

6 Click the border of the WordArt text.

7 Click the Home tab.

8 Click the Font down arrow.

9 Click the font that you want.

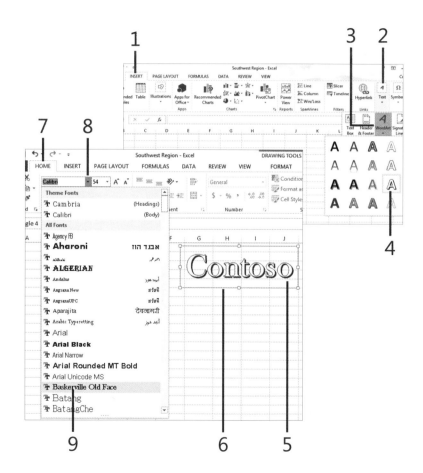

Change WordArt text colors

1 Click the border of the WordArt that you want to format.

2 Click the Home tab.

3 Click the Font Color down arrow.

4 Click the color that you want.

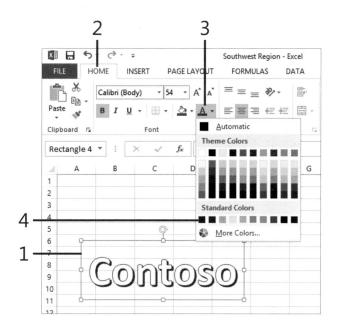

Inserting clip art into a worksheet

If you want to include a worksheet in a presentation that you give to your colleagues or in a report that you make available on your company's website, you can add images from the clip art collection that comes with Office to accent your worksheet.

You can manage your clip art by using the Clip Art task pane, whether that means searching for clip art on your computer or on the web.

Add clip art

1 Click the Insert tab.

2 Click Illustrations.

3 Click Online Pictures.

(continued on next page)

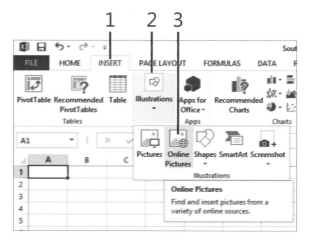

Add clip art *(continued)*

4 Type a description of the clip art that you want.

5 Press Enter.

6 Click the clip art that you want to insert.

7 Click Insert.

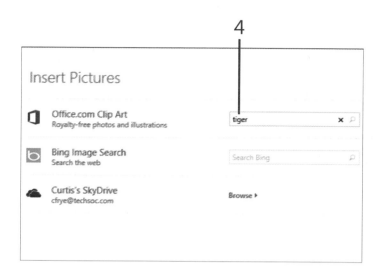

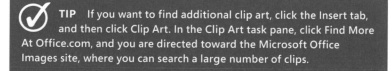

TIP If you want to find additional clip art, click the Insert tab, and then click Clip Art. In the Clip Art task pane, click Find More At Office.com, and you are directed toward the Microsoft Office Images site, where you can search a large number of clips.

Inserting and changing a diagram

A number of diagram types are probably familiar to most business people: the pyramid, which shows a hierarchical relationship; the target, which uses a ring of concentric circles to display the approach to a target; the Venn diagram, which shows the intersection of items in various sets; and the cycle,

which displays the steps in a repeating process. Rather than create these diagrams on your own, you can have Excel create the basic diagram, and then you can fill in the details. After you create the diagram, you can apply an AutoFormat to alter its appearance.

Insert a diagram

1 Click the Insert tab.

2 Click Illustrations.

3 Click SmartArt.

4 Click the category of SmartArt that you want to create.

5 Click the specific diagram that you want to add to your worksheet.

6 Click OK.

(continued on next page)

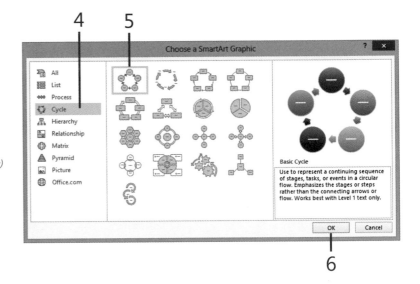

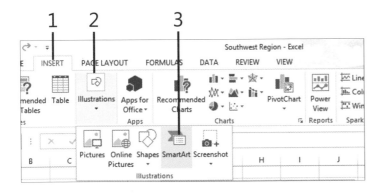

Insert a diagram *(continued)*

7 Click a text box to add text to your diagram.

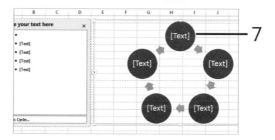

Change the style of a diagram

1 Click the diagram that you want to change.

2 Click the Design tab.

3 In the Layouts group on the ribbon, click the layout that you want to apply to the diagram.

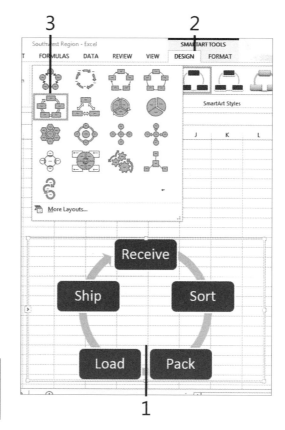

> ✓ **TIP** A preview of the new format appears when you hover the mouse pointer over a layout in the Layouts gallery—feel free to experiment!

Creating an organization chart

One of the most important tools in any business is the organization chart, which shows the reporting relationships between employees and their supervisors. Creating the base of an organization chart is simple, as is adding employees to the chart.

After you create the chart, you can change the chart's direction so that the relationships run from left to right and not up and down. You can also apply an AutoFormat to change the chart's appearance.

Create an organization chart

1 Click the Insert tab.

2 Click Illustrations.

3 Click SmartArt.

4 Click Hierarchy.

5 Click the first graphic in the Hierarchy group.

6 Click OK.

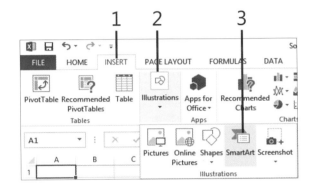

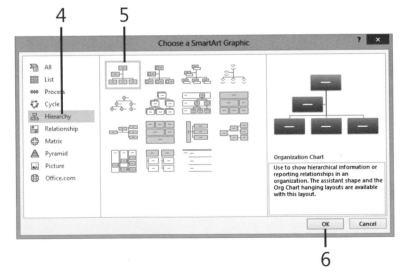

Add a shape

1 Click the shape that you want to add a shape above, under, or next to.

2 If necessary, click the Design tab.

3 Click Add Shape.

4 Click the option that reflects where you want to add the shape in the chart.

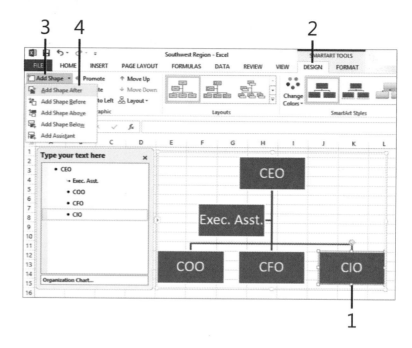

TIP Click Add Assistant to place the shape below the current shape with an elbow connector.

Changing the layout and design of a SmartArt graphic

Each class of SmartArt graphics is built on an underlying model and has a standard design. Any changes that you make to your SmartArt graphics' layout take place within that model. You can move individual shapes within a SmartArt graphic, or you can change the graphic's layout all at once by selecting a predefined layout. Similarly, you can edit each object's appearance separately, or you can change the entire graphic's appearance at once.

Alter the layout of your organization chart

1 Click the organization chart.

2 Click the Design tab.

3 Click a new layout for your organization chart.

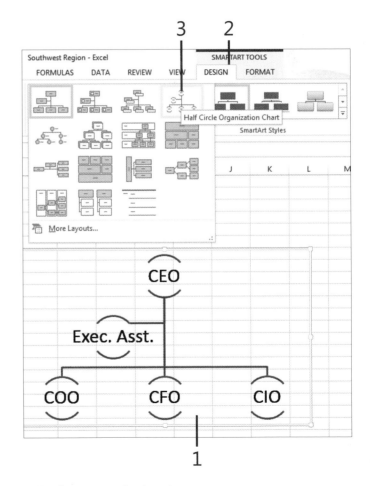

Change the design of your organization chart

1 Click the organization chart that you want to change.

2 Click the Design tab.

3 Click Change Colors.

4 Click the color scheme that you want.

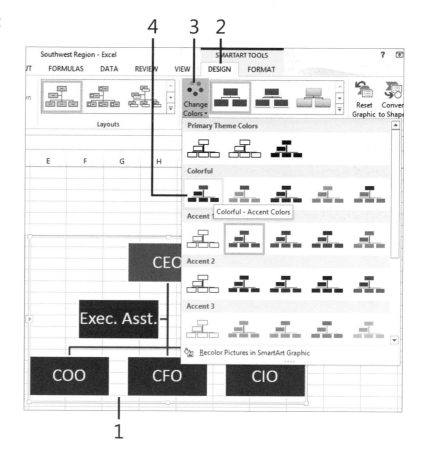

Adding an equation to a shape

You can use Excel 2013 to analyze your data in many ways, but it can be difficult to understand exactly how your formulas calculate their values. If you want to display the equation that you use to calculate a value, you can add that mathematical equation to the interior of a shape. To add an equation to a shape, click the shape, and then click the Insert tab. In the Symbols group, click Equation, and then click the Equation Tools Design tab on the ribbon to display the equation-editing interface.

Add a model equation

1 Click the shape to which you want to add an equation.

2 Click the Insert tab.

3 Click Symbols.

4 Click the Equation button's down arrow.

5 Click the equation that you want to add.

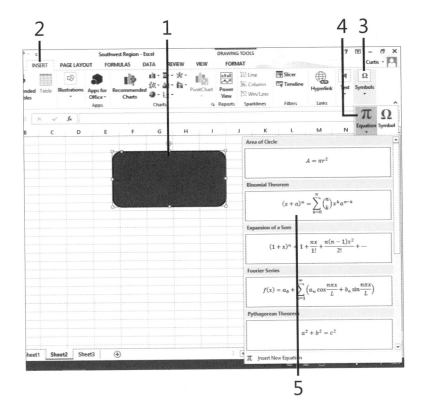

TIP You can edit the model equation's elements after you create the equation.

Add a custom equation

1 Click the shape to which you want to add the equation.

2 Click the Insert tab.

3 Click Symbols.

4 Click the Equation button.

5 If necessary, click the Design tab.

6 Click the type of equation structure that you want to create.

7 Click the specific structure to use for your equation.

8 Type the equation elements into the structure's boxes.

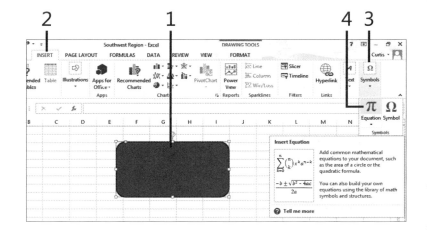

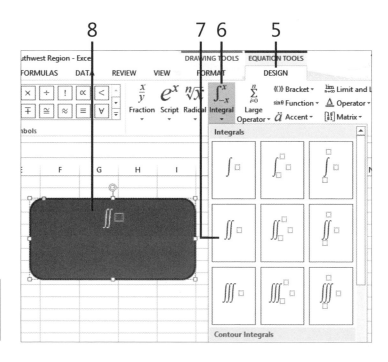

TIP By clicking the symbol or operator in the Symbols gallery, you can add symbols such as the infinity sign or arithmetic operators such as plus, minus, multiply, and divide.

Reordering objects

Objects in an Excel worksheet exist in layers. The worksheet layer holds the worksheet's cells, the background layer holds any images that you display behind the worksheet, and the drawing layer holds items such as shapes and clip art. When you add an object such as a shape or image to a worksheet,

Excel places that object on the drawing layer and in front of all existing objects. That's why moving a newer object into the same space as an older object obscures the older object. You can change the order of objects on the drawing layer to get the effect that you want.

Change the order of objects

1 Click the object that you want to move.

2 If necessary, click the Format tab.

3 Follow either of these steps:

   a Click the Bring Forward down arrow, and then select whether to bring the object to the front of the stack or to move it up one place.

   b Click the Send Backward down arrow, and then select whether to send the object to the back of the stack or to move it back one place.

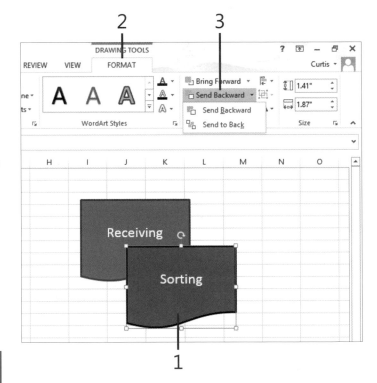

> **TIP**   When you click the Bring Forward arrow, you will also see the Bring To Front option, which moves a selected object in front of all other objects. Similarly, clicking the Send Backward arrow shows the Send To Back option, which sends the selected object to the back.

Sharing Excel data with other programs

14

Microsoft Excel 2013 is a powerful program, but it doesn't try to do everything. Other Microsoft Office 2013 programs have complementary strengths: Microsoft Access 2013 is ideal for working with large data collections; Microsoft PowerPoint 2013 lets you create attractive presentations to print or project onto a screen; and Microsoft Word 2013 is great for creating text documents. You can include files created in other programs in your Excel workbooks or create links to them. Also, if a colleague uses a database or spreadsheet program that can write its data to a text file, there's a very good chance that you can bring that data into Excel.

In this section:

- Linking and embedding other files
- Exchanging table data between Excel and Word
- Copying Excel charts and data into PowerPoint
- Exchanging data between Access and Excel
- Importing a text file

Introducing linking and embedding

Excel works wonderfully as a stand-alone program, but it really shines when you use it in combination with other programs. One way to use Excel in conjunction with other programs is to include in your worksheets files created in other programs, such as graphics, Word documents, or PowerPoint presentations. You can add these objects to your workbooks through linking and embedding.

Keep in mind several important things when you consider whether to link to an object or embed it in a worksheet. As the name implies, embedding an object stores a copy of the object in the workbook. For example, if you want to add a company logo to an invoice generated from table data, you can identify the graphic and indicate that you want to embed

it in the file. The advantage of embedding an object in an Excel file is that you don't have to worry about the graphic, chart, or image not being available because the person who created the workbook didn't include the graphic. If you create a workbook with embedded files, you can open your workbook anywhere and be certain that your graphics are available.

A disadvantage of embedding objects in workbooks is that the embedded files can be large and can dramatically increase the size of your workbooks. Although a single low-resolution logo meant to be viewed on a computer monitor probably won't have much of an impact on your file's size, the same image rendered at a resolution suitable for printing

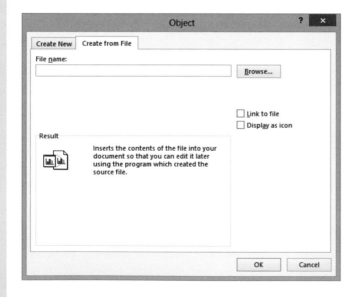

might double the size of the workbook. If you embed more than one image—or more than one copy of the same image—you might make your file unworkably large.

When you want to include more than one image or external file in an Excel workbook, you should consider creating a link to the files. For example, rather than embed many copies of a high-resolution logo in your worksheets, you can save the logo file on your hard disk and link to the file's location on your computer. Excel uses the reference to find the file and display it as part of the workbook. The workbook will be no larger than it was originally, and you won't need multiple

copies of the same file if you link to it more than once. The advantage of linking is that you save disk space, but the disadvantage is that moving the workbook from computer to computer can be difficult unless you have the extra files when you travel or distribute the workbook to colleagues.

In general, embedding an object in an Excel workbook works best if you use the object only once in the workbook and if you have room to store the workbook with the embedded object. Otherwise, such as when you use the same file multiple times in the same workbook, you need to link to the file instead.

Linking and embedding other files

Excel workbooks can hold a lot of data, and you can make your data even more meaningful when you include files created with other programs. For example, you might have a Word document with important background information or a PowerPoint presentation that puts your data into context for your colleagues. You can include those files in your worksheets by linking or embedding the files as objects.

Embed a file in a worksheet

1 Click the Insert tab.

2 Click Text.

3 Click Object.

4 Click Create From File.

5 Click Browse.

6 Navigate to the folder that contains the file that you want to embed.

7 Double-click the file that you want to embed in your worksheet.

8 Click OK.

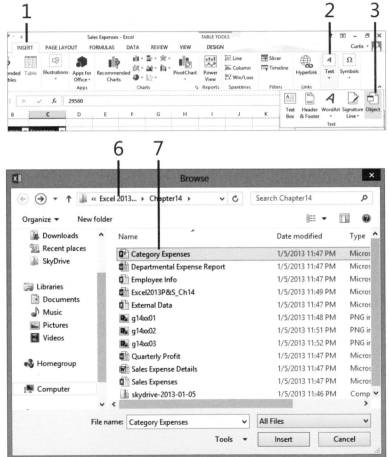

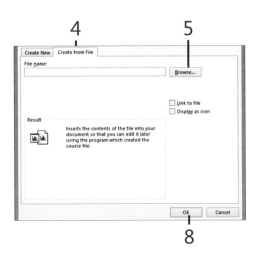

Link to a file

1 Click the Insert tab.

2 Click Text.

3 Click Object.

4 Click Create From File.

5 Click Browse.

6 Navigate to the folder that contains the file that you want to link to.

7 Double-click the file that you want to link to.

8 Select the Link To File check box.

9 Click OK.

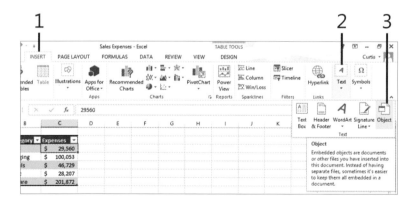

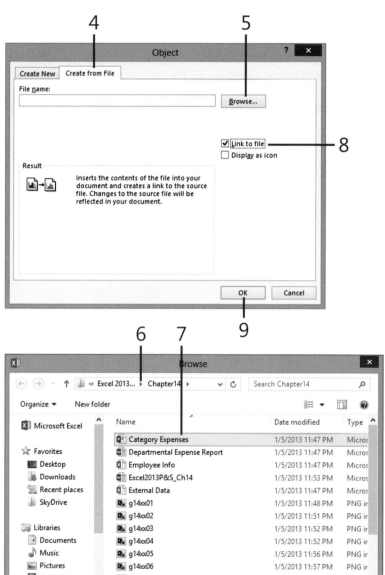

> ✓ **TIP**   If you want the file you've linked to or embedded to take up as little room as possible in your workbook, select the Display As Icon check box in the Object dialog box.

Exchanging table data between Excel and Word

Just as you can create workbooks to store and manipulate financial and other data in Excel, you can use Word to create reports and other text documents to interpret and provide valuable context for your worksheet data. Word documents can also present data in tables, which are arranged in rows and columns like a worksheet. For example, if you receive a report from a traveling colleague in which she created a table listing the prices of popular products at a competitor's store, you can copy the data from the Word document to an Excel worksheet for direct comparison. You can also go in the opposite direction, copying Excel data to a table in Word.

Paste Word data into Excel

1 In Word, select the table that you want to import into Excel.

2 Click the Home tab.

3 Click the Copy button.

4 In Excel, click the cell in which you want the upper-left table cell to appear.

5 Click the Home tab.

6 Click Paste.

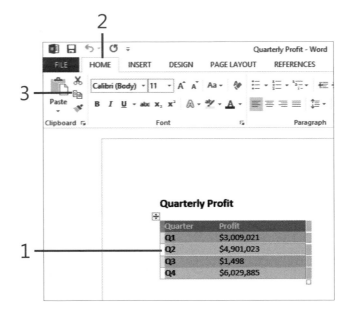

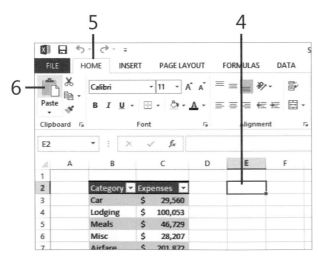

Copy Excel data to Word

1 In Excel, select the cells that you want to export.

2 Click the Home tab.

3 Click the Copy button.

4 In Word, click the location where you want the pasted cells to appear.

5 Click the Home tab.

6 Click Paste.

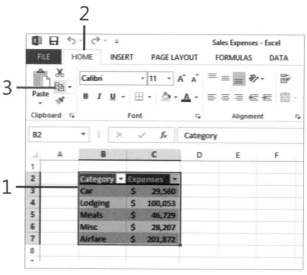

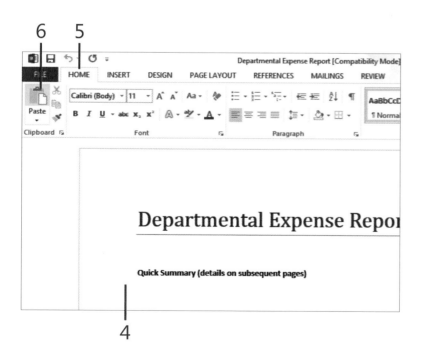

Copying Excel charts and data into PowerPoint

It's possible to present Excel data to your colleagues by using Excel exclusively, but if you're developing a formal presentation, you might want to use PowerPoint. Because presentations often contain graphical representations of numerical data, it's easy to include your Excel data in a PowerPoint presentation.

When you copy an Excel chart into a PowerPoint presentation, you can select how you want PowerPoint to manage the chart

and its data. If you don't make any changes, PowerPoint creates the chart and maintains a link to the workbook from which it came. You can also choose to paste the entire workbook into PowerPoint or to paste a picture of the chart's current state.

Move Excel data to PowerPoint

1 In Excel, select the cells that you want to export.

2 Click the Home tab.

3 Click the Copy button.

4 In PowerPoint, click the location where you want the pasted cells to appear.

5 Click the Home tab.

6 Click Paste.

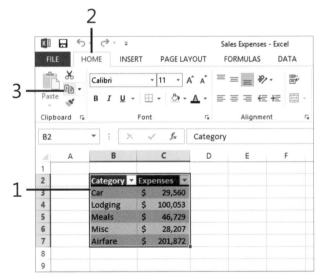

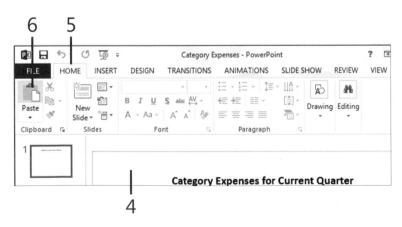

Copy an Excel chart to PowerPoint

1 In Excel, select the chart that you want to export.

2 Click the Home tab.

3 Click the Copy button.

4 In PowerPoint, click the location where you want the pasted chart to appear.

5 Click the Home tab.

6 Click the Paste button's down arrow.

7 Follow any of these steps:

    a Click the Chart (Linked To Excel Data) option to paste the chart into the presentation and retain a live link to the source workbook.

    b Click the Excel Chart (Entire Workbook) option to paste the chart and a copy of the workbook to the presentation.

    c Click the Paste As Picture option to paste an image of the chart into the presentation.

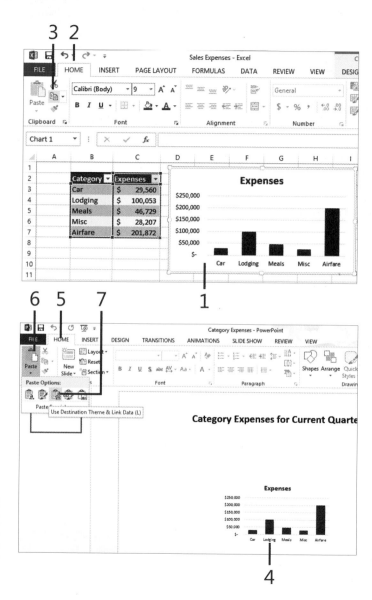

> ⚠ **CAUTION** Neither of the latter two options in step 7 maintains a live link between the chart and its original workbook. In the first case, you paste a copy of the data into the PowerPoint presentation; in the second, you just take a picture of the chart and paste that into the presentation.

Exchanging data between Access and Excel

No other Microsoft Office 2013 programs have as much in common as Access and Excel, but each program retains its unique strengths. Where Excel offers a wide range of data analysis and presentation tools that you can use to summarize your data, Access is designed to let you store, manipulate, and ask questions about large data collections. You can also use Access queries to locate and summarize table data. Although it is possible to look up data in an Excel worksheet, it's much easier to do in Access.

Paste Access table data into an Excel worksheet

1   In Access, display the table from which you want to copy the data.

2   Select the table cells that you want to copy.

3   Click the Home tab.

4   Click Copy.

5   In Excel, click the cell where you want the first table value to appear.

6   Click the Home tab.

7   Click the Paste button's down arrow.

8   Click the Match Destination Formatting icon.

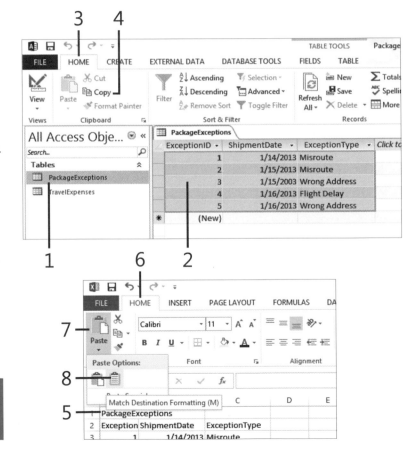

> **TIP**   When you position your mouse pointer over the Match Destination Formatting icon, Excel 2013 displays a live preview of how the data will appear when you paste it into your worksheet.

Send Excel data to Access

1 In Excel, select the cells that you want to copy.

2 Click the Home tab.

3 Click the Copy button.

4 In Access, display the table that you want to receive the pasted data.

5 In the (New) record row, select as many cells as there are columns of data to be pasted.

6 Click the Home tab.

7 Click Paste.

8 Click Yes to acknowledge that you want to paste the worksheet data into the table.

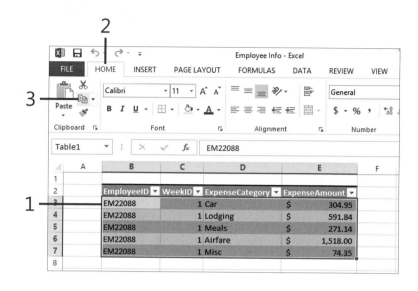

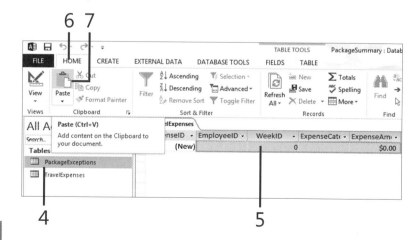

⚠️ **CAUTION** If you click only a single cell in the Access table's New record row, you'll paste all your worksheet data into a single table cell, making the new data worthless.

Importing a text file

Excel can read data from quite a few other spreadsheet and database programs, but you might have a colleague who uses a spreadsheet or database program that creates files that you can't read with Excel. If that's the case, you can ask your colleague to save the file as a text file, using a comma, tab, or other character (called a delimiter) to mark the end of each cell's data. Even if you can't transfer data any other way, you can always read spreadsheet data if it's presented to you in a text file. Any formatting and formulas are lost, but the data will be there for you to analyze.

Paste text into Excel

1 Click the Data tab.

2 Click Get External Data.

3 Click From Text.

4 Navigate to the folder that contains the text file that you want to import.

5 Double-click the text file.

(continued on next page)

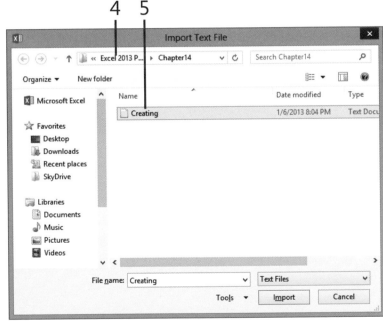

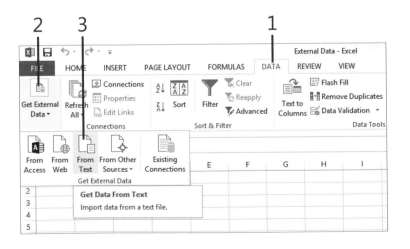

TIP If you can choose whether to have a text file created so that it contains fixed-width or delimited values, ask for the delimited values. Character delimiters are much easier for Excel to detect, which means less work for you when you want to import the data.

Paste text into Excel *(continued)*

6 Select the Delimited option.

7 Click Next.

8 Select the file's delimiter character.

9 Verify that the data appears correctly in the Data Preview pane.

10 Click Finish.

11 Click OK.

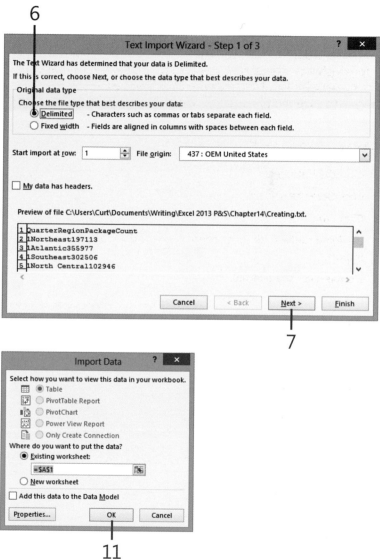

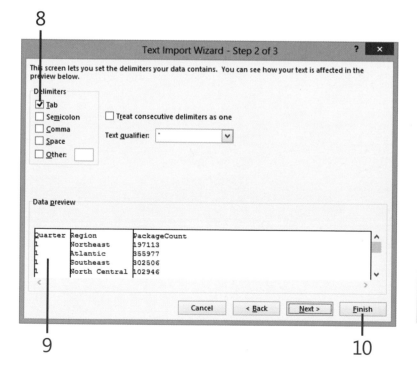

Using Excel in a group environment

15

Even though single individuals might be in charge of managing a company's financial data and related information, there is usually a group of folks who either enter data into workbooks or have input into future revenue or growth projections. You and your colleagues can add comments to workbooks to describe their contents and to offer insights into how certain values are derived. If you and your colleagues need to open or edit a workbook at the same time but from different computers, you can turn on workbook sharing so that more than one person can have the workbook open at a time. You can view any changes that your colleagues make and then accept or reject those changes to produce a final version of a workbook.

Microsoft Excel 2013 also takes full advantage of XML (the Extensible Markup Language). XML is a content markup language, meaning that an XML file has information about the data contained within it, not just how the data should be displayed. Not only is the Excel 2013 file format based on XML, but you can also save your Excel workbooks as StrictOpenXML-Spreadsheet files, which means that your Excel data can be read by a wide range of programs, not just those programs listed in the Save As dialog box's Save As Type drop-down list.

In this section:

- Sharing workbooks in Excel
- Commenting in cells
- Tracking changes in workbooks
- Accepting or rejecting changes
- Saving worksheets to the web
- Dynamically updating worksheets published to the web
- Retrieving web data from Excel
- Modifying web queries
- Interacting over the web with XML
- Saving data to the cloud using SkyDrive
- Editing a workbook in the Excel Web App
- Sharing Excel workbooks on the web
- Sharing a Worksheet online using Lync

Sharing workbooks in Excel

When you want to enable more than one individual to work with a workbook simultaneously, you must turn on workbook sharing. Workbook sharing is perfect for mid-sized businesses in which employees need to look up customer, sales, and product data frequently. In larger companies, turning on workbook sharing makes it possible for coworkers at different offices to add values to a workbook that's used to develop a cost estimate or to maintain expense reports.

Turn on workbook sharing

1 Click the Review tab.

2 Click Share Workbook.

3 Select the Allow Changes By More Than One User check box.

4 Click OK to close the dialog box.

5 Click Save to save the workbook.

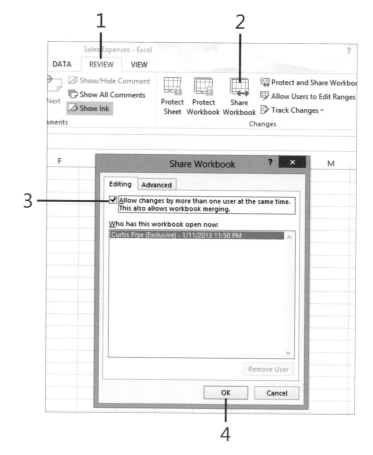

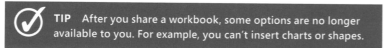

TIP After you share a workbook, some options are no longer available to you. For example, you can't insert charts or shapes.

CAUTION You can't share a workbook that contains an Excel table. If you want to share a workbook that contains an Excel table, you must convert the table to a normal range. The error message that appears explains how to convert the Excel table to a normal range.

Adding and viewing cell comments

When you and your colleagues share responsibility for creating a workbook, you might want to add comments to some cells to suggest modifications to a formula, ask whether a cell's contents might be formatted differently, or provide an updated value for a workbook's owner to add after the owner verifies the data. Excel 2013 marks cells that contain comments by placing a red flag at the top-right corner, making it easy for you and your colleagues to identify which cells have additional information available. For example, you could add a comment to a sales worksheet explaining that two exceptionally large purchases pushed one hour's sales way beyond the norm.

Add a comment

1 Click the cell to which you want to add a comment.

2 Click the Review tab.

3 Click New Comment.

4 Type the comment that you want.

5 Click anywhere outside the comment to stop adding text.

> ✓ **TIP** By default, Excel displays the red flag at the top-right corner only for cells that contain comments. If you want a cell's comments to be shown the entire time that your workbook is open, right-click the cell with the comment and then click Show/Hide Comments on the shortcut menu. If a cell's comments are shown the entire time, you can return to showing only the indicator by right-clicking the cell and then clicking Hide Comment. You can also click the Show All Comments button on the ribbon to show or hide all comments.

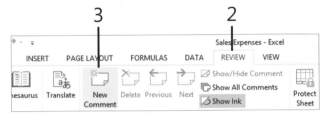

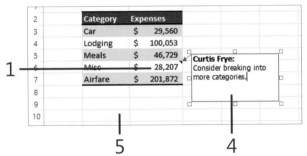

View a comment

1 Hover the mouse pointer over a cell with a red triangle in the top-right corner.

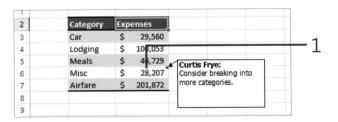

Editing and deleting comments

Comments in Excel workbooks are often used to add information during the creation and editing process. You might have an opinion about estimates of future sales, to share suggestions about how to format worksheet data, or to indicate that additional information should be included in your analysis. As you and your colleagues address these issues, you should either change or eliminate the comments related to them.

Edit a comment

1 Select the cell that contains the comment.

2 Click the Review tab.

3 Click Edit Comment.

4 Edit the comment text.

5 Click anywhere outside the comment box to stop editing.

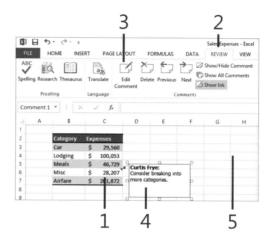

Delete a comment

1 Select the cell that contains the comment.

2 Click the Review tab.

3 Click Delete.

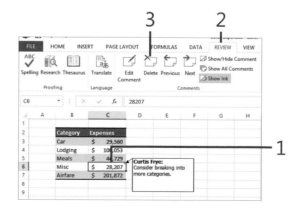

> ⚠️ **CAUTION** The name attributed to a comment might not be the same as the person who actually created it. Instead, a comment reflects the name of the person who was logged on to the computer on which the comment was made.

Tracking changes in workbooks

Whenever you collaborate with a number of your colleagues in producing or editing a workbook, you should consider tracking the changes that each user makes. When you turn on Track Changes, Excel 2013 highlights any changes made to the workbook in a color assigned to the user who made the changes. When you have a question about a change, you can quickly identify who made it and verify that it is correct.

Turn on Track Changes

1 Click the Review tab.

2 Click Track Changes.

3 Click Highlight Changes.

4 Select the Track Changes While Editing check box.

5 Click OK.

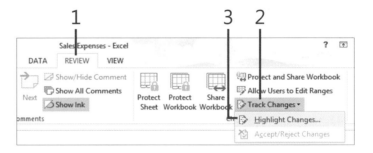

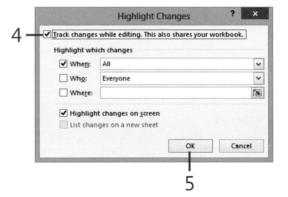

TIP If your workbook's changed cells aren't marked, you can have Excel display them by clicking the Review tab, clicking Track Changes, clicking Highlight Changes, selecting the Highlight Changes On Screen check box, and clicking OK.

Accepting or rejecting changes

When you and your colleagues have made your changes to a workbook, you can go through the workbook and accept or reject those changes. The best way to accept or reject changes is to move through them one at a time. Examining each change in a large document can be tedious, but it's far less of a hassle to take an hour to finalize a workbook than it is to spend a day reconstructing a workbook after you accidentally accept every change. If you want to keep track of every change, you can have Excel create a new worksheet named History and list every change made since you last saved. Whenever you save your workbook, Excel deletes the History worksheet.

View a change

1 Hover over a cell with a blue triangle in the top-left corner.

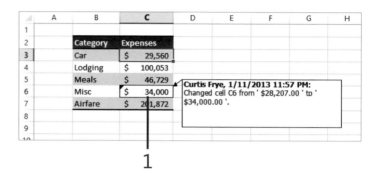

Review changes

1 Click the Review tab.

2 Click Track Changes.

3 Click Accept/Reject Changes, and then click OK to save your workbook.

(continued on next page)

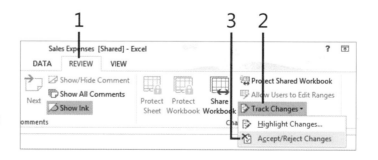

Review changes *(continued)*

4 Select the Who check box.

5 Click the Who down arrow.

6 Click Everyone.

7 Click OK.

8 Do any of the following:

   a Click Accept to accept the current change.

   b Click Reject to reject the current change.

   c Click Accept All to accept all the changes.

   d Click Reject All to reject all the changes.

   e Click Close to stop reviewing changes.

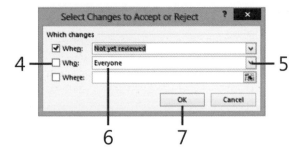

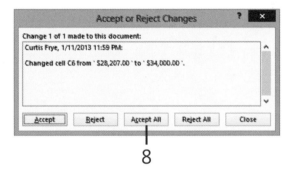

⚠️ **CAUTION** You should consider making a backup copy of your workbook before accepting any changes. Having a record of what changes were made in case something goes wrong is never a bad idea.

✓ **TIP** If you want to review only those changes made after a specific date, click the When down arrow in the Highlight Changes dialog box, click Since Date, and type the date in the When box.

Maintaining a change history

When you edit a workbook over a period of time or as part of a group, it can be useful to maintain a record of who made which changes and when. This information helps you evaluate each change, take into account the perspective of the individual who made the change, and determine whether certain changes reflect information not available to other commenters.

Create a change history

1   Make changes to a workbook that has Change Tracking turned on.

2   Click the Review tab.

3   Click Track Changes.

4   Click Highlight Changes.

(continued on next page)

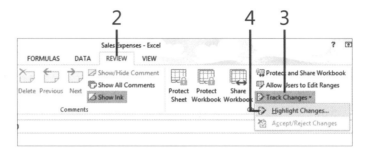

 TIP   When you turn Change Tracking off, Excel deletes the change history worksheet.

Create a change history *(continued)*

5 If necessary, select the When check box and set the value in the When list box to All.

6 Select the List Changes On A New Sheet check box.

7 Click OK.

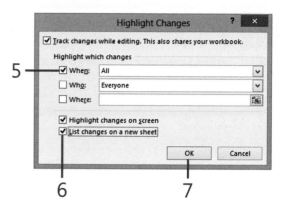

Saving worksheets to the web

Exchanging data with traveling colleagues presents a real chal-lenge to all organizations. Writing the data to a webpage means that you don't have to send the entire workbook to travelers. In fact, your colleagues don't even need Excel on their machines!

Saving workbooks as webpages also enables you to make data available over a corporate network (an intranet). As long as your company's network supports web connections, you can make your data available to any authorized user.

Save a workbook to the web

1 Click the File tab.

2 Click Save As.

3 Click Computer.

4 Click the Browse button.

(continued on next page)

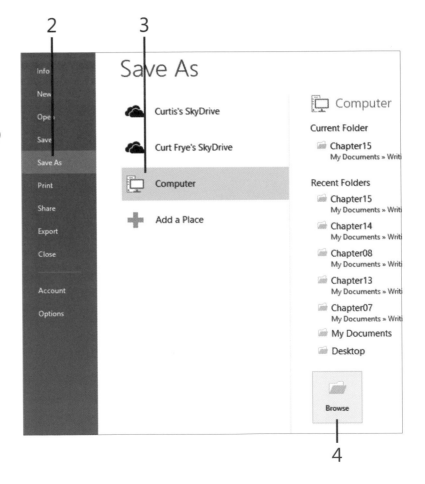

Save a workbook to the web (continued)

5 Click the Save As Type down arrow.

6 Click Web Page.

7 Navigate to the folder where you want to save your workbook.

8 Type the file name that you want.

9 Click Save.

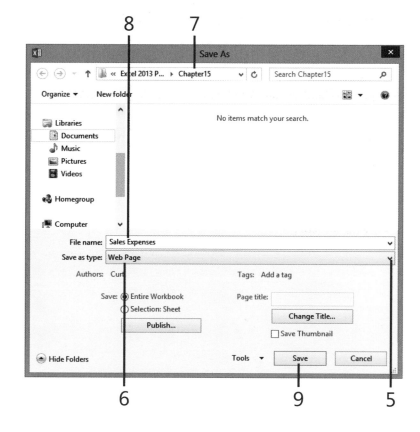

✓ **TIP** You can change the text that appears on the title bar of the Excel document's web page by clicking the Change Title button in the Save As dialog box.

Dynamically updating worksheets published to the web

One advantage of working with Excel over the web is that you and your colleagues can interact with Excel worksheets that you have published on the web. By adding interactivity to your worksheet, you and your colleagues can edit cell values, sort the values in the worksheet, apply a filter, or create formulas. You can also use interactivity to update an Excel-based web page whenever there is a change in the workbook on which the file is based.

Update worksheets published to the web

1 Click the File tab.

2 Click Save As.

3 Click Computer.

4 Click Browse.

(continued on next page)

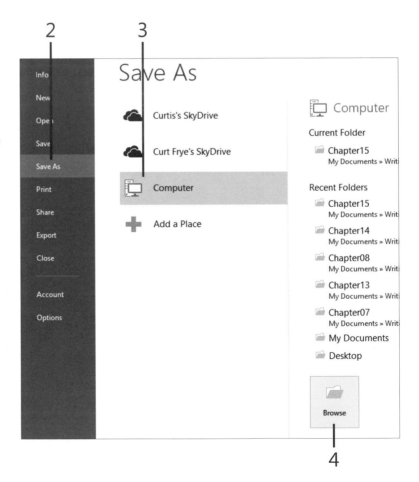

Update worksheets published to the web

(continued)

5 Click the Save As Type down arrow.

6 Click Web Page.

7 Click Publish.

8 Click the Choose down arrow.

9 Click the sheet that contains the data that you want to update.

10 Click the element that you want to publish.

11 Select the AutoRepublish Every Time This Workbook Is Saved check box.

12 Click Publish.

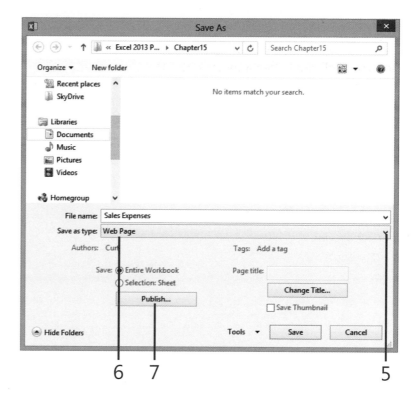

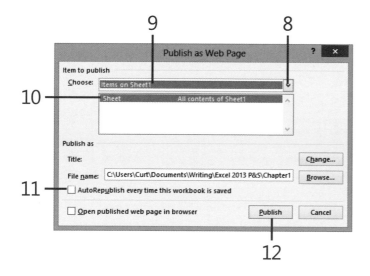

Retrieving web data using Excel

The World Wide Web is a great source of information. From stock quotes to product descriptions, many companies publish useful information on their websites. The most common structure used to present financial information is the table, which,

like a spreadsheet, organizes the data into rows and columns. Excel 2013 makes creating a web query easy by letting you copy data directly from a web page into Excel and then create a query to retrieve data from the table that you copied.

Retrieve data from web pages

1 Click the Data tab.

2 Click Get External Data.

3 Click From Web.

4 Type the address of the web page you want.

5 Click Go.

(continued on next page)

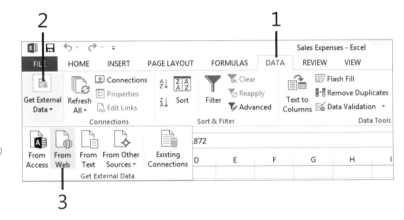

Retrieve data from web pages *(continued)*

6 Click the yellow boxes with black arrows to specify which tables you want to import.

7 Click Import.

8 Click OK.

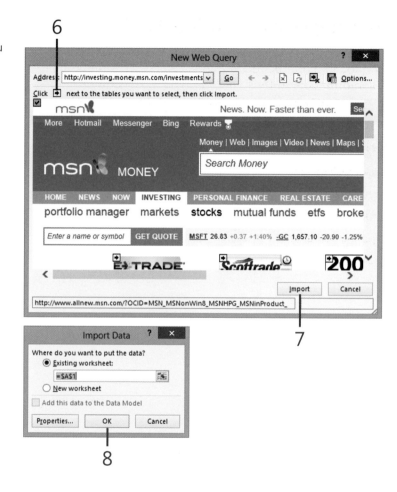

 TIP When you click a yellow box with a black arrow, it changes into a green box with a check mark.

Copying web data to Excel

Many web pages are created in a way that lets you copy data to your clipboard and then paste it into an Excel workbook or other file. In many cases, you can highlight the data you want using the mouse pointer and then copy and paste the data as you would any other file contents.

Copy data from the web to Excel

1 In your web browser, type the URL that you want to visit.

2 Select the data that you want to copy into Excel.

3 Press Ctrl+C to copy the data to the Clipboard.

4 In Excel, click the cell where you want to paste the data.

5 Click the Home tab.

6 Click Paste.

> **TIP** When you are ready to paste data from the web into Excel, you can click the Paste button's down arrow to display a list of options. The last option is Create Refreshable Web Query, which displays the New Web Query dialog box.

Modifying web queries

When you create a web query, you make it possible to use data from tables on your company's intranet or the Internet in your worksheets. However, financial data can change, so you should use the buttons on the Data tab on the ribbon to change how Excel deals with data drawn from other sources. One way that you can ensure that the external data is current is to have Excel refresh the data regularly.

Schedule web query data refreshes

1 Click the Data tab.

2 Click any cell that contains query data.

3 Click Properties in the Connections group.

4 Select the Refresh Every check box.

5 Type the number of minutes between refreshes in the Minutes box.

6 Click OK.

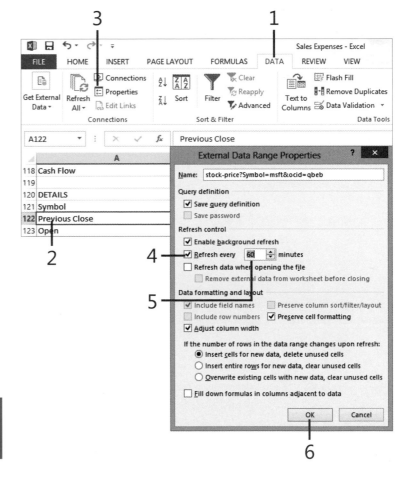

> ✓ **TIP** To have Excel refresh the data every time you open your workbook, select the Refresh Data When Opening The File check box.

Introducing XML

Although the Hypertext Markup Language (HTML) is great for describing how a web page should be displayed in a browser, the language isn't designed to communicate anything about the contents of a document. For example, telling Internet Explorer to display a worksheet as an HTML table tells you nothing about the data shown on that web page. However, when you save your worksheet data to an XML document, Excel annotates the data with tags describing which program generated the data, the name of the worksheet, and the data that belongs in each cell. With that information, Excel or another spreadsheet program that understands XML can read your worksheet data and retain your original meaning.

Although a full discussion of XML is beyond the scope of this book, the following bit of XML code shows how to identify an Excel workbook in XML:

```
<?xml version="1.0"?>

<Workbook xmlns="urn:schemas-microsoft-
com:office:spreadsheet" xmlns:o="urn:schemas-microsoft-
com:office:office" xmlns:x="urn:schemas-microsoft-
com:office:excel" xmlns:ss="urn:schemas-microsoft-
com:office:spreadsheet" xmlns:html="http://www.w3.org/TR/
REC-html40">
```

Also, XML can identify rows and cells within the spreadsheet, as in the following example:

```
<Row>
<Cell><Data ss:Type="String">Atlantic</Data></Cell>
<Cell><Data ss:Type="Date">1/1/2013</Data></Cell>
<Cell><Data ss:Type="Number">2013</Data></Cell>
<Cell><Data ss:Type="String">January</Data></Cell>
<Cell><Data ss:Type="Number">1</Data></Cell>
<Cell><Data ss:Type="Number">2</Data></Cell>
<Cell><Data ss:Type="String">Tuesday</Data></Cell>
<Cell><Data ss:Type="Number">120933</Data></Cell>
</Row>
```

The preceding XML code fragment represents the high-lighted row in the following worksheet.

	A	B	C	D	E	F	G	H
1	Center	Date	Year	Month	Week	Day	Weekday	Volume
2	Atlantic	1/1/2013	2013	January	1	1	Tuesday	120933
3	Atlantic	1/2/2013	2013	January	1	2	Wednesday	52979
4	Atlantic	1/3/2013	2013	January	1	3	Thursday	45683
5	Atlantic	1/4/2013	2013	January	1	4	Friday	53152

Saving data to the cloud using SkyDrive

As information workers become increasingly mobile, they need to access their data from anywhere and to have a single version of a file to which they can turn. Excel 2013 is integrated with SkyDrive, a Microsoft cloud service that stores your files remotely and lets you access them over the Internet. To use SkyDrive, open Internet Explorer and visit *http://www.skydrive.com*. You will need a Microsoft account to use SkyDrive.

Save a file to SkyDrive

1 Open *http://www.skydrive.com* in your web browser.

2 Click the Upload item on the ribbon.

3 Navigate to the folder that contains the file that you want to upload.

4 Click the file.

5 Click Open.

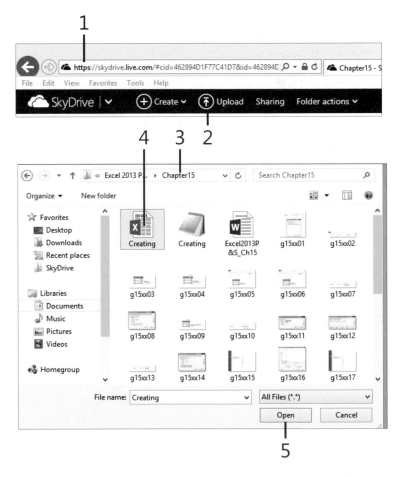

Interacting over the web using XML

The goal of XML is to be a universal language, allowing data to move freely from one application to another. That means that saving an Excel worksheet as an XML document allows any other spreadsheet program to read the XML file, separate out the cell names and data, and use the annotations to re-create the worksheet. By the same token, you can take a worksheet saved as an XML file and, regardless of the program in which the file was created, import it into Excel.

Save a workbook as a Strict Open XML Spreadsheet file

1 Click the File tab.

2 Click Save As.

3 Click Computer.

4 Click Browse.

5 Click the Save As Type down arrow.

6 Click Strict Open XML Spreadsheet.

7 Type the file name that you want.

8 Click Save.

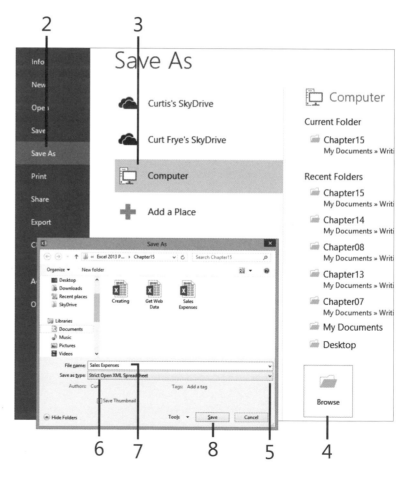

Import an XML spreadsheet file

1 Click the File tab.

2 Click Open.

3 Click Computer.

4 Click Browse.

5 Navigate to the folder containing the XML document that you want.

6 Double-click the XML document.

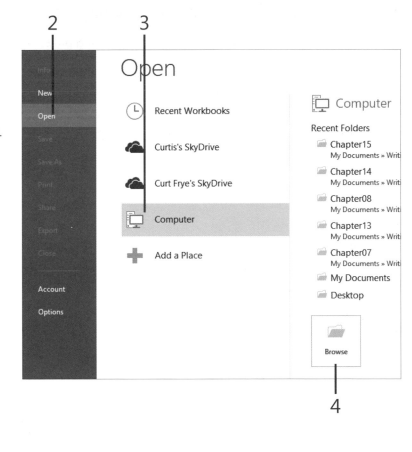

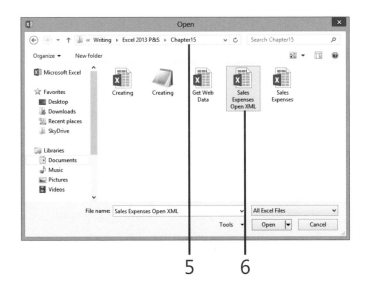

TIP If you don't see any XML documents in the Open dialog box, click the file type button and click All Excel Files.

Editing a workbook in the Excel Web App

The SkyDrive service and Microsoft Office 365 provide access to the Office Web Apps, which let you create and edit Office documents in your web browser. The Microsoft Excel Web App provides a rich set of capabilities that you can use to create new workbooks and edit workbooks that you created in the desktop version of the application. If you find you need some features that aren't available in the Excel Web App, you can open the file in the Excel 2013 desktop application.

Edit a file in the Excel Web App

1 In your web browser, visit *http://www.skydrive.com*.

2 Navigate to the folder that contains the file that you want to edit.

3 Click the tile of the file that you want to edit.

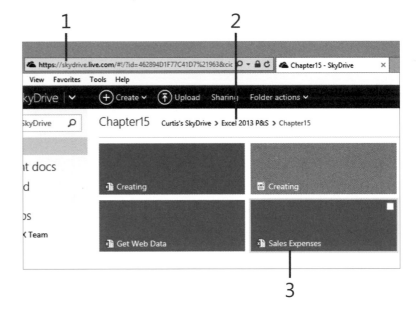

⊘ TIP The Excel Web App saves your workbook every time that you edit a cell, so there's no Save button on the Quick Access toolbar.

Open a file in the Excel desktop application

1 In your web browser, visit *http://www.skydrive.com*.

2 Navigate to the folder that contains the file that you want to open.

3 Right-click the tile of the file that you want to open.

4 Click Open In Excel.

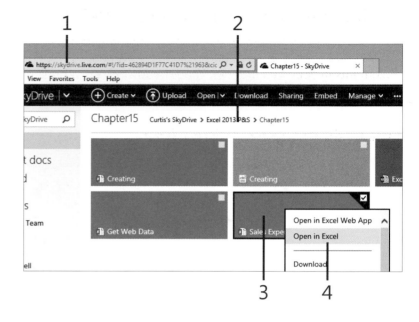

TIP Your computer will display a series of warning messages indicating that it is trying to open a file from the Internet. You will need to confirm the action and possibly reenter your SkyDrive login information.

Sharing Excel workbooks on the web

Both SkyDrive and Office 365 let you create and edit Excel workbooks in your web browser. You can also share your workbooks on the web, either by embedding a worksheet in a webpage or by creating a link to a public file stored in your SkyDrive account. In both cases, anyone with the web address of the file can view it, so you should either be sure that the page is available on a secure corporate network or that the data is safe to share with the public.

Embed a workbook in a webpage

1 In Excel Web App, display the workbook that you want to embed in a webpage.

2 Click Home.

3 Click Share.

4 Click Embed.

5 Click Generate.

(continued on next page)

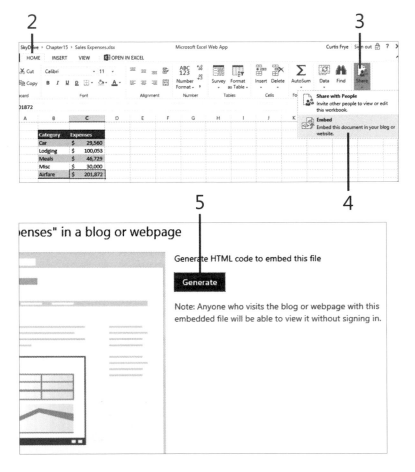

Embed a workbook in a webpage *(continued)*

6 Select the display and interactivity options for the workbook.

7 Click Copy.

8 Paste the code into an HTML document.

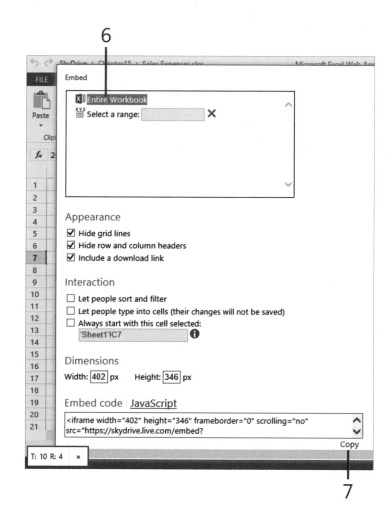

Making workbooks available on the web

When you work as part of a team, you need to be able to share your Excel files in a way that lets your colleagues edit your files. You can share individual files stored on SkyDrive by sending your colleagues an email message with a link to the file. In addition to sharing the file, you can choose whether each individual can edit the file and if they need to log in to their Microsoft Account to do so.

Make a workbook available on the web

1 In Excel Web App, display the workbook you that want to embed in a web page.

2 Click Home.

3 Click Share.

4 Click Share With People.

5 Type or select the email addresses of the people that you want to edit the workbook.

6 Type a personal message.

7 Click Share.

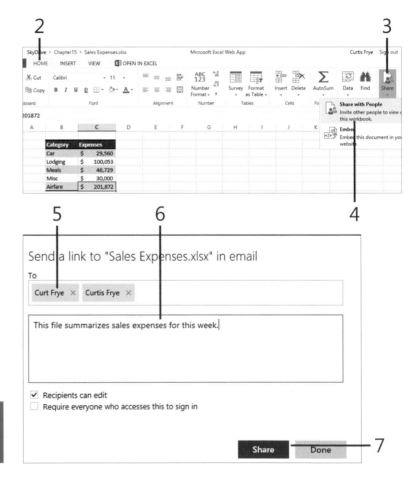

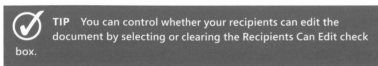

TIP You can control whether your recipients can edit the document by selecting or clearing the Recipients Can Edit check box.

Sharing a worksheet online using Lync

As Excel users become more mobile, the need to share worksheets and communicate effectively when your team isn't in the same room takes on increased importance. Microsoft Lync enables users to communicate securely anywhere that they have network connectivity. Lync integrates voice and video calls, Lync Meetings, and instant messaging in one application. Lync offers a consistent and familiar experience that's optimized for the device, operating system, or browser being used, including Windows 7 and Windows 8, Windows Phone, iOS, and Android smartphones.

In addition to secure communication, Lync enables teams to share programs, such as Excel, or their entire desktop with other meeting participants. When it's best for your colleagues to see your entire desktop, you can share a single workbook. In other circumstances, such as when you're drawing data from multiple sources to create a workbook, you can share your entire desktop. Desktop sharing is also useful for

co-editing scenarios, desktop support, troubleshooting, and real-time demos.

The meeting presenter can give and take control over desktop and file sharing. Participants can request control at any time and, when given permission, can edit documents and pass control to other users. This fluid sharing environment is perfect for informal collaborations where the users are commenting on and editing a document in a live setting.

Meeting hosts and presenters can also make documents available to meeting participants. Beyond simple sharing, the presenters and organizers can assign permissions for individual documents based on several criteria. For example, they can limit documents to the owner, only to co-presenters, or make the documents available to all attendees. All of the content and the associated permissions remain available and in effect until the expiration date set by the meeting host.

Index

About the Author

Curtis Frye is a writer, speaker, and performer who lives in Portland, Oregon. He is the author or coauthor of more than 20 books, including *Microsoft Excel 2013 Step by Step*. In addition to his writing, Curt presents keynote addresses on Excel and motivational topics.

What do you think of this book?

We want to hear from you!
To participate in a brief online survey, please visit:

microsoft.com/learning/booksurvey

Tell us how well this book meets your needs—what works effectively, and what we can do better.
Your feedback will help us continually improve our books and learning resources for you.

Thank you in advance for your input!